CONSTRUCTING CUBAN AMERICA

HISTORIA USA
A series edited by Luis Alvarez, Carlos Blanton, and Lorrin Thomas

Books in the Series

Oliver A. Rosales, *Civil Rights in Bakersfield: Segregation and Multiracial Activism in the Central Valley*
Luis Alvarez, *Chicanx Utopias: Pop Culture and the Politics of the Possible*
Felipe Hinojosa, *Apostles of Change: Latino Radical Politics, Church Occupations, and the Fight to Save the Barrio*
Patricia Silver, *Sunbelt Diaspora: Race, Class, and Latino Politics in Puerto Rican Orlando*
Cristina Salinas, *Managed Migrations: Growers, Farmworkers, and Border Enforcement in the Twentieth Century*
Perla Guerrero, *Nuevo South: Latinas/os, Asians, and the Remaking of Place*

CONSTRUCTING CUBAN AMERICA

Race and Identity in
Florida's Caribbean South, 1868–1945

ANDREW GOMEZ

University of Texas Press   Austin

Copyright © 2024 by the University of Texas Press
All rights reserved
Printed in the United States of America
First edition, 2024

Requests for permission to reproduce material from this work should be sent to permissions@utpress.utexas.edu.

♾ The paper used in this book meets the minimum requirements of ANSI/NISO Z39.48-1992 (R1997) (Permanence of Paper).

Library of Congress Cataloging-in-Publication Data

Names: Gomez, Andrew, author.
Title: Constructing Cuban America : race and identity in Florida's Caribbean South, 1868–1945 / Andrew Gomez.
Other titles: Race and identity in Florida's Caribbean South, 1868–1945
Description: First edition. | Austin : University of Texas Press, 2024. | Includes bibliographical references and index.
Identifiers: LCCN 2023047508 (print) | LCCN 2023047509 (ebook)
   ISBN 978-1-4773-2975-7 (hardcover)
   ISBN 978-1-4773-2976-4 (pdf)
   ISBN 978-1-4773-2977-1 (epub)
Subjects: LCSH: Cuban Americans—Race identity—Florida, South—History—19th century. | Cuban Americans—Race identity—Florida, South—History—20th century. | Cuban Americans—Florida, South—Social conditions—History. | Florida, South—Race relations—History—19th century. | Florida, South—Race relations—History—20th century.
Classification: LCC F320.C97 G66 2024 (print) | LCC F320.C97 (ebook) | DDC 975.9/06004687291073—dc23/eng/20231115
LC record available at https://lccn.loc.gov/2023047508
LC ebook record available at https://lccn.loc.gov/2023047509

doi:10.7560/329757

To my parents

CONTENTS

Acknowledgments ix

Introduction
Retracing Race in Cuban South Florida 1

1. Multiracial Democracy and Radical Reconstruction
   Cubans in Key West, 1868–1888 17

2. Liberty and Labor in Cuban South Florida 41

3. The Specter of Jim Crow and the Limits of Interracial Democracy 63

4. "Two Cultures at the Same Time"
   Blackness and Whiteness in Cuban South Florida 87

5. Cuban Americans, the Depression, and World War II 113

Epilogue
Memory and Historic Cuban America 133

Notes 143

Index 185

Acknowledgments

This project began during my time as a graduate student at UCLA. Many of the people I met there have shaped fundamental aspects of this project. Stephen Aron, Robin Derby, Raul Fernandez, and Tobias Higbie all advised on the original version of this project. Toby has been a fantastic mentor, and his supportive nudges about this book over the years were much appreciated. Raul, in addition to providing important insights on the project, helped create one of the most supportive academic communities I have ever been a part of in UC-Cuba. He, along with Anita Casavantes Bradford, Emilio Bejel, Nancy Burke, and the rest of UC-Cuba's leadership group, have done an incredible job of building a little academic oasis that I and this book greatly benefited from. Lastly, Jorge Carlos Arias, Jessica L. Harris, Preeti Sharma, Nickolas de Carlo, and Devin McCutchen have all been remarkable friends and colleagues who since we met at UCLA have lent their support in ways too numerous to name.

This project was made possible by several generous sources of funding and the expertise and support of several archives and libraries. At UCLA, this project was funded by the Graduate Division, the History Department, the Latin American Institute, and the UC-Cuba Initiative. At the University of Puget Sound, the project was supported by the History Department and a grant from the Andrew W. Mellon Foundation. The research for this book was largely based on archival work in several Florida archives and shorter visits to the Biblioteca Nacional de Cuba José Martí and the Archivo Nacional de la República de Cuba in Havana. While it would be impossible to list all of the people that have helped me along the way, I would like to give special thanks to Andy Huse, Tom Hambright, Breana Sowers, Belkis Quesada, Tomaro Taylor, Richard Phillips, Terry Eagan, Corey Malcom, Emerson Elliott, and Rachel Thompson. You all made working on this project a joy.

For the last eight years, I have been lucky enough to be surrounded by a remarkable group of colleagues at the University of Puget Sound. The encouragement of my colleagues in the history department has been invaluable, and I am honored to be surrounded by such a talented group of educators and scholars. My colleague John Lear has been an especially important mentor, reading and commenting on various iterations of this project and providing valuable advice along the way. I would also be remiss if I did not mention the wonderful students who have been in my classes during my time at Puget Sound. They are my favorite part of my job, and they have been a constant source of inspiration. I would especially like to thank the many students who have shown so much interest in learning about Cuban and Cuban American history from our little slice of the Pacific Northwest.

The University of Texas Press has been an ideal partner for this book. Kerry Webb has been a fantastic advocate for the project, and she made what could have been a labyrinthian process for a first-time author a simple and supportive process. Christina Vargas and Robert Kimzey have similarly helped me navigate the many steps that inevitably come up while finishing a book. I would also like to thank Sandra Spicher, who took a detailed look at the book and provided the index. Lorrin Thomas, who is one of the series editors for Historia USA, provided me with important guidance and encouragement. Her thorough notes and thoughtful suggestions on my original manuscript greatly aided me in my final edits. My two readers—who waived their anonymity—were Dalia Antonia Caraballo Muller and Jesse Hoffnung-Garskof. Their keen insights, thoughtful critiques, and remarkable expertise greatly improved this manuscript. Along with Lorrin, they modeled a type of scholarly generosity I can only hope to provide for others in the future. Many, many thanks.

My parents and partner, Caroline, have been remarkable sources of support in writing this book. My parents remain the most significant lottery I have ever won. In addition to providing me with endless reservoirs of love and support, they were my first and most beloved teachers of Latin American history and culture (y mamí, I promise the next project will involve Honduras). Caroline has been a constant source of solace, care, and joy through this entire process. She has made the most stressful moments of writing this book bearable, and I (and our dear Luna) are forever indebted to her for her kindness, brilliance, and love. Gracias, mi amor.

CONSTRUCTING CUBAN AMERICA

INTRODUCTION

Retracing Race in Cuban South Florida

A Tampa, Florida, park at the intersection of 8th Avenue and 13th Street bears the unique distinction of being the property of the Cuban government. The park, Parque Amigos de José Martí, is located within Tampa's Ybor City district. Referred to colloquially as José Martí Park, the property was owned by various Cuban families, dating back to the nineteenth century. In 1956, Manuel Quevedo donated the park to the Cuban government to create a "garden and sanctuary" in honor of Martí—the famed Cuban writer and revolutionary—that would include imported royal palms and a shrine made from marble gathered from the Isle of Pines.[1] Designed as a collaboration between city officials in Tampa and the Cuban government, then Cuban president Fulgencio Batista served as the group's honorary chairman. It was Batista's tenure as Cuba's president that would soon throw the park's future into disarray. Batista famously fled the island on New Year's Eve in 1958 following Fidel Castro's Cuban Revolution. Amid confusion over the future of the park, project leaders such as Tony Pizzo were still able to build a José Martí statue and an explanatory plaque during the early 1960s.[2] While the park became a site of political confrontation during its early years, it has continued to be one of the more public symbols of Cuban South Florida.[3]

The park itself is sparsely designed. The Parque Amigos largely consists of a statue of José Martí, a bust of Antonio Maceo, and an informational plaque.[4] Martí and Maceo were two of the more central figures of Cuba's nineteenth-century independence movement. Martí, an influential poet and journalist, was one of the leading architects of the Cuban Revolutionary Party and the Cuban War of Independence. Maceo was one of the movement's key generals and one of the most influential Cubans of color on the island. The plaque, however, explains the origins of Cuban Ybor City and the role of Tampa in Cuba's independence movement. Titled "La Casa de Pedroso 1893," the plaque reads:

> Paulina Pedroso was one of the great women patriots of Cuba. After an attempt on the life of Jose Marti, the Pedroso House became his refuge. Whenever Marti stayed here the flag of the budding Republic of Cuba fluttered outside. Evenings, the Cubans formed groups outside the little house to watch the Apostle of Freedom through the windows. Marti's room remained lighted until late at night, and at times, in the silence, the scratching of his pen could be heard. An intruder would have found Ruperto, Paulina's husband, on guard duty.

Paulina Pedroso was reflective of the thousands of Cubans throughout exile centers that actively supported the Cuban independence movement throughout the nineteenth century.[5] As a Black Cuban, she also underscored the multiracial nature of the independence movement and the many ways in which Black Cubans contributed to the cause of a free Cuba. Moreover, her husband, Ruperto, spoke to another important aspect of Cuban South Florida. As a cigar maker, Ruperto belonged to an industry that became the economic backbone for much of South Florida at the turn of the century and provided stability for thousands of Cuban families in the region.

An older Cuban landmark that is part of this same narrative can be found a few hundred miles south, in Key West, Florida. For much of the twentieth century, Key West was designed as a military hub and a tourist destination, boasting landmarks such as the La Concha Hotel and various sites tied to US luminaries such as Harry Truman and Ernest Hemingway. Duval Street, one of Key West's major arteries, traverses much of the island city and houses many of its more famous tourist attractions. However, at 516 Duval Street, a two-story Baroque structure points to an older period when Key West was a manufacturing town, the largest city in Florida, and was better known to many of its inhabitants as Cayo Hueso. El Instituto San Carlos was founded in 1871 by Cuban émigrés following the outbreak of the Ten Years' War. Thousands of Cubans soon populated the Florida city, where they became an influential voice in local politics and the city's cultural life. Founded as a multipurpose facility, the San Carlos became a key meeting place for revolutionary luminaries such as Martí, possessed one of the largest theaters in the city, and included one of the few interracial schools in Reconstruction-era Florida.[6] Throughout its early history, the San Carlos represented many of the most aspirational aspects of the Cuban independence movement in regard to working-class support and interracial democracy. While the San Carlos has gone through several iterations and buildings, it continues to stand as one of the oldest and most enduring Cuban institutions in the United States.[7]

By the early twentieth century, however, the Cuban communities that surrounded the Pedroso house and the Instituto San Carlos had changed considerably. The current Instituto San Carlos building was rebuilt in 1924. When a beauty contest was being organized that year to celebrate the opening of the building, a local newspaper reported on the conditions and prizes of the competition. The first requirement noted that to be a contestant, "se necesita ser blanca."[8] The contest's requirement for white participants was a mere footnote that reflected a much broader shift that had taken place over decades in Cuban South Florida. Near the end of the nineteenth century, the framework of Florida's Jim Crow system was crafted by Democratic lawmakers. Segregationist policies around marriage, schooling, and transportation were written into state and local law. Initially, it was unclear how these changes would affect the multiracial Cuban enclaves of South Florida. Beginning with marriage cases and later extending into nearly every facet of daily life, Jim Crow segregation soon became an integral part of life in Key West and Tampa. Cigar factories remained integrated, but few other facets of South Florida life did. While many of these changes were spurred by broader changes in the American South, Black Cubans also suspected that a shift in perception had taken place among white Cubans. Evelio Grillo, a Black Cuban raised in the Ybor City neighborhood that would later house the Parque Amigos, was keenly aware of these shifts as a child. Growing up in the 1920s, he remembered that his mother's white Cuban friends from the local cigar factory did not interact with her outside of work. Similarly, he recalled that "I don't remember playing with a single white Cuban child."[9]

In analyzing the roots of Cuban South Florida, a central goal of this book is to explore the chasm between the idealism symbolized by the aforementioned Cuban American landmarks and the racial separatism that people such as Evelio Grillo experienced. This text tracks how Cubans in Key West and Tampa navigated the turbulent racial politics of South Florida from the beginning of Cuba's Ten Years' War to the conclusion of the Second World War. During the earlier period of Cuban South Florida—1868 to 1885—Cubans were able to take many of the multiracial and egalitarian ideals of the Cuban independence movement and model them in South Florida, even as they continued to wrestle with the role of racism within their own communities. However, from 1885 onwards, the Cuban experience in South Florida became increasingly separated by race. Gradually, Black Cubans were legally grouped alongside African Americans and other Black residents while white Cubans became integrated into American society as white Cuban Americans. While the Jim Crow system accelerated many of these changes, this analysis also underscores the role that white Cubans played in distancing themselves from their Black counterparts and integrating into South Florida society.

Studies of these communities have generally focused on the nature of the Cuban independence movement and the cigar industry. In the case of the former, various scholars have written about Key West and Ybor City in relation to the broader rise of the Cuban independence movement, El Partido Revolucionario Cubano (Cuban Revolutionary Party), and the émigré press.[10] In this context, the Cuban communities of Key West and Tampa have been written about within the framing of Cuban nationalism and the broader migrant networks that made independence possible. The economic driver of both cities—the Clear Havana cigar industry—has also been a topic of interest.[11] In particular, scholars have looked at the many forms of activism that were organized in South Florida as well as the dynamics among the multiethnic work force in Ybor City.[12] Moreover, recent work on other Cuban enclaves during the independence era—such as those in New York City and Veracruz, Mexico—have also illustrated similarities and differences among the exile and cigarmaking communities of the late nineteenth century.[13] This book continues to frame the cigar industry as an essential component of Cuban South Florida, but it also thinks about how other institutions and social dynamics influenced the development of Cuban American identity and conceptions of race.

In addition to the aforementioned studies, this book also looks to build on the work of previous scholars that have used aspects of race to analyze Cuban South Florida during the late nineteenth and early twentieth centuries. While Key West has been scantly studied in this regard, scholars such as Winston James, Nancy Raquel Mirabal, and Susan Greenbaum have written various works on Black Cuban identity in Ybor City.[14] Similarly, Nancy Hewitt's work on women in Tampa often connected the roles of race and ethnicity on women's activism at the turn of the century.[15] While distinct, all of these works have considered the ways in which Jim Crow segregation led to fundamental changes in the Black Cuban community while also nodding to the broader fractures in Cuban American society. The role of La Unión Martí-Maceo—the best-known Black Cuban institution in Tampa—plays an important role in many of these studies.

One way in which this book expands on these works is by exploring the long arc of race in Cuban South Florida from 1868 to 1945. The longer chronology allows for a full retelling of Cuban South Florida, from the idealism of interracial democracy in the independence era to the racial separatism of the Jim Crow South. Beginning with Reconstruction-era Key West allows for a depiction of the early Cuban independence movement and a case study in how early émigrés attempted to put the ideals of interracial democracy into practice. Doing so also underscores how elements of racial separatism were still present in this community, even as many other Cubans began to build multiracial coalitions. In general, Key West remains one of the least studied communities in Cuban South Florida, and the Reconstruction-era focus also establishes early linkages with African American and Afro-Bahamian communities.[16] The subsequent founding of Ybor City and West Tampa became an extension of these ideals. When Martí would later proclaim in Tampa that "to our fatherland crumbling to pieces down there, and blinded by corruption, we must take the devout and farseeing country being built here," he conceded the role of émigré centers in modeling the social and political goals of a future Cuban republic.[17]

The majority of the text then grapples with the role of racial discrimination and its gradually intensifying influence on Cuban American communities. Near the end of his chapter on Afro-Cubans in Florida, Winston James noted that Jim Crow alone was an insufficient explanation for the racial separation that occurred between white and Black Cubans during the early 1900s—an explanation that failed to take individual agency into account, and the broader history of Cubans in South Florida challenging authority in other ways.[18] James, like Greenbaum, Hewitt, and Mirabal, offered possible explanations that this book looks to expand on. In addition to thinking about the role of segregationist policies, and other topics addressed by some of the aforementioned scholars, the later chapters also point to a number of other factors rarely discussed: the initial push of Jim Crow policies in Cuban Key West regarding intermarriage cases, the limits of the independence movement's color-blind ideology in South Florida, fraternal orders, voting rights, Americanization efforts, World War II, and other developments that point to the many ways that various systems and institutions altered civic and social life in South Florida. In addition to thinking about Jim Crow as a system that imposed a set of legal and social practices on the Cuban American community, these chapters also examine Cuban American agency—both white and Black—as a means of understanding how Cuban Americans navigated these systems via cultural institutions, activism, celebrations, local politics, and myriad other factors. This analysis also allows for a broader retelling of race in Cuban American communities and builds on works that deal with related issues within the context of Cuban New York by Jesse Hoffnung-Garskof, Nancy Raquel Mirabal, and Christina D. Abreu.[19]

Unlike many other studies on race in early Cuban America, this book analyzes the simultaneous racial formation of white and Black Cubans. This is especially important given the relative paucity of scholarship that has considered the relationship between the two groups and the nascent development of white Cuban identity in the United States. In addition to painting a more comprehensive picture of the Cuban American experience, exploring the two groups also underscores how they were inextricably linked. During the independence era, white and Black Cubans often stressed racial unity as a way of envisioning a burgeoning Cuban nationalism. However, over time, white Cubans began to articulate a particular form of Cuban whiteness in the US that was actively contrasted from Black Cuban identity and linked increasingly with European immigrants and the local Anglo community. Similarly, the weakening bonds between Black and white Cubans led Black Cubans to find new alliances with local African American communities, forging a new identity for young Black Cubans that were raised amid both cultures. Frank Andre Guridy has underscored various connections between Black Cubans and African Americans in other locations during this period—this text adds to the growing understanding of the linkages between Black Cubans and African Americans during the early twentieth century.[20]

In analyzing the relationship between white and Black Cubans in early Cuban South Florida, the role of anti-Blackness is a persistent theme. As Miriam Jiménez Román and Juan Flores asserted in their *Afro-Latin@ Reader*, one of the most significant lenses for understanding the Afro-Latino experience has been "the anti-Black racism within the Latin@

communities themselves."²¹ In the case of Cuban South Florida, white Cubans formed political alliances, personal relationships, and social customs that regularly excluded Black Cubans. In her recent book on legal manifestations of Latino anti-Blackness, Tanya Katerí Hernández has used the phrase "racial innocence" to underscore how white Latinos in particular have in many cases reinforced aspects of anti-Blackness within the United States.²² That white Latinos have been marginalized in specific ways in the United States has not kept them from reinforcing existing racial hierarchies in the nation. As Hernández notes, "A Latino claim of racial innocence in the racist world White non-Hispanics created in the United States is a thin reed of moral superiority when a Latino hand is the one forcefully slamming the door to Black inclusion."²³ This text looks to further historicize this concept by looking at the earliest Cuban American communities in Florida and showing how assertions of white Cuban identity were sometimes predicated on upholding systems of racial separatism.

This book also seeks to expand on previous scholarship in terms of analyzing these communities as a distinct region. Works on early Cuban South Florida have typically been filtered through the lens of a specific community, be it West Tampa, Key West, or Ybor City. While aspects of each community were distinct in terms of chronology, scale, and local governance, Key West and Tampa were deeply tied to one another via the cigar industry, steamship travel, and migratory labor. During the late 1800s and early 1900s, it was especially common for Cuban families to have spent time living and working in both cities. Additionally, broad trends regarding race, identity, and class were largely mirrored in both Tampa and Key West. This could be seen in factors such as organizing for Cuban independence, Jim Crow policies, changes in the cigar industry, and other developments. A simultaneous examination of both cities allows for an understanding of the relationship between the two communities and the many links between them.

With this in mind, I will sometimes refer to the region as the Caribbean South. This framing owes a debt of gratitude to previous scholars who have looked beyond national borders to understand Cuba and the broader Caribbean. Dalia Antonia Caraballo Muller's "Gulf World"— itself a nod to Mexican scholars and the "complejo Golfo-Caribe"—and Frank Andre Guridy's "U.S.-Caribbean world" are two recent examples of this type of lens.²⁴ While distinct, both of these framings pointed to the role of commerce, revolution, and diaspora in articulating the ways

Cubans engaged with the broader world during the late nineteenth and early twentieth centuries. This text's use of the Caribbean South echoes some of the same themes but is also meant to narrow in on the role of race and racialization in understanding the experiences of Caribbean people in the US South. Cuban migrants during this period make up a unique chapter in the history of the US South, but they are also part of a much broader narrative.[25] While Caribbean populations have shaped other parts of the US South, such as New Orleans, their connection to Florida has been particularly pronounced. The periodization in this text reflects the first large-scale wave of Caribbean migration to South Florida after statehood in 1845. Key West in particular was considerably shaped by Bahamian and Cuban migration during the late nineteenth century. Later, the text covers the expansion of Cuban South Florida into various parts of Tampa. In all of this analysis, race is central to understanding how Caribbean people and Cubans in particular navigated their place in the US South. Beginning with Reconstruction and ending with the Jim Crow period, understanding the racial dynamics between Cuba, the Bahamas, and the United States is crucial to contextualizing the experiences of Caribbean South Floridians. While Guridy similarly noted the "cross-fertilization between Cuban and US conceptions of race," this text looks to expand on this by simultaneously understanding how Cuban whiteness and Blackness were negotiated between Cuba and the United States.[26]

While the narrative of this project ends in 1945, Caribbean populations have continued to shape other parts of the Caribbean South in the proceeding decades. The development of modern Miami in the 1920s spurred additional Caribbean migration with the notable addition of Caribbean tourists as well.[27] Similar trends have continued for decades: seasonal Bahamian workers in early 1900s Florida, the well-known Cuban migratory wave to Miami following the Cuban Revolution, Haitian refugees during the Duvalier era, and a broader panoply of other Caribbean migrants who relocated to Florida during the late twentieth century. The recent movement of thousands of Puerto Ricans to Central Florida in the wake of Hurricane Maria is but the most recent in a long history of Caribbean people remaking the Caribbean South.[28]

CHAPTER OVERVIEWS AND THEMES

Chapter 1 covers early Cuban migration to Key West and how Cubans navigated Reconstruction-era Florida. Following the beginning of the Ten Years' War in Cuba, thousands of Cubans relocated to Key West, replanting a significant share of the Cuban cigar industry along with them. Cubans were migrating to the US's southernmost city at a time of considerable political change. As was true throughout the US South after the Civil War, fundamental changes to the terms of citizenship and political participation transformed South Florida. In Key West, a newly enfranchised African American community alongside Caribbean migrants from Cuba and the Bahamas significantly changed the development of the island city. After considering these developments, the chapter goes on to explore how Cubans played active roles in shaping the local economy and the region's politics. A central consideration in this section looks at the Republican Party and its Monroe County coalition of Anglos, African Americans, Cubans, and Bahamians. Members of each group played active roles in party leadership and regularly occupied various city and statewide positions. Cubans, largely allied with the Republican Party, secured several important posts, culminating in the election of Carlos Manuel de Céspedes y Céspedes as mayor in 1875. While each ethnic group had unique sets of concerns, there were also active ties between them, as they organized together, labored in many of the same settings, and socialized in multiethnic and multiracial Key West. However, this chapter also underscores the smaller number of white Cubans that allied themselves with the Democratic Party and points to other ways in which aspects of racial separatism were still present in Cuban Key West. The chapter considers how the ideals of the Cuban independence movement shaped this period of Key West as many émigrés in Key West debated and modeled what a future Cuban republic might be.

A concurrent development in Cuban South Florida was the rise of the Cuban Revolutionary Party and labor militancy more generally—the two represented some of the most significant forms of interracial organizing in late-1800s Cuban South Florida. Chapter 2 first considers the role of interracial independence organizations within Key West and Tampa during the late nineteenth century. Looking at the work of local activists and key leaders, the chapter considers the ways in which discourses over race and "racelessness" shaped these communities. The chapter later details the interracial labor unions that characterized Cuban South Florida and the many challenges they faced during the late nineteenth and early twentieth centuries. In particular, anti-labor violence in the post-Reconstruction period was part of a broader wave of targeted assaults of radical labor unions and other interracial institutions. With the founding of Ybor City in 1885, South Florida possessed two of the largest Clear Havana centers, producing millions of dollars in revenue.

Workers, in turn, developed some of the largest labor unions in the state, which recruited regardless of race and gender. Sections of the chapter also explore the founding of these unions and their relationship to the Cuban independence movement. While revolutionary leaders such as José Martí ultimately secured the support of most Cuban cigar makers in South Florida, the 1880s and 1890s also reflected tensions within the Cuban independence movement and its color-blind rhetoric.

The latter half of the chapter considers the violent suppression of the Cuban-led labor movement in South Florida after the Cuban War of Independence. The crucial years after 1898 represented both the peak and unraveling of some of the most radical cigar unions in South Florida. Led by Anglo city leaders and some manufacturers, anti-union campaigns and vigilante violence became normalized during this period. Similarly, the Cigar Makers' International Union (CMIU) looked to gain control of organizing in the region by promising a more palatable labor movement. With an image of Anglo leadership, the CMIU used racial tropes about Cubans that were prominent in the post-1898 era, and it ultimately secured a foothold in the region. In the process, Cubans lost one of the more important forums for interracial organizing in South Florida.

Chapter 3 considers how the expansion of segregationist policies took root in Cuban South Florida over time. With the end of Reconstruction and the federal power that undergirded it, leaders of the Democratic Party began to control major political offices in Florida. This movement weakened the state Republican Party and Black political power in particular. Beginning with a new state constitution in 1885, a series of laws regarding intermarriage, social segregation, and voting became the building blocks for the Jim Crow system in Florida. This chapter considers some of the earliest indications of how Jim Crow laws would change Cuban enclaves by looking at the removal of Monroe County judge James Dean under the accusation that he was marrying interracial couples that involved Cuban spouses. The chapter then explores how reforms to the Democratic Party, voting, and public transportation further segregated Key West and Tampa. The latter half of the chapter explores how the Cuban community responded to these changes. White Cubans began to segregate mutual-aid societies and other organizations while continuing to take part in political organizations and fraternal orders that barred Black membership. For Black Cubans, they began to form their own associations, such as Tampa's La Unión Martí-Maceo, in response to the region's new racial order.

The end of the chapter also considers how flaws in the aspirational ideas of multiracial democracy became increasingly pronounced in both South Florida and Cuba. The founding of the Partido Independiente de Color (PIC / Independent Party of Color) in Cuba—a group that united some Black Cubans in calling for a series of national reforms and equitable policies—is a key institution for this analysis. The PIC's founding drew condemnation from the Cuban government and US publications that printed sensationalist claims regarding the group's plans and motivations. In South Florida, many of these trends were echoed with local publications covering the tumult on the island and local Cubans similarly debating the merits of the group. Tensions between the Cuban state and the PIC reached their peak when the Cuban military targeted and killed PIC members in 1912. This moment is examined as a way of showing how Black Cubans were marginalized and viewed as suspicious in both Cuba and South Florida during this period.

The second generation of Cubans in South Florida were raised in a society that was considerably different from that of their parents. The Jim Crow system became fully entrenched during the 1920s and 1930s, with political institutions, social life, and many local customs strictly defined by racial separatism. These changes led to further divisions among Cubans by race. Chapter 4 opens by analyzing how Black Cubans adjusted in terms of institutional affiliations and outreach to the broader Black community in both Key West and Tampa. While Black Cubans were initially reluctant to collaborate with African Americans due to cultural and linguistic barriers, the two groups were brought together by intermarriage, schooling, entertainment, and other facets of daily life. The chapter also considers how women's activism and community work became essential to bringing the Black Cuban and African American communities together in these endeavors. White Cubans, conversely, became further entrenched as part of South Florida's white community. White Cubans attended schools with local Anglos and other white immigrants, continued to be influential in local politics, and retained few connections with Black Cubans in the region. While exoticized and seen as ethnic others, white Cubans firmly established themselves as an essential constituency to life in South Florida during this period. Prominent Cubans in particular established active connections with South Florida's Anglo community. Moreover, white Cubans increasingly devoted themselves to "Americanization" efforts that were meant to spur their integration into US society. The chapter also considers the ways that white Cubans justified their distance from Black Cubans as a means of examining older prejudices that clearly continued to guide many white Cubans in South Florida.

Chapter 5 considers the ways in which the Great Depression and World War II further shaped both communities in relation to Cuba, economic strife, and wartime service. In Key West and Tampa, the Great Depression triggered a near collapse of the Clear Havana cigar industry. In Key West, where the cigar industry had been slowly contracting for years, the Depression assured its transition from a cigar town to a military and tourist-driven economy. Tampa, whose cigar industry would continue for decades, was nonetheless also profoundly altered as the industry lost its dominance in the region. Coupled with the era's Jim Crow policies, the Black Cuban communities of both Cuban enclaves dwindled during this period. White Cubans remained an important social and political force in the region, but with migration similarly slowing during this period, white Cuban Americans began to adapt to new identities. In particular, this chapter looks at the case study of the Instituto San Carlos to see how the institution transformed into a symbol of Cuba-US relations and a multigenerational Cuban American community. Lastly, this chapter will consider the ways in which World War II shaped Key West and Tampa as well as veterans who served. For many white Cubans, the war represented a full engagement with US ideals as American citizens and further established white Cubans as accepted members of US society. For some Black Cubans, however, the war also served as a catalyst for activism in Florida and spurred a call to redouble efforts to organize alongside the African American community. These divergent approaches to engaging with or confronting US ideals spoke to the differing paths that white and Black Cubans charted over multiple generations.

RACE AND IDENTITY IN SOUTH FLORIDA

Race is a crucial analytical lens employed throughout this text. As with many works on race and identity, a recurring tension lies between the social construction of race and its real consequences for the populations in question. Moreover, as Petra R. Rivera-Rideau, Jennifer A. Jones, and Tianna S. Paschel have underscored, the study of this type of diasporic population requires an understanding of competing conceptions of race between nations.[29] The timeline of this book coincides with a period of significant change in both Cuba and the United States in regard to its racial politics. In Cuba, this period begins with debates over independence and slavery and ends with the early republic and the struggles of Black Cubans to secure representation and power in Cuba. As discussed above, the debates surrounding these shifts were often echoed in Cuban communities in South Florida. The book's timeline begins with Reconstruction in the United States and the first large-scale effort to build a multiracial democracy in the US South. By the 1940s, Cubans in Florida had experienced decades of a Jim Crow system that disenfranchised Black Americans and used extralegal means to segregate Southern society.

As a result, the book reflects these evolving histories of racial conception and terminology. When referring to Cubans of African descent, I will invoke a variety of phrases: Cuban of color, Afro-Cuban, and Black Cuban, among others. The phrases "Black Cuban" and "Cuban of color" largely mirror the Spanish terms *raza de color*, *clase de color*, and *negro* that were widely used in both Cuba and South Florida during the late nineteenth and early twentieth centuries. Moreover, I will also at times quote the wording used by Black Cubans themselves or by outsiders who attempted to categorize Cubans of color—both often revealing for different reasons related to identity, perception, or biases. In many cases, shifts in terminology also sometimes reflected generational divides and broader evolutions regarding self-identification. While Black Cuban migrants like Rafael Serra actively employed the language of *raza de color* and *negro*, this was not necessarily common among the second and third generations of Cuban Americans, who grew up in the United States and increasingly spoke English as their dominant language. One of the most prominent Black Cuban families in Tampa points to this development. Francisco Rodríguez Sr. was an early member of La Unión Martí-Maceo— an organization that looked to represent the interests of Tampa's *clase de color*. La Unión's founding was in part spurred by Black Cubans being barred from joining El Círculo Cubano, another Cuban mutual-aid society whose antecedent organization was racially integrated. During these early years, La Unión made few overtures to the local African American community and was a largely insular organization. The experiences of Francisco Rodríguez Jr. were decidedly different. Raised in Jim Crow Florida, during the early twentieth century, he defined himself as a "black Latin."[30] More than a label, the younger Rodríguez viewed this idea as central to his identity, as his own life navigated the path between his Cuban heritage and the African American community he was raised alongside in the American South. While inevitably imperfect, this text attempts to chart these shifts and capture the range of terminology that Black Cubans used to define themselves.

The evolving concept of whiteness is similarly essential to understanding the experience of white Cubans in South Florida. In recent years, a variety of works have focused on the evolution of whiteness in the United States. Typically focused on European immigrant communities, many of these works have highlighted how a growing number of ethnic groups over time have been able to claim whiteness in the United States, often by adopting the nation's racial binary and racial hierarchy. White Cuban Americans underwent similar shifts during the timeline of this book, though their experience was unique in important ways. White Cubans were exoticized and seen as a foreign element in South Florida. Nevertheless, they were also essential to South Florida's economy, and prominent white Cubans became mainstays of the most influential fraternal orders, the Democratic Party, and other power structures in both Key West and Tampa. As a result, white Cubans were treated as white citizens, which had significant consequences for voting, schooling, medical care, and a range of other factors that permeated daily life in South Florida.

Cuban whiteness was nevertheless unsteady, with working-class white Cubans ostracized at various moments. In some ways, the white Cuban experience shares similarities to other Latin Americans in the United States during the nineteenth and early twentieth centuries. Following the signing of the Treaty of Guadalupe Hidalgo in 1848, many Mexican nationals transitioned into becoming US citizens. While Mexican Americans could technically claim US citizenship and some aspects of whiteness, these changes were counteracted by many other forms of discrimination that working-class Mexican Americans experienced. As Ernesto Chávez has noted, this led to an "unstable whiteness" that required the vigilance of Mexican Americans.[31] Laura Gómez similarly observed an "off-white" status of Mexican Americans in New Mexico who were able to claim some aspects of whiteness even as they were not socially accepted as white.[32] Glenn Chambers, in his analysis of Caribbean and Central American New Orleans in the early 1900s, noted similar trends among non-Black migrants from Central America. While some white and mestizo migrants from Central America attempted to distance themselves from Black migrants in Louisiana and claim aspects of whiteness, they were still sometimes cast as a racial "other."[33] Intersections between race, education, and class were central to understanding these dynamics.[34] While wealthier white Cuban Americans in South Florida could claim aspects of whiteness via class, interethnic marriage, and ties to dominant power structures, these privileges were not necessarily extended to working-class Cubans. While not as widespread as abuses against Mexican and Mexican American workers, the white Cuban working class was also cast as a foreign element that was sometimes subjected to various forms of discrimination. However, as noted in chapter four, prominent white Cubans also played an important role in challenging caricatures and slights lobbed toward the working-class population.

Throughout the book, Cubans of European ancestry will be referred to as white Cubans—a phrasing that serves as a direct translation of the *cubano blanco* wording that would have been used during this period. However, just as with Black Cubans, I also examine the other ways that white Cubans referred to themselves over time. In the case of Tampa, white Cubans referred to themselves as part of the city's "Latin" population alongside Italians and Spaniards. While technically including Black Cubans as well—as seen in Francisco Rodríguez Jr.'s self-classification—white Cubans often invoked the phrase as a means of pairing themselves alongside European immigrants. As noted in chapter 4, many Cubans invoked the concept of a Latin identity as a means of tying themselves to a broader narrative about immigration to the United States—one that was nearly always absent of Black Cubans when undertaking collective efforts in Tampa's Latin community.

Ultimately, racial terminology is one of several ways of analyzing changes to South Florida's Cuban communities. Beginning with Key West in 1868, earlier migrants employed language that was closer to Cuban ideas of race and reflected the aspirational concepts of the Cuban independence movement. Over time, these terms adjusted to the unique community dynamics of South Florida and the racial separatism that defined the era. For Black Cubans, their relationships to other Black Caribbean people and African Americans led to shared experiences that brought them closer to one another in terms of language and community. Conversely, white Cubans began to adopt ideas and language that positioned them closer to white South Floridians. While these ideas were certainly present in the earliest Cuban-American communities in South Florida, they became more pronounced over time. In the process, white and Black Cubans led lives that were significantly different from the ones they founded together in exile during the late nineteenth century. Examining how and why these shifts occurred is one of the central goals of this text.

· I ·
MULTIRACIAL DEMOCRACY AND RADICAL RECONSTRUCTION

Cubans in Key West, 1868–1888

Narciso López sailed from Mexico's Contoy Island in 1850 with the intent of freeing Cuba from Spanish tyranny. Traveling on the *Creole* with several hundred men, the ship likely boasted a newly designed "lone star" flag. Created by Miguel Teurbe Tolón, the flag became the symbol of Cuban revolutionaries for decades and has now served as the official flag of the Cuban republic for well over a century. The expedition's ambition was befitting of its architect. López, born in Venezuela to a wealthy family, became a fixture of the Spanish military as a young man. By the 1840s, he became swept up in the nascent Cuban independence movement and fled to the United States to further plot an insurrection.[1] He found many sympathetic friends in the United States.[2] Part of this stemmed from existing constituencies in the United States that wished to see Cuba under US influence. President James K. Polk, like several US leaders before him, had already attempted to purchase Cuba outright from Spain.[3] Southern plantation owners coveted an additional slave state, and Northern businesspeople saw the economic possibilities of working closely with a newly independent Cuba. López was able to secure financial backing from various American interests before attempting his filibuster.

López's filibuster was an abject failure. He arrived in Cárdenas and confidently proclaimed an independent Cuba. He envisioned that Cubans would be swept up in the emotion of the movement and fight alongside his forces. This vision did not come to fruition. Within a day, López and his men were chased out of Cuba and fled toward Key West. Tailed by a Spanish warship, they safely arrived at the United States' southernmost point and disbanded.[4] The filibuster became a national scandal back in the United States. Many Americans sympathized with López's efforts, others following the story were amused by López's quixotic folly, while others became alarmed by potential violations of the United States' Neutrality Act. Political scandal soon followed, and one of López's primary backers, John Quitman, was forced to resign as governor of Mississippi over his involvement. López attempted another filibuster the following year. He was captured by Spanish forces and executed in front of a crowd of thousands for his efforts.[5]

As errant as López's attempts may have been, efforts for Cuban independence bore fruit in proceeding decades. His escape to Key West became a symbolic exodus that would repeat itself for decades among fellow Cubans fleeing the Spanish Empire. Over the next fifty years, Key West became a key launching point for the Cuban independence movement and its war against Spain. The independence movement went through myriad changes during this period. It is instructive that López began his efforts as a wealthy military man, a supporter of slavery, and a clear admirer of the United States. By the end of the century, Key West's independence movement was fueled by its working-class population, Cuba's abolition movement, and a revolutionary poet who cautioned Cubans about the imperial ambitions of their northern neighbors. As the Cuban independence movement shifted through various iterations, Key West was frequently essential to these developments.

Key West's trajectory in the late nineteenth century was defined by two seminal events: the Cuban independence movement and Radical Reconstruction. Beginning in 1868 with the Ten Years' War, the Cuban insurgency launched a thirty-year campaign to capture its independence from the Spanish Empire. The Ten Years' War triggered the first of several exile waves to the United States, with Key West serving as one of the first and largest homes to Cuba's exile community. Key West was composed of the transplanted cigar industry that began to take root in South Florida and some of the most active revolutionaries that had been previously imprisoned by the Spanish. The other defining factor in Key West's nineteenth-century history was Radical Reconstruction. Dating from 1867–1877, Radical Reconstruction was the first concerted effort in United States history to support and produce an interracial democracy in the American South. Led by the power of the federal government and energized by African American activists, Radical Reconstruction marked the beginning of Black office-holding in the South and the widespread proliferation of Black educational institutions, medical facilities, and other essential services. In Key West, the guiding principles of Radical Reconstruction were clearly present as Cubans, African Americans, and Bahamians became critical to the Republican Party's power on the island. Moreover, and unlike many other areas of the South, fundamental aspects of Radical Reconstruction were present in Key West as late as the 1880s.

This chapter argues that these unique circumstances allowed for Cubans in Key West to simultaneously build a radical outpost of Cuban independence while also working alongside African Americans and Afro-Bahamians to model how an interracial democracy might flourish in Cuba. It is important to note that the beginning of this timeline, 1868, represents a precarious moment in Cuban history. Nearly two decades before the full abolition of slavery in Cuba, the Cuban insurgency of 1868 was composed of a contradictory coalition of former enslavers demanding outright abolition, the nascent radical working class of Havana, rural farmers, and other elite enslavers that argued for a more gradual approach on the question of race. In many respects, Key West represented the vanguard of this debate, even as racial inequities could still be seen in Cuban Key West. As a working-class community with a substantial Black Cuban population, Key West leaders like Martín Morúa Delgado and Guillermo Sorondo placed Black Cubans at the center of the independence movement and argued that any vision of a free Cuba that did not fully absorb and embrace Black Cubans was a farce. Meanwhile, Cubans in Key West also became an active part of the literary and political life of the city. Working alongside Afro-Bahamians and African Americans, Cubans built a political coalition that regularly elected members of their own communities to serve in office and fundamentally reoriented the cultural identity of the city. Elements of racial separatism could be still be seen in some political and social organizations, but there was still a significant coalition of Cubans that worked to create a more ambitious alternative. As independence leaders argued throughout the late 1800s, exile communities represented a critical way to place the ideals of the Cuban independence movement into practice. As Diego Vicente Tejera noted to an audience in Key West's Instituto San Carlos in 1887 regarding Cubans and their time in the United States, "these immigrants will take back to their homeland the habits acquired in this great school of democracy."[6] Key West represented one of the most ambitious examples of this type of work.

A RADICAL VISION OF CUBAN INDEPENDENCE

On October 10, 1868, Carlos Manuel de Céspedes planted his own Cuban flag in Yara, a small town in Cuba's Granma province, and declared open rebellion on the Spanish Empire. This marked the early stages of the Ten Years' War and the broader thirty-year struggle to gain Cuban independence. Céspedes's proclamation came with much greater support than López's. Decades of revolutionary organizing led wealthy landowners, the abolitionist movement, Cubans of color, and the urban working class to all consider revolution a viable option. In his "Grito de Yara" proclamation, Céspedes declared an independent Cuba and also outlined the eventual abolition of slavery. This vision of gradual abolition quickly gave way to more radical proposals toward abolition by 1869 that drew greater numbers of Black Cubans to the revolutionary cause.[7] In the years that followed, Cubans waged a brutal war against the Spanish while Cubans within the insurgency continued to debate the movement's composition and aims.

In the early years of the Ten Years' War, Key West became a critical site of reunion and reconciliation amid the tumult of the conflict. The Figueredo family serves as a typical example. Candelaria Figueredo's father, Pedro "Perucho" Figueredo y Cisneros, was one of the original architects of the Ten Years' War, and Candelaria herself became an ardent proponent of Cuban independence. By 1871, following her capture by Spanish forces, she was forced to flee Cuba. In her autobiography, she remembered the experience of arriving in Key West and "finding myself in the arms of my poor mother after fourteen months of separation, which for me seemed like fourteen centuries. There we stayed and there I endured the cruel pain of seeing how the people closest to my heart were disappearing."[8] Juan Pérez Rolo, who arrived in Key West as a child in 1869, remembered a similarly supportive Cuban community that greeted the arrival of new émigrés with chants of "¡Cuba Libre!"[9]

Key West soon became one of the most militant outposts for Cuban independence and posited a vision of Cuban independence that was one of the most inclusive among émigré communities.[10] In the United States, Key West and New York City were the most influential Cuban communities. Though united in their broad aims, the two major Cuban enclaves were different in composition. While New York City did possess a smaller working-class core of Cubans that grew over time, the city became a haven for many of the revolutionary intelligentsia, merchants, and other white, wealthy Cubans during the 1860s.[11] Key West, conversely, made up the working-class core of the exile population with greater racial and socioeconomic diversity. Key West's Cuban population was a reflection of the Cuban cigar industry that drove the city's growth. Shortly after the Ten Years' War began, manufacturers and thousands of Cuban cigar makers migrated to Key West in an effort to replant the industry. Manufacturers shipped raw Cuban tobacco to Key West and hired an overwhelmingly Cuban work force to produce their cigars. This became the basis of the Clear Havana cigar industry that became the largest employer of Key West and attracted thousands of workers regardless of race and gender.

At the forefront of working-class organizing and interracial work forces, cigar workers had a different set of concerns when compared to wealthier revolutionaries. Dating back to its origins in Havana, cigar-making was an urban industry. As other scholars have shown, the anonymity offered by nineteenth-century urban centers allowed Cuban artisans the ability to form workers' associations, mutual-aid societies, and other unique cultural markers.[12] These opportunities presented both a boon to the multiracial work forces of cities and a threat to colonial authorities attempting to tighten control of imperial possessions. As a result, the cigar workers that moved to Key West were composed of a diverse subset of Cuban working-class society and viewed themselves as having a different outlook on Cuban independence when compared to wealthier insurgents.[13] The Cuban cigar industry that was formed in the early nineteenth century was primarily in Havana and from the beginning possessed a multiracial work force—including Chinese-born cigar makers—composed of free and unfree laborers. Jean Stubbs's analysis of Cuban factories in the 1830s revealed that out of 2,234 cigar workers, 1,622 were free laborers, while 612 were enslaved people.[14] While statistics on enslaved people in particular were harder to verify over time, it was clear that Black cigar workers—free and unfree—were an integral part of the Cuban industry.[15] Collaborations between some of these workers became common, and cigar-maker unions were among the first attempts at organized labor in Cuba. These trends continued in Key West. By the 1870s, La Unión de Tabaqueros was organized by Key

West's cigar makers and represented one of the first of many cigarmaking unions that would become the norm in Cuban Florida.[16]

The radicalization of cigar workers in many ways began with the very structure of the industry and the factory floor. In the workplace, the *lector* was responsible for the informal education of nearly every cigar worker. The lector was a skilled orator that read to cigar workers during the workday.[17] The lector role was repressed by the Spanish in Cuba during the Ten Years' War, but it was quickly replanted in émigré centers like Key West.[18] While reading lists could vary, the lector of a typical Key West factory would have likely been reading from a mixture of émigré newspapers such as the local *El Republicano* or *El Yara*, political texts, and classic works of fiction.[19] Cubans, regardless of race, were captive audiences for the lector. As Joan Casanovas has noted on the Cuban factories that preceded the Floridian industry, "The *lectura* also helped to blur divisions of race and status among workers. Since free and unfree laborers worked together in tobacco manufacturing, slaves, indentured Chinese, free blacks, apprentices, and *dependientes* became part of the audience."[20] The lector was part performer, part teacher, and part scholar. In 1874, a *New York Times* writer described this unique position in the factory:

> This "reader" is a most valuable and well-stored personage. He reads rapidly and loudly, first a newspaper and then a letter, and he is so well supplied with reading matter, either in print or manuscript, that he goes on all day without exhausting his material. He commences with the stock in his hat, then descends through the pockets of his coat, vest, and pantaloons.[21]

The lector in many ways reflected the varied aims and interests of Cuban Key West. Radical politics, the Cuban independence movement, and a broad knowledge of classic literature made up the core of the city's working-class intellectualism.

While radical in many respects, Key West's cigar factories and other aspects of the independence movement still reflected racial and gender inequalities in more subtle ways. Cubans of color made up a substantial percentage of cigar factory workers on the island, but this did not translate to some of the higher-paid positions in the factory. Cubans of color made up roughly 15 percent of the city's cigar workers in 1885, but the more specialized and well-paid roles of manufacturer, selector, and lector generally went to white Cubans.[22] As an example, Martín Morúa Delgado was an influential journalist and lector in the city, but his status as a Black lector was a rarity in Key West and other cigar centers in Florida. Similarly, women's roles in revolutionary Key West were more limited. In the factory, Cuban women worked almost exclusively as stemmers—this was an early part of the cigar process that involved workers separating the tobacco leaf from the stem and was one of the lower-paid positions in the factory.[23] Similarly, women played roles in the local independence movement in Key West but were often relegated to fundraising efforts and charitable work.[24] By the turn of the century, more militant labor unions offered greater possibilities to Black Cubans and Cuban women. Stemmers' unions in particular were among some of the most militant labor organizations in Florida during the early twentieth century. However, the early years of Cuban Key West still reflected the hierarchical nature of the cigar factory that sometimes limited opportunities for Black and women workers.

Nevertheless, debates over race and racial equality were readily apparent in Cuban Key West outside of cigar factories as well. By 1880, just over 20 percent of the city's Cuban exile community was Black or multiracial.[25] Both Black and white Cubans articulated the importance of racial solidarity on the island. The Afro-Cuban Martín Morúa Delgado was representative of this type of discourse. At various times in his life, he served as a writer, labor organizer, translator, and later, as a senator in the early Cuban republic. While in Key West during the 1880s, he served as a cigar factory lector, translator, and journalist. Moreover, he was an editor for *El Pueblo* and *La Revista Popular*—both of which gave a platform to other Cubans of color such as Joaquín Granados, Juan Bonilla, Margarito Gutiérrez, and Emilio Planas.[26] During a period where the Cuban insurgency was fractured in regard to the role of Black Cubans going forward, Morúa was a persistent proponent of full inclusion. Writing for *El Separatista*, he noted that "freedom does not allow for compromise. One cannot be half free, like one cannot be half enslaved."[27] Black Cubans in South Florida were also actively tied to revolutionary publications such as *La Fraternidad* that actively connected Black Cubans in Cuba with Black Cubans in émigré centers in South Florida and New York City.[28]

White Cubans like Diego Vicente Tejera echoed similar sentiments about the need to fully include Cubans of color. His most notable address on the topic, "Blancos y Negros," was delivered in Key West in 1897.[29]

He also addressed related issues of equality during the 1880s. In an 1887 Key West address on the importance of democratizing educational access and on the deleterious effects of Spanish colonialism, he wondered, "Didn't we maintain a rancid preoccupation with caste, affirming that in society two types of individuals exist, those that are our equal and those that are inferior, and the first should be treated with consideration and the latter with disdain, so as to keep them at a distance?"[30] Going forward, he noted, "now, we should do exactly the opposite."[31]

No institution spoke to the multiracial ideals of the Cuban independence movement like the Instituto San Carlos. Dating back to its inception, the San Carlos was designed to be a multiuse facility that combined a free school for Cuban children, a cultural institution, and a general home for supporters of the Cuban independence movement.[32] Founded in 1871 by Cuban émigrés, the Instituto became a key symbol of interracial organizing in the independence movement. Orators such as Diego Vicente Tejera and the Afro-Cuban Rafael Serra—who also briefly served on the San Carlos board of directors—lectured on a wide range of issues at the Instituto, with race being one of the recurring themes.[33] The Instituto also boasted an interracial school—a rarity in the American South, even during Reconstruction. Emilio Planas, a Black Cuban who would later become a journalist, was one of the school's early pupils, graduating at the top of his class.[34] The San Carlos boys' school opened in 1871, with a girls' school opening in 1874.[35] One observer noted that one of the school's tasks was to form citizens "for the republic of tomorrow."[36] As with many aspects of Cuban Key West, the San Carlos was intended to model the future Cuban republic and its ideals. While the San Carlos was occasionally plagued by funding issues, the school was one of the more lasting institutions in Cuban Key West and reflected many of the most aspirational aspects of the Cuban independence movement.

The San Carlos also hosted major figures of the Cuban independence movement, some of whom spoke to the Black Cuban experience. One of the San Carlos's most celebrated nights involved the 1885 visit of Antonio Maceo Grajales.[37] Maceo, the multiracial military figure and one of the key leaders of the independence movement, was universally revered by Cuban insurgents.[38] His visit to the San Carlos was centered on various aspects of the independence movement, with the role of Black Cubans raised by several speakers. As one speaker noted, "We who feel pride to belong to that noble race, victims of the cruelty and humiliation of Spanish tyranny, protest with all the fervor of offended dignity."[39]

As the victims of slavery and ongoing marginalization, Cubans of color understood Spanish repression in a distinct manner. The same speaker noted that "we Cubans of color are part of one whole, named Cuba, and in virtue of it, before being a factor that benefited that infamous government that exploited and exploits with cruelty, we are and will be their most bitter enemies."[40]

RECONSTRUCTION-ERA FLORIDA AND MULTIRACIAL KEY WEST

Cubans began to settle in significant numbers in Key West during a period of considerable flux for both Key West and Florida more generally. Only three years removed from the Civil War and a year after the passage of the Reconstruction Acts, the island was undergoing significant shifts in terms of demographics, political representation, and the regional economy.

In Florida and Key West, the possibilities and limits of these changes became evident throughout the 1860s and 1870s. Black officials like Josiah T. Walls, Jonathan C. Gibbs, and William Bradwell became mainstays of Florida's Republican Party, and were leaders of a larger cluster of elected and appointed Black officials in the state. The political successes of many of these Black representatives, including Walls's ascendance to the House of Representatives, would have been inconceivable decades earlier. Similar stories littered this period of Florida's political history. Thomas W. Long and Robert Meacham were both born enslaved, later served in various capacities in Florida politics, and were also instrumental in the expansion of Florida's public schools.[41] These successes were marked by considerable struggles along the way. From the beginning, white Republicans in Florida often opted for more moderate policies and proposals that left Black Republicans on the margins.[42] Moreover, Black Floridians were regularly targeted by the Ku Klux Klan (KKK) and other white supremacists, often suffered voter intimidation and discrimination, and had a litany of rights threatened or questioned, such as the right to bear arms.[43]

While Key West Republicans certainly experienced challenges in incorporating more radical proposals around land and labor reform, the multiracial and multiethnic history of Key West during Reconstruction was a notable departure from much of the rest of the state. While anti-Black violence pervaded large swaths of Northern Florida, Key West's Cuban, African American, and Afro-Bahamian community played a decisive role in the city's politics and were represented in nearly every local office—from the mayoral seat to the city's alderpeople. Even more jarringly, this dominance persisted well into the 1880s, over a decade after the end of Reconstruction and the rise of Democratic control in Florida. This was reflective of the many ways in which these communities shaped the city and the region. Aside from politics, they were ingrained in the city's cultural institutions and charitable efforts. As contemporary observers noted, while Key West was the largest city in Florida, it felt fundamentally apart from the rest of the state and more closely resembled the Caribbean. In a *New York Times* article titled "A Queer Town," one writer was struck by the dominance of Spanish on the island, the "odd lot" of residents from "all qurters [sic] of the globe," and the unique climate and flora of the city.[44]

The activism and discourse over racial equality did not occur in a vacuum in Key West—these were parts of larger discussions over race that were raised by the city's African American and Afro-Bahamian communities before the large-scale arrival of Cuban migrants. The African American community of late nineteenth-century Key West was composed of multigenerational Florida families, freedmen, veterans of the Civil War, and other African Americans who relocated to Key West in the post–Civil War era.[45] Similarly, Black Bahamians planted roots in Key West decades before the Ten Years' War. Although many of the first Bahamians in Key West were white, Black Bahamians defined much of the city's Bahamian growth throughout the nineteenth century. The growth of maritime industries such as salt raking and sponging led to increased numbers of Afro-Bahamians moving to Key West throughout the nineteenth century. By 1868, Black Bahamians were a generation removed from the abolition of slavery on the Bahamian islands. However, inequality and discrimination persisted in the Bahamas, and Black Bahamians increasingly viewed Key West as a city that presented greater access to workers' rights and racial equality.[46] Bahamian politics in Key West were deeply informed by these experiences.

In Key West, African American and Bahamian officials greatly influenced Key West institutions and politics. Born in St. Augustine, Florida, in 1848 and raised in Key West, Nelson English represented the city's Black middle class. Born to a free, property-owning family from St. Augustine, Nelson English was trained as an accountant and became a mainstay of Key West's political life in the late nineteenth century.[47] Both he and his father, James D. English, held public office in Key West—Nelson as postmaster and James as a county commissioner.[48] Robert Gabriel's life was similarly shaped by the opportunities offered during Reconstruction.

FIGURE 1 *Serving in various positions beginning in the 1870s, Robert Gabriel had one of the longest careers among Black officials in Key West. He served on Key West's city council as late as the early 1900s. (Key West Art and Historical Society Collection. Image courtesy of the Florida Keys History Center, Monroe County Public Library, Key West, Florida.)*

Born in Key West in 1854, Gabriel was able to serve in a variety of political positions throughout his career—by the end of his life, he had the distinction of serving in federal, state, and county posts (fig. 1).[49] Similar developments took place in Key West's Bahamian community. William Artrell, an Afro-Bahamian born in 1836, was central to the expansion of Black education in Key West. Trained as an educator in the Bahamas, with previous experience running the Woodcock Foundation schools in Nassau, Artrell moved to Key West in 1870 and served as the first principal of the public Frederick Douglass School in Key West.[50] The Douglass School became a bedrock of Key West's Black community until the 1960s and was a crucial site for bringing together the island's multiethnic Black population.

Along the way, some Black Americans began to make connections between the Black struggle in the Americas and the Cuban independence movement. Born to Louisiana Creole parents, John Willis Menard later moved to Florida during the 1870s.[51] By 1882, Menard was running the *Key West News*, part of a rich array of Black newspapers that were founded in late nineteenth-century Florida.[52] Menard was shaped by several experiences in the Caribbean and bridged discussions between Black equality and Cuba.[53] It was in Key West that he became a supporter of the Cuban independence movement. Indeed, while serving as a customs inspector in Key West in 1884, he was removed from his position under accusations that he was supporting Cuban filibuster expeditions against the Spanish crown.[54] While Menard denied these charges, his support for abolitionist causes in the Caribbean and his poems on Cuba and its future pointed to his clear sympathy for Cuban independence.[55] Similar connections were fictionalized in James Weldon Johnson's *Autobiography of an Ex-Colored Man*, which mirrored several facets of Johnson's life and experience. Johnson, the son of a Bahamian mother and an African American father, was born and raised in Jacksonville, which contained a smaller Cuban cigarmaking community. At one point in the novel, the unnamed multiracial narrator ingratiates himself in the Cuban community and takes up work in a cigar factory, where he notes that "cigar-making is the one trade where the color-line is not drawn."[56] Johnson's narrator learns Spanish and becomes keenly interested in the Cuban independence movement. As the narrator noted when speaking to a Cuban coworker, the Cuban "sat there . . . telling me of the Gomezes, both the white one and the black one, of Maceo and Bandera, he grew positively eloquent."[57] Just as with Menard, Johnson drew parallels between liberation struggles, abolition, and the broader bonds of the Black experience in the Americas. This echoed other national African American movements and organizations that drew active connections to Caribbean struggles and Cuban solidarity movements in particular.[58]

THE CULTURAL AND POLITICAL COALITIONS OF CARIBBEAN KEY WEST

The strongest evidence of the multiracial coalitions that were built in Key West were seen at the ballot box. During the 1870s and 1880s, Key West, and Monroe County more generally, elected a rich panoply of Cuban, Bahamian, and African American representatives. For Bahamian and Cuban immigrants, this was greatly aided by the voting laws of the era. Immigrants who resided in the state for a year could vote in state elections, while only six months of residency were required to vote in local elections.[59] In Reconstruction-era Key West, the Republican Party was dependent on the coalition of Cubans, African Americans, and Bahamians to achieve electoral success, and they became a critical voting bloc that also fielded several candidates for citywide elections.[60] While each ethnic group tended to have their own Republican club, the groups frequently collaborated with one another and boasted a vision of a multiethnic and multiracial Republican Party on the island. In this spirit, the city's Bahamian Republican Club noted in a resolution that "as Republicans we desire and respectfully request the hearty co-operation of all good Republicans irrespective of race, color, religion or birthplace."[61] Black Key West residents not only participated in these efforts but often served as elected representatives. Well over a dozen Black Key West residents were elected into office in the late nineteenth century. These included the Afro-Bahamian Robert W. Butler, who served as county commissioner; Charles R. Adams and the aforementioned William Artrell, both Afro-Bahamians that also served on the city council; and possibly included the Cuban-born José Juan Figueroa, who served as city councilman.[62] Factoring in white Cubans, another dozen or so officials served in posts ranging from county judges to customs officials.[63]

Many of these trends reflected a demographic reality. By 1870, of the 5,657 permanent residents of Monroe County, nearly half were foreign-born.[64] Of the foreign-born population, Cubans made up 42 percent of the city's immigrants, while non-Cuban migrants categorized as being from the "West Indies"[65] made up an additional 40 percent of Monroe County's foreign-born population.[66] By 1880, Monroe County's population had nearly doubled to 10,940 inhabitants, with the county becoming majority immigrant.[67] Similarly, the city's multiethnic Black population rose from 18 percent to 29 percent of the county's population between 1870 and 1880.[68]

One of the most fertile periods for this type of multiracial organizing occurred between 1875 and 1876. These were crucial years in the Reconstruction history of the nation and in Florida. One of the last substantial pieces of legislation to pass during the Radical Reconstruction era was the 1875 Civil Rights Act, which forbade discrimination in various public settings. As South Carolina's Robert B. Elliott noted during the bill's 1874 debate, the bill spoke to a broader reckoning that "American citizenship carries with it every civil and political right which manhood can confer."[69] When the bill passed in March of 1875, a massive celebration took place in Key West. The nature and composition of the crowd spoke to the diverse political allegiances at play in the island city. After a crowd led by the city's Black population gathered at the local courthouse, the group led the first of two marches through Key West. The procession was led by the famed Key West Cornet Band and two flag bearers—one hoisting a United States flag while the other lifted the Cuban flag. They were followed by large clusters of the city's respective ethnic groups, a Douglass School group led by William Artrell, and a young African American girl riding a chariot and dressed as the "goddess of Liberty."[70] Returning to the courthouse, one member of the crowd read the bill aloud before several speakers—spanning a wide sampling of Key West's ethnic communities—spoke regarding the bill's passage.[71] The converging symbols of African American liberation, Cuban independence, Black education, and Republican politics spoke to how Key West's ethnic communities found their struggles bound to one another.

Soon after, the Republican coalition would reshape the city's politics in other ways. Perhaps the largest demonstration of political influence was the election of Carlos Manuel de Céspedes y Céspedes as mayor of Key West in 1875. Céspedes was the son of Carlos Manuel de Céspedes, the Cuban revolutionary that famously began the Ten Years' War with the "Grito de Yara." After Céspedes's Republican candidacy was announced, there were reports of "great excitement" over the nomination and the upcoming election.[72] Céspedes ultimately won the election, reflecting the growing importance of the Cuban vote in Florida's largest city and the broader Republican coalition.[73] For years to come, the Cuban vote was considered essential in local elections. Coupled with the economic importance of the Cuban cigar industry, Cubans became an essential group in Key West's cultural, political, and economic life. More importantly, Céspedes's election, and others like it, charted a path for Cubans to be devoted to the cause of Cuban independence while also being attentive to their adopted home in Key West.

Céspedes's tenure produced a particularly surreal scene that summed up the unique racial and ethnic dynamics of Key West. July 4, 1876, marked the centennial of the United States' independence. Towns across the country planned celebrations to commemorate the event. While celebratory in nature, Fourth of July festivities also revealed a great deal about racial and ethnic politics in a given city.[74] In some parts of post–Civil War Florida, white residents tried to curtail Black participation in Fourth of July festivities.[75] In this way, the holiday sometimes became a reflection on Civil War memory and the ability to claim US identity and rights in public. Key West's celebration was decidedly different from northern parts of the state and firmly reflected the unique dynamics of the Caribbean South. City leaders in Key West planned an entire day's worth of celebrations that consisted of parades, public speeches, and performances. Black Key West residents were represented in various ways alongside Key West's other communities. The night ended with a series of plays performed at the Instituto San Carlos interspersed with speeches made in both English and Spanish.[76] The celebration and the scene were fitting: on the day that the United States celebrated its one-hundredth anniversary, the largest city in Florida, led by a Cuban revolutionary mayor working in concert with a city council composed of Bahamians, Cubans, African Americans, and Anglos, celebrated the US centennial in the halls of an institution that boasted an interracial school and proudly hung a Cuban flag outside of its building.

Cubans and their allies were also willing to use their power to challenge Republican Party officials when they felt their voices were being marginalized. This was a persistent issue throughout Florida during the Reconstruction era. While Black officials became increasingly common throughout the state, the party's leadership structure was still overwhelmingly white.[77] In Key West, Frank N. Wicker was a mainstay of the Republican Party's white leadership, at times serving as the head of Monroe County's Republican Executive Committee.[78] In 1876, Republican officials were preparing to send county representatives to the state convention in Madison, Florida. Traditionally, a mass meeting would have been held to nominate delegates for the convention. When Wicker attempted to buck this trend by asking the city's Republican clubs to send ten representatives to the nominating meeting, many of Key West's Caribbean residents were infuriated. Bahamians and Cubans were organized in distinct Republican societies, and they likely believed that their voices would have been minimized in the nominating convention by diluting the number of members present. Both groups stormed the nominating meeting and demanded to receive greater representation in the nominating process. The group ultimately left to the Instituto San Carlos, created an executive committee that included William Artrell, then mayor Carlos Manuel de Céspedes y Céspedes (fig. 2), and a group of other Republicans that likely included the Afro-Cuban Carlos Borrego, and passed a series of resolutions protesting the county party.[79]

An even larger confrontation occurred with Wicker in 1882 over a state senate seat.[80] Wicker, once again controlling the nominating process, nominated John Jay Philbrick, with the clear majority of Republicans in the district instead favoring George W. Allen, who had previously held the state senate seat.[81] The city's multiracial coalition soon launched a bilingual rally and campaign for George W. Allen's candidacy.[82] Allen, essentially running as a second Republican on the ticket, easily carried

FIGURE 2 *Carlos Manuel de Céspedes y Céspedes was elected mayor of Key West in 1875 as a Republican Party candidate. His election represented the growing importance of Cuban voters in Key West and became one of many electoral positions and appointments that Cubans secured in Reconstruction-era Key West. (Image courtesy of Florida Keys History Center, Monroe County Public Library, Key West, Florida.)*

the election. While a multiethnic coalition placed Allen in office, the *Key of the Gulf* made special notice of the role Cubans played in the election. Noting that Cubans had "contributed to the wealth and prosperity of this island more than any other class," the writer asserted that the election also showed that Cubans "now give fair warning to all, that they will act in a solid body on all occasions where it is their interest to do so."[83]

Key West's social and educational institutions underscored points of interracial collaboration while still promoting many organizations that were specific to ethnic groups in the city. The Instituto San Carlos was one such institution that balanced aims specific to the Cuban community while also catering to Key West's interracial population. The San Carlos school was interracial and was noted for admitting students "of all classes," but its ties to the Cuban revolutionary movement and the Spanish language meant that the school generally catered to Cuban students.[84] However, the San Carlos connected with a broader set of Key West's community in other ways. Politically, the San Carlos sometimes hosted meetings of the Cuban Republican Club as well as broader meetings that brought together the party's multiracial and multiethnic coalitions.[85] Most significantly, the San Carlos's theater bridged many social and racial gaps on the island. Lauded in the city, the San Carlos theater was a cultural center of Key West that housed countless traveling troupes and theater companies as part of the Caribbean entertainment circuit.[86] The San Carlos would continue to be one of the city's main theaters for decades and was one of the most important ways that the Cuban community regularly interacted with other residents of the island.

Another important, and scantly studied, aspect of this community was the interpersonal ties that bonded Cubans, Bahamians, and African Americans. Analyzing census data from the 1870s and 1880s points to the widespread integration of Key West neighborhoods and the sheer volume of interethnic and sometimes interracial relationships. An analysis of the 1880 census shows that of the thirty-one streets that Cubans lived on, twenty-one of them had multiracial populations.[87] Using census data during this period presents a series of unique challenges. Race was ultimately determined by the census taker, but a glance at the 1885 census points to a wide variety of personal connections between Key West's various ethnic and racial groups. The residence at 72 Whitehead Street was occupied by José Lago, a white Cuban; his Afro-Bahamian wife, Elizabeth Lago; and their four Key West–born children and Bahamian mother-in-law.[88] The house at 61 Petronia Street was occupied by Alfred Delgado, categorized as a Black Cuban, and his wife, Margaret Delgado, identified as a Black Bahamian.[89] Some households even point to a diasporic history between Cuban families that previously resided in the Bahamas. The home at 1 Angela Street was headed by the multiracial Guillermo Sorondo, likely the same Guillermo Sorondo that helped found Colegio Unificación in Key West, who lived alongside a range of family members born in both Cuba and the Bahamas.[90] Most marriages on the island remained within the same racial and ethnic group, and interracial marriages were quite rare. Nevertheless, the sheer volume of interethnic relationships and the smaller number of interracial relationships point to the relative tolerance of Key West during this period.

Census data also reflected the interracial and multiethnic composition of cigar factories. In Tampa, Ybor City's cigar factories have long been remembered for their multiethnic work force.[91] However, less attention has been paid to similar dynamics in Key West's factories years before Ybor City's founding. Cigar factories possessed workers with many different specialties and titles, but "cigar maker" was by far the most common title, covering the bulk of cigar rollers on the factory floor. In the 1885 census, 1,760 cigar makers were enumerated, with 21 percent of cigar makers identified as Black or multiracial. Within the category of Black or multiracial workers, 72 percent were Cubans, 20 percent were

Bahamians, and 7 percent were likely African American.⁹² Similar distributions could be seen among stemmers, over 90 percent of whom were women. Stemmers of color made up 20 percent of the work force. While no African American workers were identified, stemmers of color were 74 percent Cuban and 26 percent Bahamian.⁹³ The relatively high numbers of Bahamian cigar workers are in some ways unsurprising. A souring Bahamian economy led many Black Bahamians to move to Key West for the purpose of being hired as cigar workers in the late nineteenth century.⁹⁴ However, the data does reflect some of the limits of nineteenth-century Key West. The more lucrative and prestigious positions in the factory tended to go to white Cubans. Moreover, African Americans were underrepresented in the factories given their overall population. Nevertheless, a substantive percentage of cigar workers belonged to the city's multiethnic Black and multiracial population. Cigarmaking was a skilled trade that provided stable wages for generations of South Florida cigar workers. Given that well-paid, autonomous work was a rarity among Black workers in Florida, this remained a significant development and another source of interethnic collaboration.

ETHNIC TENSIONS, ANGLO KEY WEST, AND THE DEMOCRATIC PARTY

While interethnic collaborations were common during this period, there were still disagreements and discord between Cubans, African Americans, and Afro-Bahamians. During the early 1870s, tensions between African Americans and Black Bahamians—possibly spurred by issues of class and economic competition—occasionally became public.⁹⁵ Similarly, in the late 1870s, the African American alderman Robert Gabriel reportedly made remarks against Bahamian immigrants when discussing a potential plan to improve communications between Key West and the Bahamian islands. The comments drew sharp rebuke from a local newspaper that asserted, "We would very much like to know from the gentleman whose votes sent him to Tallahassee and whose votes gave him a seat in the council chamber, if not the Bahamian majority!"⁹⁶

In the case of schools and religious institutions, some of the separation was also structural. While Cuban Key West had access to the San Carlos school, the Frederick Douglass School became the central educational institution for African Americans and Afro-Bahamians. Founded in the 1870s, the Douglass School went through various iterations and struggles but would continue to be the city's main Black educational institution well into the twentieth century.[97] During Reconstruction, it also served as a meeting place for the Episcopal St. Peter's Parish.[98] The aforementioned William Artrell and John Lewis Menard served as principals during the late nineteenth century.[99] Artrell in particular was closely associated with the school during the 1870s, and he was regarded as one of the city's best and most influential teachers.[100] Religious schools such as St. Francis Xavier's also offered alternatives for Black families on the island.[101] Religious institutions were similarly aligned by race and ethnicity in other ways. As early as 1876, Cubans led by Carlos Manuel de Céspedes y Céspedes and Reverend Juan Baez were attempting to build additional religious services that would specifically cater to Key West's Cuban population.[102] St. Paul's Episcopal Church opened its doors to all members of Key West society, but it offered separate services for Cuban, Anglo, and Black parishioners, with Baez leading the Cuban services.[103]

Fraternal orders became another arena of racial and ethnic separation, with some cases pointing to the role that racism continued to play within the city's ethnic communities. Cuba Lodge No. 15 of the Independent Order of Odd Fellows was led by prominent Cubans on the island such as Carlos Recio and Angel de Loño.[104] These lodges sometimes reflected aspects of white Cuban racism toward Black Cubans in Key West. As Jesse Hoffnung-Garskoff has noted, one Cuban-founded lodge in 1872 "voted to exclude men of color from initiation" and also barred discussions about race.[105] An Abraham Lincoln Masonic Lodge was founded by Black Cubans, although it is unclear if other Black residents were members as well.[106] Similarly, a St. Michael's Lodge of the Grand United Order of Odd Fellows was a likely alternative for the city's Black residents.[107] The Afro-Bahamian educator William Artrell also took part in temperance organizing, which allowed for women's participation but had a more complicated track record of recruiting Black members.[108] Source material on many of these lodges is quite limited. Nevertheless, it does point to the ways in which fraternal orders were often defined around the strictures of ethnicity and race. In the case of the Cuban community in particular, it also underscored how the revolutionary rhetoric of the independence movement sometimes lived alongside aspects of racial separatism that were present within other aspects of daily life.

In addition to these internal divisions, white Key West residents grew wary of the relative growth in political power from the Cuban, Bahamian, and African American coalition. In particular, the validity of Cuban and Bahamian voting rights was questioned at various points. In an 1876 newspaper exchange, two Floridians questioned whether or not recent immigrants in Florida could legally vote. The second respondent clarified that immigrants were eligible to vote in local elections after only six months of residence but also noted that "the idea that foreigners, seeking a temporary refuge on our shores from oppression, should be allowed to control our State, is revolting and antagonistic to every feeling of free and popular government."[109] A similar exchange in a Democratic newspaper took place in 1882 within a broader discussion about whether foreign-born Black residents could become naturalized citizens. As the writer in the *Key West Democrat* snidely noted, "If this be true it would seriously affect the Republican party of this County, since fully half of their voters are naturalized Nassau and Cuban Negroes."[110]

Democratic operatives were especially worried that Cubans would form a permanent and lasting alliance with the Republican Party and Key West's multiethnic coalition. In an 1883 article defending Cuban voters, the *Key of the Gulf* listed the many contributions Cubans had made to Key West and noted that "all they ask is, to become faithful citizens, and to govern themselves as such."[111] In response to this piece, the *Key West Democrat* grew concerned about Cubans voting as a uniform bloc. Given the importance of the Cuban vote and Cuban business on the island, the newspaper was more guarded in addressing the broad Cuban population. Nevertheless, when writing about the possibility of Cubans unifying in their voting, the *Democrat* asserted that the "race issue engenders bad blood and sooner or later leads to clannism, and makes hard and bitter feelings between people, who by every tie on earth should live in peace and harmony."[112] The article also pointed to how Cubans had been welcomed in Key West, asking, "Have they not found wives among the older settlers and the Americans? Who can number the children born to Latin fathers and English speaking mothers, or *vice versa*."[113]

Over time, one of the strongest threats to multiracial unity in Key West was driven by the Democratic Party's attempts to court the Cuban vote. Cuban voters were strongly allied with the Republican Party during this era, but the connection between some Cuban voters and the Democratic Party portended future trends among wealthier Cubans during the Jim Crow era. Much of this began in the 1870s with the founding of the Cuban Democratic Club.[114] Angel de Loño, a local judge and supporter of Cuban independence, became one of the leading voices among Cuban Democrats. For many Cubans, voting with the Democratic Party became one way of voicing dissatisfaction with the national Republican Party when it came to pro–Cuban independence policies. However, the Democratic Party in Florida could not be separated from efforts to violently suppress and disenfranchise Black voters. In 1880, a Democratic "torchlight procession" took place throughout the streets of Key West, at one point clashing with Black Key West residents opposed to the Democratic Party.[115] The Democratic crowd eventually ended at "Delgado's piazza" with de Loño providing one of the evening's speeches. Later commenting on the march, a local Democratic newspaper noted that the upcoming election would be "the full zenith of its glory, a token of a redeemed South and a guarantee of Southern prosperity."[116] The "Redeemer" ideology, deeply tied to Black suppression in the US South, revealed a great deal about the party's aims in Monroe County and throughout the region.

Cuban supporters of the Democratic Party elucidated a great deal about the racial dynamics of the city. It is true that Cubans, regardless of race, were often exoticized as an ethnic and racial other during this period in Key West history. Speaking of the Cuban "race" or of the "Latin race" in the city became a fairly common shorthand among the city's Anglo population.[117] Race in this context was often a confluence of biological markers, ethnicity, and class. However, the racial status of fair-skinned Cubans was especially negotiable, as many wealthier white Cubans were able to intermix with elite Anglo society in the city. The aforementioned note from the *Key West Democrat* writer about "children born to Latin fathers and English speaking mothers" pointed to how intermarriage was already becoming another means of integrating into white society.[118] In regard to party support, some white Cubans were motivated by broader Democratic proposals that backed a more aggressive Cuba policy that would support the Cuban insurrection. However, this was a luxury that Black residents of Key West likely did not have. The bulk of Black Cubans, Afro-Bahamians, and African Americans could hardly afford to support a Democratic Party that was actively dismantling Black rights throughout the state. White Cubans that joined the Democratic Party during this moment were joining a party that was unambiguously tied to anti-Blackness throughout the region.

Additionally, just as in the case of fraternal orders, affiliations with the Democratic Party likely underscored how some white Cubans continued to hold racial prejudices that were replanted in the United States. As Ada Ferrer has shown, while the anti-racist framing of the Cuban independence movement was revolutionary, every major phase of the movement continued to possess elements of anti-Blackness.[119] Elements of this were inevitably seen in Cuban South Florida. Therefore, while aspects of racial separatism became amplified by the end of the nineteenth century via Jim Crow policies, it is also important to emphasize earlier moments where white Cubans attached themselves to movements dismantling Reconstruction and Black rights. Doing so underscores the ways in which the Jim Crow system that was imposed years later had antecedents in Cuban South Florida.

While Democratic officials were often quite cautious about how they depicted Cubans, they were much more brazen in their characterizations of African American officials. John Willis Menard and Robert Gabriel were common targets in the *Key West Democrat*. The newspaper used various racial tropes to demonize both men, referring to Gabriel at one point as an "ill-mannered son of Ethopia [sp]."[120] The *Democrat*, however, was notably more cautious in its approach of Cubans. When it grew worried of accusations that Democrats in the city were antagonistic to Cubans, they published an article in both English and Spanish attempting to assuage Cubans by asserting that Democrats were among the closest allies to the Cuban people.[121] Cuban support to the Republican Party during this period was quite faithful, but the Democratic Party's overtures toward Cubans spoke to ethnic and racial dynamics in the city that would grow more pronounced as Florida's segregationist policies became absolute.

THE HOPE AND REALITY OF 1888

Even with the growth of the Democratic Party in the state, the Reconstruction-era coalition of Key West's Republican Party continued throughout the late 1870s and 1880s. Statewide, Florida Democrats captured control of the governorship and the major legislative bodies by 1876.[122] In much of the state, this meant rolling back many of the gains made during Reconstruction, particularly in regard to Black Americans. While Democrats wielded considerable power in Monroe County during this period, Republicans were still able to be a viable force that continued to elect Black officials. This distinction did not go unnoticed. The African American *New York Age* and its Key West correspondent, L. W. Livingston, noted in a series of 1888 articles that Key West seemed to "hardly . . . remind one of any other town in the United States."[123] In describing the town's confluence of Bahamian Conchs,[124] Cubans, African Americans, and other groups, Livingston noted that "it is impossible to determine where the line begins and where it ends."[125] In specifically looking at the Cuban population that dominated the island, he noted that "the Cubans probably have the same reason for being prejudiced as the Southern whites" but observed that a white Cuban would treat a Black Cuban or African American "with the same respect and civility that he treats a white Cuban gentleman, a white American gentleman or any body [sic] for that matter."[126] While this chapter underscores the complicated politics of some white Cubans during this period, Livingston's remarks do point to the ways in which many white Cubans committed themselves to the multiracial project of democracy in Key West and within the independence movement.

For Livingston, the unique racial and ethnic composition of the city and its power structure made for one of the most radical expressions of multiracial democracy in the American South. A November 1888 article in which he declared Key West the "Freest Town in the South" underscored this particular point.[127] He described the jubilant mood among Key West's multiethnic coalition following various victories in local elections. In particular, Livingston drew attention to the election of two Black officials—James Dean as Monroe County judge and Charles DuPont as Monroe County sheriff. These victories were deeply symbolic and also spoke to the continued power of Black voters and their allies. The judicial and law enforcement systems in Florida, and in the South more generally, had long been the tools of suppressing Black freedom. Indeed, white Redeemers were already using the power of state governments to reassert these norms in the post-Reconstruction South. Within this context, the ascension of Dean and DuPont in 1888 were acts of radical defiance. As Livingston asserted, Black Americans in Key West "act their sentiments, with none to molest or make them afraid."[128] However, Dean's tenure as judge would be one of the final victories of the Caribbean South's multiracial coalitions in Key West. Democrats in power would eventually rewrite the state's constitution, implement a rigid Jim Crow system that permeated the entire state, and specifically target men like Dean.

Nevertheless, the coalitions built by Cubans, African Americans, and Afro-Bahamians during the 1870s and 1880s reflected the unique intersections of the Caribbean South during this period. Informed by international debates over emancipation and civil rights, members of all three communities found common cause in Key West. The timing of this convergence was equally important. Backed by Radical Reconstruction—including changes to naturalization laws that made Black migrants eligible for citizenship in 1870—these multiethnic coalitions were able to use voting and officeholding to their advantage. In the most populous city in Florida, they were able to control significant portions of local government and create a political system that reflected the city's various ethnic groups. In this respect, Key West represented an example of multiracial democracy in practice.

For Cubans, their early history in Key West pointed to the ways in which they continued to take part in independence-era politics while still shaping their new communities. While previous examinations of Cuban Tampa have noted the interracial politics of the independence movement, the example of Key West points to one of the most radical manifestations of these types of collaborations. Key West was fundamentally reshaped in the late 1860s by the mass arrival of Cuban exiles in the city. Once there, they founded a robust cigarmaking industry and launched one of the most important sites of Cuban independence. As Cuban exiles were themselves debating the future of race in Cuba, they established a community in a United States city that was radically revising its own relationship between race and power. Black Cubans in particular asserted their rights and claimed a place in both the independence movement and Key West's political life. From this adopted home, Black and white Cubans debated and modeled what a Cuban republic might be. As was true in the independence movement in Cuba, issues of racism and racial inequity persisted in Key West. Nevertheless, significant numbers of Cuban exiles were able to build a community that was devoted to the cause of Cuban independence while also living up to many of the independence movement's ideals.

· 2 ·

LIBERTY AND LABOR IN CUBAN SOUTH FLORIDA

The life of Francisco Rodríguez Sr. intersected with many essential moments in Cuban and Cuban American history. Born in Cuba's tobacco capital of Pinar del Río in 1888, he moved to Tampa in 1909. Learning of Tampa from cigar lectores in Cuba, he moved to the United States in hopes of greater "progress" and opportunities.[1] Between the period of his birth and his migration to the United States, Cuba and South Florida underwent significant changes. In South Florida, the 1890s represented one of the more vibrant periods of Cuban American life. Rodríguez's birth roughly coincided with the founding of Tampa's Ybor City, the second major Cuban American cigarmaking enclave, which became the multigenerational home of the Rodríguez family. Like Key West, Tampa would become the site of a radicalized working-class town that led some of the most powerful unions in Florida during the 1880s and 1890s. Moreover, Cuban Americans in Key West and Tampa became essential contributors and leaders of the Partido Revolucionario Cubano (PRC), which helped fund and carry out the last war for Cuban independence.

In Cuba during this period, the island insurgency achieved a bittersweet independence. Black Cubans guided and led significant aspects of the Cuban War of Independence, which lasted from 1895 to 1898. They did so as part of a broader fight to secure and build upon essential rights in a new Cuban republic. Rodríguez, who lived in Cuba during the early years of the republic, would have witnessed this firsthand. As he would later assert, "The influence of Black Cubans in the political matters of the island of Cuba has been very large."[2] Nevertheless, post-1898 Cuba struggled to secure the type of independence that a previous generation of Cubans had fought for. On the brink of victory, the United States intervened in the conflict following the explosion of the USS *Maine*. The US government would become a mainstay of Cuban life and politics for decades. Moreover, the economic devastation of the war led some Cubans to migrate away from the island nation, a likely development that informed Rodríguez Sr.'s own decision to migrate.

By the time Rodríguez arrived, however, the interracial democracy and labor organizing that defined the region at the turn of the century had largely dissipated. In the case of the former, Rodríguez played a leading role in La Unión Martí-Maceo, a mutual-aid society organized for Black Cubans. The existence of the organization was a byproduct of Black Cubans being forced out of the larger Círculo Cubano by its white members. The Martí-Maceo name—an acknowledgment of the multiracial coalition that made Cuban independence possible—was also a forceful reminder of how South Florida's exile communities were changing. In the case of labor organizing, many of the most radical South Florida unions that promoted organizing within an interracial framework were attacked by city leaders, dissolved, and replaced by more conservative unions. When later recalling strikes over union recognition in Tampa, Rodríguez asserted flatly that whenever the union was recognized, "the Black [worker] has been discarded . . . Black cigarmakers have never wanted that union."[3]

Understanding the limits of the Cuban independence movement's interracial framing and the active dismantling of South Florida's radical labor movement is critical for understanding race relations in Cuban South Florida at the turn of the century. The intertwined issues of race, independence, and labor created opportunities for collaboration and fissure throughout this period. In the case of the insurgency, Black Cubans were central to nearly every facet of the Cuban independence movement of the 1890s. As soldiers, intellectuals, fundraisers, and workers, Black Cubans asserted their full dignity and place within Cuban identity. Similarly, the 1890s and the period immediately after the Cuban War of Independence produced some of the most effective labor unions in the history of Cuban South Florida. Influenced by socialism and anarchism, South Florida's cigar unions became among the most powerful organizations in the state and supported union locals that organized across race and gender.[4]

However, there were key limits to these gains that became clearer over time. The promises of racial equality were rooted in a vision of a raceless society that limited Black Cubans. Therefore, while their contributions became essential to the war effort, they were overlooked in both Cuba and Cuban American communities following Cuba's conditional independence. Labor remained one of the most effective sites of interracial organizing immediately after 1898. Particularly in Tampa, the creation of La Resistencia—a powerful labor collective—represented one of the most militant periods of South Florida's labor history. However, this too came under threat. These unions soon became ostracized by larger US-based labor federations such as the American Federation of Labor (AFL) and became victims of vigilante violence throughout South Florida. In the process, a particular vision of Cuban American identity was created that stressed US integration, eschewing radicalism, and moving away from active discussions over the role of race in society.

FIGHTING FOR AN EQUAL CUBA

In the period between the Ten Years' War and the Cuban War of Independence, the independence movement changed in a variety of ways. Race, central in many ways to the Ten Years' War, continued to shape the insurgency. Most significantly, the discussion shifted from one that was often centered on abolition to a broader discussion about the place of Black Cubans in the republic. As noted in chapter 1, Key West residents—and Black Cuban residents in particular—had been raising this issue for years. Over time, these ideas grew to be fundamental to the Cuban independence movement on the island as well as in exile centers. Moreover, an increasing number of Cubans began to have concrete discussions about the future of race relations in Cuba and the need to address historical inequities. As Diego Vicente Tejera asserted in an 1897 speech on race in Key West, Cubans would be culpable for allowing racial antagonisms to plague the republic of Cuba if they did not "begin from now to prevent those ills" and discuss issues of race openly.[5] In South Florida, this occurred along two tracks. Black Cubans asserted their own visions of becoming equal partners in the future republic and became ardent supporters of the final push for independence. Black Cubans were far from a monolith in this regard. While they argued for a more equal society, Black Cubans sometimes disagreed over tactics and race-based organizing. The other thread of this discourse in the region was driven by white Cubans, who often posited their vision of a multiracial Cuba. As Francisco Rodríguez Sr. later noted, this period was largely remembered for a "grand fraternity" that existed between Black and white Cubans.[6] However, there were also limits to this racial discourse that were evident at the time and would continue to be a source of tension in the future.

Black Cubans asserted themselves in nearly every facet of the Cuban independence movement in South Florida. Figures such as Joaquín Granados, Margarito Gutiérrez, Paulina Pedroso, Juan Bonilla, Rafael Serra, Emilio Planas, and others were instrumental to the Afro-Cuban community in Tampa and Key West during the late nineteenth century. Their lives also reflected the shifting nature of the Cuban diaspora during this period. Some, such as Planas and Bonilla, came of age in places like Key West and Tampa, while others, such as Serra, lived for a brief time in South Florida before spending much of their life in New York City.[7] Nevertheless, Black Cubans were active members of the central institutions of Cuban South Florida during the late nineteenth century. Rafael Serra served on the board of directors at the San Carlos during his brief stay in Key West.[8] Moreover, figures such as Emilio Planas were educated in the San Carlos school as children.[9] The Liceo Cubano in Tampa became a similar site where Black Cubans such as Julian Gonzalez spoke to local community members.[10] Indeed, both institutions became key sites for discussions surrounding Cuban independence while also addressing slights aimed at Black Cubans. In 1880, for instance, Margarito Gutiérrez played a leading role in organizing a mass meeting at the San Carlos to criticize recent comments made by prominent Spaniards that tried to paint the Cuban Little War—the conflict between the Ten Years' War and the Cuban War of Independence—as a Black uprising aimed at killing off white residents of the island.[11]

The revolutionary press was one of the more active sites of Black Cuban work during the late nineteenth century. Particularly by the 1890s, there were dozens of exile newspapers in Cuban American enclaves. Black Cubans were frequent contributors and creators of said newspapers. Martín Morúa Delgado was one of the most notable Black Cubans in South Florida during this period. While well-known for his later life as a senator in the early Cuban republic, Morúa was an active revolutionary in late 1800s South Florida. His influence on the exile press was pronounced. In 1899, Teófilo Domínguez—who himself founded *El Sport*—published a book of brief biographies related to prominent Afro-Cubans in the United States.[12] The text catalogued the devotion of Black Cubans to the independence movement and listed their many contributions to Cuban American communities.[13] Morúa was a prominent fixture of the book, providing platforms for many of the other Black Cubans profiled in it. Morúa's *El Pueblo* and *La Revista Popular* published the work of Black authors such as Joaquín Granados, Juan Bonilla, Margarito Gutiérrez, and Emilio Planas.[14]

The émigré press actively reported on the central work being accomplished by Black Cubans in Cuba and the broader diaspora. Publications such as *Revista de Cayo Hueso* in Key West published articles and artwork that spoke to the work and legacy of Antonio Maceo, Jesús Rabí, and Juan Gualberto Gómez. A December 1897 issue, for instance, was devoted mostly to the memory of Antonio Maceo one year after his passing. While many articles recounted his military exploits and long history as a leader of the independence movement, Esteban Borrero Echeverria also situated him within the centuries-long battle that Black Cubans had waged against enslavement and colonialism. Borrero noted Maceo's role in inspiring current and future Cubans—including Black Cubans—to support independence. As Borrero noted, Maceo was a "man of color and Cuban at the same time."[15] Similar articles remembered Gualberto Gómez as a "warrior for liberty and human dignity" and spoke of how well he was received in South Florida.[16] While publications like *Revista de Cayo Hueso* would struggle to fully capture it, Black Cubans served at disproportionate rates in the Cuban military, and their exploits were well known in Cuba and the broader diaspora. One drawing in the *Revista* pictured a charging Jesús Rabí with the caption "brilliant charge by the intrepid General Jesús Rabí."[17] Occasionally, Cuban publications were reprinted in South Florida that detailed the work of Black Cubans, such as José Miró's *Muerte del General Maceo*.[18] The admiration Cubans expressed for many Black leaders during the Cuban War of Independence was also noticed by outsiders. One African American soldier in Cuba during the conflict recalled an adoring crowd when Rabí rode in: "It was surprising how the Cubans turned out to do homage to that black Cuban general. It was the best of people who turned out. There was no color line drawn there."[19]

The independence movement also created a series of spaces for Cuban women. While there were definite limits to this type of activism, Cuban women and girls in South Florida participated as fundraisers, orators, writers, and performers and also provided essential goods for the war effort in Cuba. Following the model outlined by the PRC in the 1890s, many Cuban women organized into small groups and devoted themselves to a particular goal. Groups such as Discípulas de Martí, Club

Emilio Nuñez, and many others were founded in the 1890s in Key West and Tampa promoting the cause of Cuban independence.[20] For groups like Discípulas de Martí, this involved fundraising events where proceeds went directly to the insurgency.[21] Moreover, some women's clubs reflected the multiracial vision of Cuban independence. The Key West–based Club Mariana Grajales de Maceo, named after Antonio Maceo's mother, was seen as creating a club without "distinction of classes, categories, or colors."[22] In a nod to a famed José Martí speech in South Florida, one writer asserted in a write-up of the group that "this is Cuba, *with all and for all.*"[23] In Tampa, the Estrella Solitaria club also had a multiracial membership.[24] Founded by Mercedes Dueñas, the club hosted events to support the independence movement and at one point donated $100 a month to the Cuban insurgency.[25]

One of Tampa's best-known Afro-Cuban women during the revolutionary period was Paulina Pedroso (fig. 3). While many details of her early life are unclear, she was born in 1855, likely to enslaved parents in Pinar del Río, Cuba.[26] She moved to Key West in the 1880s, marrying Ruperto Pedroso in 1886 in Monroe County.[27] It was her time in Tampa during the 1890s that cemented her legacy within the independence movement. She helped operate a boardinghouse with her husband, Ruperto Pedroso, and became close friends with José Martí, who would stay with them while in Tampa. As a result, the home often became a meeting place during Martí's visits, which would draw independence leaders such as Ramón Rivero as well as prominent Afro-Cubans such as Joaquín Granados, Emilio Planas, and Cornelio Brito.[28] She was a well-known organizer for events regarding Cuban independence, and Pedroso also served as treasurer and founding member of the Sociedad de Socorros La Caridad, a women's group in Tampa devoted to the insurgency.[29] Over time, she would become one of the more memorable figures of Tampa's Cuban exile community during the independence years. A 1913 *Tampa Tribune* obituary remembered her as "one of Cuba's heroines," while the aforementioned Francisco Rodríguez Sr. noted that people continued to remember her and that "she was a very brave woman who was not scared of anything."[30]

There were also inevitable tensions and disagreements within the independence movement during this period. The memory and importance of Black military service during the Ten Years' War, for instance, was actively debated by white and Black Cubans with the discussion clearly tied to future political rights.[31] There were also tensions over who

FIGURE 3 *Paulina Pedroso was one of the more notable figures in Cuban Tampa. While often remembered for her friendship with José Martí, she was also a well-known organizer in Tampa who reflected the various types of activism that Black Cuban women undertook during the 1890s. (Tony Pizzo Collection. Image courtesy of University of South Florida Special Collections, University of South Florida Libraries, Tampa, Florida.)*

would assume leadership positions within émigré independence groups. Some of this was a byproduct of the ways in which the PRC was organized. One of the most significant achievements of José Martí—one of the leading designers of the PRC—was its ability to cobble together a vast coalition of Cubans with varying interests and backgrounds. However, this also posed key problems in terms of representation. As Lilian Guerra has argued, parts of this coalition were still racist in regard to their views of Black Cubans, and key leadership positions within the PRC were still held by white, wealthy Cubans.[32]

Given that so much of 1890s discourse was centered around the future Cuban republic and how it would function, there were also disagreements over how Black Cubans should organize. One of the most notable disagreements over this was between Martín Morúa Delgado and Juan Gualberto Gómez. Morúa had written passionately about the importance of Black Cubans in the independence struggle and in Cuba going forward. However, he was opposed to organizations that were created to explicitly recruit Black Cubans, such as Gómez's Directorio de Sociedades de la Raza de Color de Cuba.[33] Gómez and other Black

Cuban intellectuals like Serra believed that this type of organizing would be critical to future efforts to secure equal power for Black Cubans.[34] Unsurprisingly, these disagreements would grow more pronounced following 1898 as decisions such as the Platt Amendment and the Morúa Law further splintered some Black leaders. Nevertheless, some of these tensions were quelled under the broader fight for independence during the 1890s.

WHITE CUBANS AND VISIONS OF A "RACELESS SOCIETY"

While the Cuban independence movement of the 1890s centered an interracial coalition as fundamental to the insurgency, Cuban leaders formulated a vision of a "raceless" society that would be interpreted in many different ways.[35] Much of this began with José Martí, the central leader of the Cuban independence movement during the early 1890s. Histories of the Cuban independence era must always wrestle with the legacy of Martí. As Lisandro Pérez recently noted—partially in jest—in his history of nineteenth-century Cuban New York, "There is no ignoring Martí, despite my efforts to do so. . . . To be sure, the man was no demigod, but he combined an unwavering commitment to a cause, one for which he was willing to sacrifice literally everything, with an exceptional talent for communicating and organizing."[36] The poet turned revolutionary became the figure most closely identified with the Cuban independence movement of the 1890s. Living much of his life in exile, with considerable time spent in New York City, Martí was also profoundly connected to the Cuban exile experience.

In November 1891, Martí visited Tampa in a much-anticipated visit.[37] By the late 1880s, Ybor City—a town later incorporated into Tampa—had become the second significant Cuban American enclave in Florida. Founded as a cigar-making town by Vicente Ybor, Ybor City became a hub for the combination of cigarmaking, radical labor organizing, and the revolutionary politics of Cuban independence. The enclave in many respects became an encapsulation of Martí's vision for the future Cuban republic. Rooted in a multiracial community centered on working-class movements, Ybor City became a reflection of the type of egalitarianism he believed to be essential to Cuba. As he noted early in his speech, "I want the first law of our Republic to be the Cuban cult of full dignity for man."[38] Martí's 1891 speech, "With All, for the Good of All," reflected many of the most essential currents in South Florida's Cuban American communities at the turn of the century. In particular, the speech outlined how to bring together the varying constituencies in Cuba around a unified republic. In his vision of a future republic, the full inclusion of Black Cubans would be essential to fostering a true democratic model. Martí's efforts were undoubtedly effective. Moreover, this stance was the byproduct of years of building multiracial coalitions in places like New York City, with Black Cubans playing a central role. As Jesse Hoffnung-Garskof has asserted about Black émigrés in New York, "Men and women in this social world did not just support Martí; they helped to create him."[39]

However, in positing a vision of racial cooperation, many white Cubans stressed ideas of a "raceless" society that sometimes minimized the role of Black Cubans in the long term. The possibilities and limits of this vision were reflected in Martí's own words, particularly when in South Florida. Many of these ideas were embedded within the aforementioned "With All, for the Good of All" Tampa speech in 1891. Among other things, the speech outlined the marginalized groups that would be essential to composing the future Cuban republic. Near the end of the speech, he outlined the ways in which many people mischaracterized the Cuban independence movement, punctuating each section with a cry of "You lie!" In one section on Black Cubans, he wondered, "Must we be afraid of the Cuban who has suffered most from being deprived of his freedom in the country where the blood he shed for it has made him love it too much to be a threat to it? Will we fear the [Black Cuban]—the noble black man, our black brother—who for the sake of the Cubans who died for him has granted eternal pardon to the Cubans who are still mistreating him?"[40]

While Martí acknowledged the role of historic oppression in race relations in Cuba, he also envisioned a society in which race would cease to be a factor. In an 1893 piece titled "My Race," Martí suggested that the concepts of race and racism would weaken under the work of independence and building the republic.[41] Martí went as far as to assert that "an affinity of character is more powerful than an affinity of color" and that "there will never be a race war in Cuba."[42] Scholars have disagreed over how to interpret this essay and his broader framing around race, with some believing that Martí was acknowledging present-day racism while hoping for a future that did not necessitate race-based organizing.[43] However, the concept of a raceless society would be deployed by others in a manner that would ignore or minimize the role of racism in Cuban and Cuban American society. As Danielle Pilar Clealand asserted in thinking about how the concept of racelessness was deployed later on, it was "used politically to . . . inhibit racial divisions and conflict," "move the conversation away from race and racism," and "discourage black activism despite a racially unequal nation."[44]

Diego Vicente Tejera, a writer and Cuban independence supporter in Key West, expressed many of the same ideas in South Florida. Born in Santiago, Cuba, Tejera similarly spent much of his life away from the island in Caracas, New York City, and Key West.[45] In 1897, he delivered a speech on race relations in Key West. Although he rarely invoked the word in his speech, Tejera was largely trying to think about the role of racism, noting how the issue needed to be addressed "before the political struggle is ignited in the future republic."[46] Tejera's conception of race, similar to many nineteenth-century writers, was an amalgam of contemporary understandings of race and ethnicity. Nevertheless, Tejera acknowledged the unique forces that Black Cubans had faced historically and in the present day. Indeed, Tejera underscored the historic role of enslavement, the ideology of white supremacy, and educational inequities.[47] Similar to Martí, he also believed that the independence wars softened racial animosity, noting that "in the forest . . . there are no whites and blacks, but soldiers."[48] He used this point to paint a forceful contrast to the United States and the Jim Crow system, remarking on the "deep and relentless antipathy, the blatant hatred, violent and aggressive, that divides blacks and whites in this land they call the throne of liberty," that was present in the United States.[49]

The potential pitfalls of the racial ideals articulated by white independence leaders in South Florida could also be seen during this earlier period. Some white independence leaders looked to the US model as something to avoid. Martí famously chronicled many aspects of US life while in exile, writing on everything from the Haymarket massacre to lynching. While he admired aspects of the United States, Martí—like other Latin American intellectuals of the period—used these as cautionary tales for thinking about the future of Cuba and Latin America in general. Similarly, Tejera noted the failings of the United States after the Civil War in truly ameliorating race relations in the country.[50] However, this also became a means of absolving issues of racism among white Cubans and in Cuba in general. Indeed, Tejera in the same speech noted that the Cuban community was "more democratic and benevolent" when compared to the US in terms of race relations.[51] Similarly, Tejera sometimes wrote of a need for Black Cubans to acclimate to or mimic white Cuban culture.[52]

Moreover, leaders like Tejera and Martí often spoke of the need to address both white and Black racism, as though they were comparable issues. In one of the only invocations of the word "racism," Tejera pronounced near the end of his speech urging that "to those who dream of impossible dominations, to the racists, to the white racist and the black racist, let us yell:—Back!"[53] Martí similarly asserted that after independence, "the white racist and the [Black] racist will be equally guilty of being racists."[54] Both sentiments ignored how centuries of racial inequality and racism continued to shape Cuban communities. In a similar vein, writer and exile Manuel de la Cruz noted how independence would bring a Cuba where ethnic and racial origins were inconsequential, as "all will be called to show aptitude" and "talents for the position which each one intends to carry out."[55] This sentiment showed a similar disregard for how historical inequalities would persist in the Cuban republic. Instead, white Cubans like de la Cruz promoted systems that reified existing racial inequality under the auspices of a meritocracy.

One of the more telling visions of Cuba's "raceless society" was found in Manuel de la Cruz's *La Revolución Cubana y la raza de color*. Published in Key West in 1895, the pamphlet gave a brief overview of the independence movement, with special attention paid to the role of Black Cubans in the independence fight and as allies in a future Cuban republic. Overall, the pamphlet tried to argue that the multiracial alliance had been critical to creating a lasting independence movement. Early on, de la Cruz openly admitted that white prejudice toward Black Cubans was one of the most significant impediments to independence: "That single fact—the fear of blacks—explains why the island of Cuba did not emancipate itself at the same time as Colombia and Mexico, and why the separatism was not honest, resolute and unanimous until the year 1868."[56] However, the pamphlet is also littered with other forms of prejudice, as he asserted that Black Cubans were more intelligent than other Black Caribbean people and African Americans, mischaracterized aspects of enslavement on the island, and at one point dismissed and demonized the role of Chinese Cubans—some of whom served valiantly for the insurgency during the Cuban independence wars—in the republican project altogether.[57]

As some Black Cubans pointed out, the vision of a raceless society soon became a weapon to silence Black Cubans, both in the United States and in Cuba. Rafael Serra was one of the most notable Black exiles during this period that worked to achieve Cuban independence. Although he spent much of his life in New York City, he also briefly lived in Key West in the 1880s, where he served on the Instituto San Carlos board of directors.[58] Serra was close with Martí and had notable disagreements with the more conservative PRC leadership that replaced him.[59] In the early 1900s, Serra analyzed the ways in which white Cubans continued to create barriers to Black Cubans in the early republic. As he noted in a 1901 article, "The war concluded. The Spaniards and Cubans embrace, the Montoro supporters kiss the Martí supporters, and they leave the blacks almost in the same condition as did the Spanish."[60] Moreover, he noted how white Cubans used the threat of further US intervention to halt racial progress, sarcastically noting that if any disagreement was shown among Cubans, "the *lynching yankees* will return to intervene in the matters of this land, where there is tyranny, but . . . we are all Cubans."[61] Serra illuminated how concepts of unity and peace could be weaponized against Black Cubans seeking equality. For Serra and his supporters, the war for independence was always meant to symbolize a broader push for equality and Black civil rights. The post-1898 period pointed to how many white Cubans developed a fundamentally different interpretation of what the war represented.

LABOR AND THE INDEPENDENCE ERA

If independence became one of the key drivers of social change in Cuban South Florida during the late nineteenth century, labor activism was the other. Cuban independence in Key West and Tampa was inextricably tied to labor and the labor radicalism that became increasingly common in Cuba and South Florida. Cigarmaking became one of the first urbanized industries in Cuba. Its work force, dating back to the mid-1800s, was composed of multiracial labor, with Black Cubans—free and enslaved—working in the industry.[62] It was in Havana cigar factories that many of the first substantive labor cooperatives were formed in the nineteenth century.[63] Unsurprisingly, some of the first labor unions founded in Key West had active ties to Havana organizations, a trend that would continue for years.[64]

The subsequent growth of South Florida's labor unions was the result of matters both practical and ideological. By the 1880s, steamships such as the *Mascotte* and *Olivette* facilitated the easy transfer of goods and people, including cigar workers traveling from Cuba to South Florida on multiple trips every week.[65] United by the steamship routes of the late nineteenth century, Havana, Key West, and Tampa became connected in many ways, and it was not uncommon to encounter cigar workers that had lived in all three cities. The other key development was the growing presence of socialism and anarchism among rank-and-file workers in Cuba and South Florida. In Cuba and in émigré communities, labor organizations during the 1880s were already being directly influenced by radical unions formed in Spain.[66] Broader influences from prominent European intellectuals such as Pierre-Joseph Proudhon and Mikhail Bakunin were already present in Cuban organizing by the late nineteenth century.[67] Over time, Cuban radicals such as Enrique Roig San Martín, Enrique Creci, and Enrique Messonier applied these ideas to Cuban organizations during the 1880s.

Moreover, South Florida Cubans would have been exposed to other prominent socialists and anarchists via other immigrants in the region. Tampa in particular would go on to be defined by its "Latin" community: the Cuban, Spanish, and Italian migrants that defined much of the city's growth at the turn of the century. Given Italy's place as one of the bastions of working-class radicalism during this period, it is unsurprising that migrants brought with them ideas and traditions that expanded on the trends already taking place in Cuban South Florida. In Tampa, members of each ethnic group went on to found their own mutual-aid societies and other community organizations. George E. Pozzetta's examination of Tampa's historic Italian Club library revealed many classic works of socialist and anarchist writings: Mikhail Bakunin, Peter Kropotkin, Luigi Galleani, Errico Malatesta, and many other prominent European radicals lined the shelves of the club's library.[68] The library also held works by Spanish anarchists and other Spanish-language works, pointing to the interethnic collaborations and exchanges that cigar workers made in Tampa.[69]

Labor unions and union activism quickly became a mainstay in Cuban American communities. As early as the 1870s, La Unión de Tabaqueros was founded in Key West by cigar workers wishing to unify workers across the entire factory system.[70] The group's motivations in early strikes would become central to union action for decades: union recognition, better wages, and basic controls over their workplaces and power structures.[71] The force of these types of actions would only grow over time. By the 1880s, Cuban socialists and anarchists were creating organizations such as Alianza Obrera in Cuba that would soon spread to South Florida.[72] One of the hallmarks of organizations like this would be the more "combative approach" that critiqued capital and the manufacturing class.⁷³ In 1885, cigar workers in Key West went on strike, pressing many of the larger factories to temporarily close. Echoing the class conflict of the era, a union posting pressed workers: "Let us wage relentless war on those who have oppressed us and now show us no mercy."⁷⁴ Unsurprisingly, future Key West organizations such as the 1887 Federación Local de Tabaqueros took on a much more radical stance when compared to their 1870s counterparts.⁷⁵

While South Florida's cigar communities were influenced by European currents regarding labor, the labor movement in the region still grew to be distinct in many ways. In particular, the twin discussions of race and independence were deeply woven within South Florida's labor movement. In the case of the former, Black Cubans were essential to the cigar industry in both Key West and Tampa. Moreover, many prominent Black Cubans were active in radical politics and union organizing. The aforementioned Morúa was a proponent of socialism by the 1880s. In an 1884 column, Morúa attempted to assuage Cuban fears of socialism and instead posited that "socialism is a leveling, not of riches, but of the rights of man to procure them, to possess them, to enjoy them. It is not the equality of fortunes, no, it is individual equality to access them."⁷⁶ Moreover, he believed that labor organizing and nationalist endeavors were compatible, as the former would prepare Cubans for a more effective republic.⁷⁷ Similarly, Joaquín Granados was defined by one contemporary as "a tireless defender of the proletariat class—to which he belongs" and was a supporter of the anarchist-influenced Círculo de Trabajadores in Havana and later of Key West's labor organizations during the 1890s.⁷⁸ Guillermo Sorondo, who was active in independence politics as well as Black Cuban organizations, was also active in labor organizing in South Florida. He was an early member of Key West's Unión de Tabaqueros, took a leadership role in the more radical Federacion Local de Tabaqueros during the 1880s, and may have played a founding role in Tampa's Liga Obrera de Trabajadores de Tampa in 1900.⁷⁹ Given the close-knit nature of South Florida's Black Cuban community, many Black Cubans had active ties to other members of the community, which often connected them simultaneously to Black educational networks, independence organizing, and labor unions. Francisco Segura, for instance, was also tied to the Federacion Local de Tabaqueros and wrote about labor in *Revista de Florida*.⁸⁰

To be sure, there were occasional clashes between the radical laborers of the region and nationalists. Enrique Roig San Martín, the most prominent Cuban anarchist during this period, viewed nationalist causes as distractions from the broader necessity for working-class internationalism.[81] In South Florida, there was an additional layer of suspicion because of the role of cigar manufacturers. Many manufacturers, even some Spanish-born owners, were proponents of Cuban independence. However, cigar makers in Key West and Tampa had long argued that some manufacturers stressed Cuban independence and unity as a means of silencing workers and dissuading them from labor activism. In particular, leaders of the independence movement would sometimes attempt to settle disputes between workers and manufacturers during this period. For some workers, they viewed this as a cynical ploy to quiet dissent in favor of the industry that helped fund the insurgency through worker donations. As Gerald Poyo has argued about how many cigar makers viewed this development, "The constant call for moderation and compromise from the nationalist leaders undermined the union's ability to decisively defeat the manufacturers and place their organizations on solid footing."[82] Throughout the 1880s, clashes between the two groups would continue to occur.

Here, again, Martí would prove decisive. In 1893 and 1894, cigar makers in Key West were once again at odds with local manufacturers. Samuel Seidenberg, one of the original Clear Havana manufacturers in Key West, soon decided to import Spanish workers to replace the striking workers of his factory, leading to charges of violating immigration laws regarding contracted labor.[83] Martí became involved in the incident, sending the PRC's lawyer to South Florida to defend the interests of Cuban cigar makers in the area. In an article on the tumult, Martí asserted both the centrality of the Cuban worker in émigré centers like Key West—"built by the poorest, neediest Cubans, along with a wealthy criollo or two"—and the broader role that émigré centers played in modeling the republic.[84] Martí also took the opportunity to highlight how the Cuban enclave differed from other parts of the United States. In thinking about race relations in Key West, he asserted that due to the "natural nobility" of Cubans, there "never was nor could have been anything like the South's barbaric lynchings or the continual murders perpetrated by men in white masks in the Northeast."[85]

Martí's intervention in the strike was part of a broader strategy to place workers as central to the future of Cuba. He had great success in recruiting even some of the most radical workers to the cause of the PRC, such as Enrique Creci, who would ultimately die during the Cuban War of

Independence.⁸⁶ As Frank Fernández has argued, while many anarchists in Cuba continued to be skeptical of the independence cause, radical exiles were much more likely to support Martí and the PRC.⁸⁷ Even after his death in 1895, Martí would continue to hold tremendous influence in South Florida. As one contemporary observed about Ybor City a few years after his death, "Even today his shadow looms over Ibor, and his name is on every lip. His words are quoted constantly. If there is an argument and someone says: He said so-and-so, then the argument is over."⁸⁸

Critical to the success of bridging labor with the cause of independence in South Florida was the role of Black Cubans. Guillermo Sorondo was among the most active exiles in South Florida's labor politics but was also seen as a trusted organizer and leader for the cause of independence.⁸⁹ Other Black leaders had similar histories tied to independence. Joaquín Granados was arrested by the Spanish in 1876 for his revolutionary activity, spurring his eventual exit to South Florida, where he then joined the Vanguardia de Crombet and Ignacio Agramonte clubs.⁹⁰ The aforementioned Pedroso family became another working-class symbol of the independence effort. By continuously staying with the Pedroso family in Tampa, Martí was echoing the idea that working-class people and Black Cubans specifically were essential to the success of the republic and émigré enclaves. Black Cubans, in turn, asserted their own visions of interracial democracy and the future Cuban republic by being active participants in both the labor movement and independence organizing. For Black workers, the labor movement provided one more avenue to class solidarity and the potential for upward mobility.

THE US LABOR MOVEMENT, NATIVISM, AND LA RESISTENCIA

While Cubans arrived in South Florida as exiles, the majority of them remained as immigrants following the conclusion of the Cuban War of Independence. Some Cubans had lived in South Florida for nearly three decades and planted roots with their families in Key West and Tampa. Moreover, the economic devastation brought on by the war led many working-class Cubans to stay given the economic conditions in the region. Additionally, workers like Francisco Rodríguez Sr., whose story started this chapter, were similarly urged to move to South Florida in the early years of the Cuban republic as a result of the same tumult and economic uncertainty. With these factors in play, cigar makers soon dedicated themselves once again to improving their conditions and organizing. During the late 1800s and early 1900s, Cuban Americans organized some of the largest and most forceful labor organizations in the state. Moreover, the unions in question were multiracial by design and represented workers regardless of race, occupation, or gender. These gains were not made without opposition. In addition to a manufacturing class that was increasingly willing to use vigilantism to quell the labor movement, large US-led labor unions also targeted the Cuban-led unions and posited a more business-friendly alternative in the region.

In particular, the Cigar Makers' International Union (CMIU) would go on to form complicated and often fractious relationships with Cuban American workers in South Florida. Affiliated with the AFL the CMIU was one of the largest cigarmaking unions in the United States, with decades of organizing history by the end of the nineteenth century. Given the growing importance of the Clear Havana industry in South Florida, the cigar workers of Key West and Tampa became important potential collaborators for the union. This type of collaboration was not unprecedented in Cuban South Florida. Earlier Cuban labor leaders had sometimes formed relationships with groups like the Knights of Labor.[91] However, by the 1880s, Cuban American workers were joining unions in the mold of Havana organizations influenced by European radicalism. The CMIU began to make increasing overtures toward South Florida workers during the 1890s. After the conclusion of the Cuban War of Independence, the CMIU's official journal reprinted an article that hinted at much of the organization's future strategy. After congratulating Cubans on their thirty-year fight for independence, the writer pivoted to the importance of having "the trade-union take the place of the junta."[92] The writer observed that "it is singular to note that, while all other nationalities have joined our works, the Cuban cigar makers have stood aloof; a few individuals have become members of the Cigar Makers' International Union, with political freedom. The 'junta' will no longer be needed here."[93] The paternalism embedded in this sentiment would reflect the coming years of conflict between the CMIU and Cuban workers.

The most radical manifestation of Cuban American cigar makers was the founding of Tampa's La Resistencia, a labor union that drew much of its strength from the cigar industry but also recruited workers in other fields. By 1900, they boasted a membership of close to five thousand, made up of cigar makers, "shop employees," and bar and restaurant workers.[94] The union's Black workers were also central to the organization. The cigar factory—one of the few institutions that continued to be interracial during the Jim Crow era—stood as a stark contrast to the changes afoot in other parts of the state. One moment that captured this tension was the 1899 Labor Day parade in Tampa. In a period where the US labor movement was still grappling with various forms of internal discrimination, the multiracial group that paraded through the city included a banner that read "Labor Knows No Color, Creed or Class."[95] A report on the parade noted that "young Cuban girls" surrounded a "Queen of Labor" who was described as "dusky."[96] The woman's race and the harmonious message about the labor movement was dissected by local press in Tampa and nearby Clearwater, the latter including openly racist characterizations about Black Tampans.[97] The brief moment reflected the bubbling antagonisms between organized labor in Cuban enclaves and white communities in greater Tampa Bay. Nevertheless, groups like Resistencia honored the decades-long tradition of multiracial organizing within the Cuban American community during the late nineteenth century. Images captured during La Resistencia's 1899 Weight Strike (figs. 4 and 5) attest to the central role that Black Cubans played within the organization.

Over time, conflicts between La Resistencia and the CMIU became more pronounced. By 1900, La Resistencia was openly protesting against "the absorbent spirit" of the CMIU that looked to displace Cuban-led unions.[98] That year, La Resistencia began to protest the presence of CMIU workers in factories and the recently created stemmers' union within the CMIU. Women typically worked as stemmers in cigar factories, and the stemmers' union represented one of the more active branches of La Resistencia. As Resistencia leaders asserted regarding the CMIU stemmers' union: "As the International never had a strippers' annex, they organized them into the American Federation of Labor, a fact opposed to all principles of trades unionism, and to the friendly spirit they should have shown toward the strippers' union already existing and affiliated with La Resistencia."[99] The historically poor record of AFL unions in regard to the recruitment of Black workers and women undoubtedly played a role in La Resistencia's distancing itself from the CMIU. In response, the CMIU increasingly relied on nationalistic, anti-Cuban arguments to position themselves within Tampa. Led by the International Trades and Labor Assembly of Tampa, AFL and other supportive unions launched a sympathy strike around the city for the CMIU.[100] CMIU officials published a statement noting that "the object of the sympathetic strike is

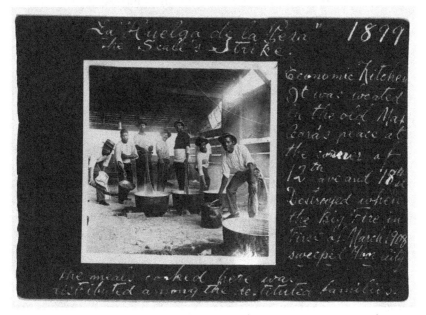

FIGURES 4 AND 5 *One of the earliest actions from La Resistencia was the 1899 Weight (or Scale) strike. These photos, taken by José Ramón Sanfeliz, show striking workers and the soup kitchens that provided food for the families of striking workers. (Tony Pizzo Collection. Image courtesy of University of South Florida Special Collections, University of South Florida Libraries, Tampa, Florida.)*

to demonstrate and educate the Resistencia people of the deep love of liberty and the right to work under American institutions that exist in the hearts of our people."[101] In another CMIU statement, leaders accused the immigrant-led Resistencia of being a "transplanted despotism" and asserted that "the men who are now engaged in striking this blow at American institutions are principally Cubans, for whose liberty America spent $400,000,000 and sacrificed 9,000 lives."[102]

Soon after, Cuban Americans would be subject to the growing trend of vigilantism. Anti-labor violence would dovetail with the racial violence that became increasingly common in South Florida at the turn of the century. As the confrontations between La Resistencia and the CMIU grew more pronounced, business interests in the city began to rally against the Cuban-led union. An early inkling of this activity could be seen in a November 1900 meeting where businesspeople, led by Hugh Macfarlane, gathered to discuss the labor troubles in the city. In articulating what they believed was a threat to the business interests of the city, the group's prepared statement noted that "the rights of each and every man guaranteed him by the constitution and laws of the state, should be protected, whether that man be laborer or manufacturer, and it is the duty of the business men to see that this is done."[103] The CMIU played into these fears by appealing to the business interests in the city and posing as the more palatable labor organization in the region.[104] In one statement, the leaders of the sympathy strike boasted of the "unanimous signed petition of the business people of Tampa" and painted La Resistencia as a "dictator" in the city.[105] Business leaders in the city soon formed a Citizens' Committee that began to take extralegal action against La Resistencia and its workers. Intimidation and forceful deportations of La Resistencia leaders became common tactics. By August 1901, a group of Resistencia leaders were "notified, very positively and unmistakably, that it would be advisable for them to leave the city within twelve hours."[106] The union's secretary, J. G. Padilla, narrowly escaped being captured by taking refuge with local Italian American friends and ultimately fleeing to Havana.[107] Others were not as fortunate. One group of Resistencia leaders was captured and forcibly deported to Honduras.[108] Alejandro Rodríguez, who stepped in as secretary when Padilla fled, was also arrested and taken away under suspicious circumstances.[109] The impunity with which the Citizens' Committee functioned pointed to a broader shift in labor and civil rights in the region.

La Resistencia's women were among the most active and scrutinized members during this period. They were central to the 1900 disputes with the CMIU, holding a mass meeting with its multiethnic membership in Tampa's Liceo Cubano and voting against recognizing the CMIU stemmers' union.[110] The stemmers' union continued to be central to many of the conflicts between Resistencia and the CMIU amid Tampa's vigilante violence. Following the spate of expulsions and arrests, Altagracia Martínez, one of the union's leaders, penned a circular that pleaded with Anglo women to curb the increasing violence in the city.[111] Nevertheless, women leaders also became targets of threats and ridicule. Luz Herrera, the stemmers' union secretary, was singled out for "inflammatory articles" that she published in the union's newspaper.[112] Joking about the wave of vigilante actions, one Jacksonville newspaper suggested that "if Emma Goldman could be deported and Carrie Nation chained, we would only have Luz Herrera of Tampa to cause us to fear any serious blow to liberty."[113] Another article in the Tampa press suggested that Martínez "was advised some days ago that it would be wise for her to cease making excitable speeches."[114]

Ultimately, La Resistencia was crushed by vigilante violence that business leaders in the city supported and sometimes led.[115] While participants in individual vigilante actions were often anonymous, Robert Ingalls has noted that "general descriptions of the group emphasized its elite origins," with the Citizens' Committee in particular "identified with the Tampa business community."[116] Vigilantes eventually raided the offices of La Resistencia's newspaper and soup kitchens.[117] The Citizens' Committee also worked with local police to intimidate and arrest striking workers on vagrancy charges.[118] Support for La Resistencia was held by fellow Cuban cigar makers in Key West, with displaced workers sometimes finding a refuge in the island city and in institutions like the San Carlos that decried the conditions in Tampa.[119] Nevertheless, the extralegal tactics employed against La Resistencia led to the gradual dissolution of the organization and were only expanded in later years.

In one of the more brazen actions of early 1900s Tampa, Francisco Milian was "abducted, beaten, and forced out of town by the Tampa police chief and an unidentified mob under a threat of death if he returned."[120] Milian was a cigar factory lector and the mayor of West Tampa at the time—a strongly Cuban city that would be incorporated into Tampa by 1925. He was targeted during this period due to being perceived as a "radical labor agitator."[121] Milian ultimately returned to Tampa, where a mass meeting decried the vigilante actions. The act was so universally deplored that even some business leaders attended the meeting and decried the abduction as antithetical to the rights of citizenship.[122] Nevertheless, vigilante violence continued to be used in South Florida in the coming years, with labor and race being central causes for its use.

By the early 1900s, two of the fundamental building blocks of Cuban American South Florida—the independence movement and the labor movement—were dissolved or diluted. The PRC structure, which connected exile centers to one another and created spaces to sometimes discuss issues like race, withered. The birth of the Cuban republic also led to an exodus of Black leadership in South Florida as figures such as Paulina Pedroso, Martín Morúa Delgado, and many others returned to Cuba.[123] In terms of the labor movement, the CMIU would go on to be the dominant force in organizing cigar makers in South Florida. Cubans would increasingly join the union, and radical labor politics continued to play a role in Cuban South Florida. However, the tools of worker suppression and vigilantism in particular became common in the region.

More importantly, the absence of the independence movement and a broadly supported radical labor movement dealt a significant blow to two of the most important sites of interracial collaboration in South Florida. Neither movement was the harmonious interracial model that it purported to be. Many aspects of white prejudice remained within the independence movement, but the broad framing of an interracial republic created openings that Black Cubans in South Florida and in Cuba actively occupied. Similarly, hierarchies of race and gender were embedded within aspects of the cigar industry. Women generally occupied lower-wage positions, and Black Cubans struggled to secure some of the more lucrative positions in factories. Even La Resistencia had Black critics such as Guillermo Sorondo, who questioned their tactics in 1901.[124] Nevertheless, the labor movement was similarly being shaped by Black Cuban workers and other laborers who were trying to craft more equitable working-class communities. Without these fundamental mechanisms, the biases and prejudices of the past became much easier to fall back on. For this reason, the South Florida that Francisco Rodríguez Sr. entered was a vastly different space. He migrated to South Florida just as Cuban institutions were formally segregating and La Resistencia was extinguished. Additionally, he entered into a society that was rapidly being shaped by a creeping Jim Crow system that would soon become a central facet of daily life in Cuban South Florida.

· 3 ·
THE SPECTER OF JIM CROW AND THE LIMITS OF INTERRACIAL DEMOCRACY

In October of 1918, the residents of Tampa faced a series of crises. On October 15th, the *Tampa Morning Tribune* reported that "with approximately 700 new cases of influenza developing in the twenty-four hours ending yesterday afternoon, and seven deaths added to the toll of the disease in Tampa, the situation here is becoming more serious and in consequence drastic steps are being taken to curb the spread of sickness."[1] Tampa, like the rest of the world, was grappling with the influenza pandemic of 1918. In Ybor City, this presented a series of challenges. Ybor City was one of the denser areas of the city, and the residents of the neighborhood made up a disproportionate number of cases during this particular wave.[2] Ybor City's signature cigar industry struggled to stay afloat amid the tumult. While the Tampa Board of Health placed requirements on business hours and ventilation in cigar factories, factories were allowed to remain open.[3] However, the sheer rates of illness forced some manufacturers to reconsider. At one point, two entire departments within the famed Sanchez & Haya factory had no healthy employees, leading to a shutdown of the factory.[4]

The manner in which the city dealt with the crisis revealed a great deal about inequality in South Florida. This was true throughout the United States, as the pandemic tended to underscore and exacerbate existing inequities regarding gender, class, and race.[5] In the midst of increasing influenza cases in Tampa, a series of temporary emergency hospitals were created. The Círculo Cubano, the city's largest Cuban mutual-aid society, housed one such hospital in Ybor City. The Círculo Cubano was a reorganized version of the original Club Nacional Cubano founded in 1899.[6] While the Club Nacional was founded as an interracial institution, the Círculo Cubano that was formed in 1902 became a whites-only organization. As a result, San Mateo hospital was created to specifically cater to Black Cubans in Ybor City during the pandemic.[7] Coupled with the Clara Frye Hospital, the two institutions were essential options for Black residents living in a Jim Crow city.[8]

The histories of institutions like the Círculo Cubano and the San Mateo pointed to the ways in which race became a significant dividing line for Cubans during the early 1900s. A significant part of this shift was due to changes happening within Florida and the US South more generally. Dating back to the 1880s, Democratic lawmakers in Florida began to rewrite the state constitution and implement aspects of what would become the Jim Crow system. While these changes did not have an immediate impact in Cuban communities, they became hardened throughout the state during the early 1900s. The brief history of the San Mateo suggested the ways in which Jim Crow segregation led to wholesale changes in daily life. Even in moments of crisis, Black and white Cubans would often navigate these challenges separate from one another.

For Key West and Tampa's Cuban communities, the consequences were stark. While segregated institutions existed in Cuban South Florida during the nineteenth century, a growing list of ethnic clubs, mutual-aid societies, schools, and other essential institutions became segregated during the early 1900s.[9] For Black Cubans, this led to the creation of new, self-sustaining organizations such as Sociedad la Unión Martí-Maceo in Tampa. The Clear Havana cigar industry—one of the most important engines of Florida's economy—was one of the few exceptions. Given its economic importance, cigar factories became one of the few sites where racial segregation did not take place. Nevertheless, life outside the factory became increasingly segregated as Black and white Cubans navigated very different realities in South Florida. This was especially true in the political sphere. The introduction of voter disenfranchisement practices such as poll taxes and the Democratic Party's all-white primary system all but ensured that Black Cubans, African Americans, and Afro-Bahamians were marginalized for decades in South Florida politics.[10]

While many of these racial policies were imposed on South Florida's Cuban communities by Florida's political leaders, changes in Key West and Tampa also reflected significant tensions within the Cuban community. Black Cubans such as Antonio Maceo, Paulina Pedroso, Rafael

Serra, Martín Morúa Delgado, and many others were able to foster a more inclusive vision of the Cuban independence movement, from both exile centers and in Cuba. By the time of the Cuban War of Independence, it was a majority-Black army that led the fight and ultimately secured the end of Spanish colonialism in Cuba. However, the proceeding periods of US occupation and the early Cuban republic did not produce the inclusive vision of Cuba that was promised during the 1890s. Black Cubans were not adequately represented in government, were still routinely discriminated against in workplaces, and were generally treated as second-class citizens. As historian Aline Helg noted about this period, "Cubans were far better at achieving unity against Spain during the War of Independence than at building equality in the new nation."[11]

The racial inequalities that were evident in Cuba were represented in other ways in South Florida. A bifurcated experience developed in South Florida, with race dictating important aspects of political and social power. While Black Cubans were experiencing various forms of disenfranchisement, many white Cubans were still able to play a role in civic life. This was the case for wealthy white Cubans that became associated with the state's Democratic Party. Moreover, Cuban debates over race occasionally spilled over into South Florida. This was especially true in regard to the founding of Cuba's Partido Independiente de Color (PIC / Independent Party of Color) in 1908 and the anti-PIC violence of 1912. Debates over the Partido became common in Key West and Tampa, with Black Cubans often being viewed suspiciously as potential coconspirators. The Partido debates in many ways reflected the impossible position that Black Cubans were placed in during the early twentieth century. In Florida, they increasingly became targets of segregationist policies and voter disenfranchisement. However, they also dealt with the reality that within their own community, white Cubans began to distance themselves from the region's Black Cuban community.

SEGREGATIONIST POLICIES AND THE DEAN CASES

As with much of the American South in the post-Reconstruction period, Florida became increasingly dominated by the Democratic Party. Democrats in the South were motivated by the "Redeemer" ideology that looked to undo many of the social and political achievements made by Black Americans during Reconstruction. Florida was no exception. Democrats recaptured the Florida governorship in 1876, triggering a period of near-total Democratic control for close to a century. By 1885, Florida Democrats proposed a new state constitution that laid out many of the building blocks of the early Jim Crow system. The constitution outlined that Black and white children could not attend the same schools and that interracial marriages between a white resident and a resident of Black heritage "to the fourth generation" would be "hereby forever prohibited."[12] Moreover, it created a path for the state legislature to authorize poll taxes in Florida counties.[13] Coupled with subsequent changes via redistricting and the party primary system, Black participation in voting and officeholding declined precipitously in the late nineteenth century.[14] Democrats argued that the new constitution did not target Black Floridians, but as one historian noted, the 1885 constitution "could well be considered a white supremacy document."[15] When paired with anti-Black legislation in the years that followed, Florida's state government created a multifaceted Jim Crow system.[16]

In 1885, it was unclear how these changes would affect everyday life in Tampa and Key West. The explicit references to white and Black residents in the 1885 constitution were meant to reflect the demographic reality that most of Florida was still centered on African American and Anglo communities. Within this context, Key West and Tampa were notable exceptions due to their large Caribbean populations, which blurred many ethnic and racial lines. The constitution's reference to Black descendance to the "fourth generation" also pointed to the arbitrary nature of policing race and marriage. This would be made even more difficult and uncertain among South Florida's multiracial Cuban populations.

Some of the earliest intersections between Jim Crow laws and South Florida's multiracial communities could be seen in the career of Judge James Dean (fig. 6). As noted at the end of chapter 1, James Dean was elected as Monroe County judge in 1888. He was one of the last publicly elected Black officials before the Jim Crow system marginalized huge swaths of the region's Black population. However, state leaders and local residents soon targeted Dean's tenure as judge. Many of the accusations made against Monroe County judge James Dean were centered on interracial marriage in Key West, especially in relation to the city's Cuban population. In a complaint to Florida's governor, one Monroe County resident asserted that Dean had "issued a license and performed the marriage between one Manuel Gonzalez [sic], a white man and a colored woman."[17] The writer also asserted that Dean signed off on the certificate after another county judge and a county clerk had refused to sanction

FIGURE 6 *James Dean was elected as Monroe County judge in 1888. He was active in Republican politics, and his tenure as judge underscored the clashes between Key West's multiracial population and the state's new segregationist policies. (Image courtesy of Florida Memory, State Library and Archives of Florida, Tallahassee, Florida.)*

the marriage.[18] The truth reflected the more complicated nuances of Key West's multiracial and multiethnic population. While Antonio Gonzales may have passed as a white Cuban, Gonzales himself later submitted that he was of multiracial Cuban heritage.[19] Echoing the broader point, Dean later asserted that a substantive percentage of Key West's Cuban population was multiracial and that many of them merely passed as white.[20] While Dean was being investigated for the charge of malfeasance, a similar case involving Dean and Florida's cohabitation laws also took place in 1889. A "Jose de Jesus Valdes"—who identified as a white Cuban—was arrested under suspicion of violating cohabitation laws by living with a Black woman named Rosa Fletcher. According to the Valdes family, Jose was taken before Judge Dean, who informed him that he would need to identify as Black and marry Fletcher to avoid legal charges.[21] Presented with the choice of identifying as a Black Cuban in Key West or going to prison, Valdes fled to Havana.[22] In response to these and other allegations, Dean was ultimately removed from his position by Governor Francis Fleming.

On August 3, 1889, a crowd of approximately eight hundred Key

West residents protested Dean's removal near the city's courthouse in Jackson Square. According to the *Florida Times-Union*, the Jackson Square protest was led by a "Jose De C. Palemino," who the writer listed as a Black Cuban[23] and was acting as chairman of the group opposed to Dean's ouster.[24] The group voiced their discontent in front of the city courthouse and passed a resolution asserting that they "hereby respectfully protest against the action of the governor of the state of Florida in this matter, and we earnestly request him to revoke said order until the said James Dean has been tried and convicted of said charge by due process of law in a court of competent jurisdiction."[25] The mixed symbols of the 1889 protest—the multiethnic and multiracial Key West crowd, the looming power of the state's Democratic Party, an African American judge, and a city square named after Andrew Jackson—summed up the countervailing forces in South Florida at the time.

The uproar surrounding Dean's tenure as judge pointed to the multiethnic coalitions that made his election possible while also underscoring the white power structures of both the Democratic and Republican Parties. In the case of the former, it was telling that the leader of the Jackson Square protest to support Dean was Cuban. It was the Republican coalition of Cubans, African Americans, Bahamians, and Anglos that made elections like Dean's possible throughout the 1870s and 1880s. As noted in chapter 1, for Black Cubans, African Americans, and Afro-Bahamians, their support of the Republican Party was tied deeply to struggles over the transnational abolition movement and civil rights. However, Dean's removal also pointed to the struggles that lay ahead regarding political power and access to its levers. In the case of the local Republican Party, the incident echoed other cases where white party leaders clashed with Black supporters over control of local politics.[26] Indeed, many Dean supporters believed that key Republican officials aided and welcomed his removal.[27] Pro- and anti-Dean factions persisted for several years afterward in Monroe County's Republican Party. For Democrats, Dean's removal symbolized the general overhaul that state party leaders sought in regard to Black voting and officeholding. In June 1889, an anonymous letter to Key West's *Daily-Equator Democrat* editor criticized Dean and his supporters while asserting that many engaged couples were purposefully marrying in other cities so that a Black judge did not sign their marriage certificate.[28] Implicit in the letter was a sharp disapproval of Black authority figures in Florida. In the years that followed, Democrats continued to use various means to disenfranchise Black voters and regional Black leaders. As the African American *Florida Sentinel* noted, many locals considered Dean's removal not a matter of procedure but "as an outrage perpetrated on [Dean] from mere race prejudice and not for malfeasance in office."[29]

The role of Angel de Loño in the Dean scandal also reflected other aspects of Cuban politics in South Florida. De Loño was a prominent white Cuban judge in Key West who had previously served as a county judge and was chosen to assume Dean's responsibilities after his removal from office.[30] As noted in chapter 1, de Loño showed how some Cubans who were fiercely devoted to Cuban independence could also side with the Democratic Party's post-Reconstruction plans. De Loño's record as a supporter of Cuban independence was unimpeachable. Born in Santiago, Cuba, to a Spanish father, his involvement with the Cuban independence movement reportedly dated back to the Narciso López expeditions.[31] After living in various parts of the United States, he relocated to Key West in the 1870s, where he was actively involved in Democratic Party politics.[32] Democratic officials had tried to recruit Cubans into the party dating back to Reconstruction, with de Loño playing a leading role.[33] While they met only limited success at the time, more Cubans would become affiliated with the Democratic Party as it became the dominant party in Monroe County throughout the 1890s and early 1900s. The appointment of de Loño, a white Cuban, to replace the African American Dean in 1889 underscored how the declining power of African Americans in Key West was not inherently tied to the Cuban experience—particularly for those that aligned themselves with the city's white power structure.

During the late nineteenth century, the Black communities of Key West and Tampa were targeted in several other ways. The state's miscegenation laws continued to be enforced. In 1899, similar charges were filed against Will Harrison and Annie Foy for allegedly marrying as an interracial couple in Key West.[34] Moreover, threats and attacks on Black institutions became more common in both Key West and Tampa. In Key West, multiple attempts were made to burn down the Frederick Douglass School in 1893.[35] In Tampa, a Catholic school for Black students was partially burned down in 1894. An inscription on a nearby tree suggested that the arson was not meant as an attack on the Catholic Church but as a response to the presence of a Black school close to white residents.[36] Perhaps the most notable event involving race relations was the Key West case of Sylvanus Johnson in 1897.[37] Johnson, an African American man in Key West, was accused of raping a local white woman. During

Johnson's court hearing, C. B. Pendleton, a local Democratic leader, reportedly shouted, "Are there enough whites in this building to aid me in lynching this negro brute?"[38] The proclamation led to days of armed confrontations between white crowds and Black Key West residents that stood guard outside of the local jail to prevent Johnson's lynching.[39] After Johnson was convicted of the crime, he was hanged in September in front of a crowd of several thousand onlookers.[40] Johnson's case reflected the growing impulse toward vigilante justice that had been commonplace in other parts of the state for decades but would become increasingly common in South Florida during the early 1900s.

In response, the Black communities of Key West and Tampa looked to one another to weather these changes. In Key West, Black leaders founded the United Republican Club of Monroe County as well as economic efforts such as the Mutual Mercantile Company, which included a leadership group with Charles DuPont and the Afro-Bahamian William Artrell.[41] DuPont would also later play a central role in founding the city's first National Association for the Advancement of Colored People (NAACP) chapter.[42] While Black officials dwindled statewide, there were some exceptional cases in South Florida. Artrell was appointed as Monroe County's internal revenue collector in 1898.[43] DuPont was elected as Monroe County sheriff in 1899 and held the position for four years, while Robert Gabriel served on the city council until the early 1900s.[44] Similarly, Black Tampans were able to hold a few positions of power in Hillsborough County during the late 1800s.[45] One of the more prominent posts held by a Black official occurred in 1895, when Levin Armwood became the county's deputy sheriff.[46] However, collaborations with Cubans—and white Cubans in particular—became increasingly scarce in the public record at the turn of the century as the multiethnic alliances of the 1870s and 1880s began to wane.

These changes also highlighted the diverging trajectories between South Florida and Cuba at a pivotal moment. It was during the era of Radical Reconstruction that Cubans were able to actively build multiracial coalitions, attain political power, and forge multiethnic support for Cuban independence. This was occurring in the 1870s, when this type of organizing would have been unthinkable in colonial Cuba. By the early 1900s, these paths inverted. Cuba would continue to struggle with racial inequality during the early republic, but basic aspects of Black political and educational rights became enshrined in the nation just as Black rights were being dismantled in South Florida.

ELECTORAL POLITICS AND EARLY JIM CROW

In Gilded Age Florida, Cubans continued to be an important force in local politics in South Florida. In 1889, two of the nine commissioners behind a new Key West charter were Cuban.[47] In an 1892 Monroe County election, a "Pompez"—almost certainly José G. Pompez—was the only Republican elected.[48] Cuban control was more pronounced in the Tampa Bay area. This was especially true in West Tampa, which operated as its own city until it was incorporated as part of Tampa in 1925. West Tampa, like Ybor City, was an overwhelmingly Cuban enclave and became one of the larger cities in Florida by the turn of the century. Led by prominent Cubans such as Fernando Figueredo, a significant share of West Tampa's city council members and mayors were of Cuban descent during the late 1800s and early 1900s.[49] Moreover, Democratic and Republican officials continued to lobby for the Cuban vote during the late 1800s. State Republicans continued to depend on historic connections with the Cuban community that had developed for decades while showing support for contemporary issues that were important to local Cubans. Eugene Locke, for instance, was an ardent defender of Cubans and tobacco interests in the state. His support led to a mass meeting at Key West's Instituto San Carlos that thanked Locke for his efforts.[50] However, Democrats also continued to make inroads with the Cuban vote. Democrat and US Senator Wilkinson Call did this through support for Cuban independence efforts during the 1890s. He, too, was honored at the San Carlos while promising his continued support of Cuban independence.[51]

The 1890s also marked an important and decisive period for voting rights in Florida that presented a series of consequences for the Cuban vote. As aforementioned, the 1885 state constitution paved a path for the establishment of poll taxes in Florida (fig. 7). By 1889, the state legislature finalized plans for the poll tax system.[52] One of the earliest considerations of how this would influence the Cuban vote was articulated by the *Florida Times-Union* in reference to Key West. After considering how Cuban voters would approach upcoming elections in 1890, the writer asserted that "the vote, however, will be greatly reduced at the next election, owing to the poll tax."[53] As the writer noted, the deadline to pay the tax had occurred two months before and only one-third of eligible voters had paid the fee.[54]

A concurrent development in voter suppression was the creation of all-white primary systems. In early Jim Crow systems across the US

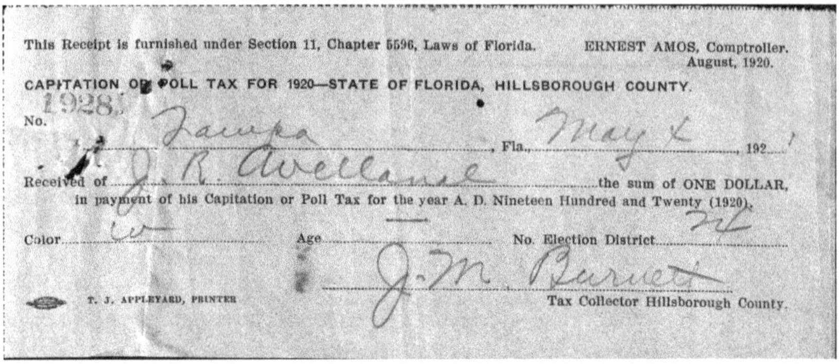

This Receipt is furnished under Section 11, Chapter 5596, Laws of Florida. ERNEST AMOS, Comptroller. August, 1920.

CAPITATION OR POLL TAX FOR 1920—STATE OF FLORIDA, HILLSBOROUGH COUNTY.

No. 1928 Tampa, Fla., May 4 1921

Received of J. R. Avellanal the sum of ONE DOLLAR, in payment of his Capitation or Poll Tax for the year A. D. Nineteen Hundred and Twenty (1920).

Color W Age — No. Election District 32

J. M. Barnett

Tax Collector Hillsborough County.

T. J. APPLEYARD, PRINTER

FIGURE 7 *By the 1890s, poll taxes became commonplace in both Monroe and Hillsborough Counties. Poll taxes became one of several tools that white Floridians used to curb Black and working-class voters. This poll tax also shows how families like the Spanish-Cuban Avellanals were classified as white on poll tax receipts. (José Ramón Avellanal Collection. Image courtesy of University of South Florida Special Collections, University of South Florida Libraries, Tampa, Florida.)*

South, party officials were given a broad ability to determine their own voters for political primaries, allowing Democratic officials to simply refuse Black voters. This was the case in Texas, which became a key battleground for the NAACP and its efforts to overturn the policy from the 1920s through the 1940s.[55] In one legal challenge over the constitutionality of Texas's all-white primary system, lawyers for a Democratic official argued that a "political party, as a private association, had the 'inherent right' to determine the qualifications of its own members."[56] By 1902, Florida's Democratic Party barred Black voters from participation in the party.[57] As one historian noted, given the growing dominance of the Democratic Party, "the candidate that emerged from the Democratic Party Primary became the *de facto* winner of state and local races before votes in the general election were cast."[58] The all-white primary system, coupled with other forms of disenfranchisement, barred a wide swath of Southern voters from the electoral process. One 1896 article on the poll tax and the relative paucity of Tampa voters that paid it noted, "Pay your poll taxes and get your passport to the Democrat paradise."[59] In Tampa, this system was combined with the creation of the White Municipal Party in 1908, which also blocked Black participation in nonpartisan municipal contests.[60] For working-class Cubans and Black Cubans especially, these reforms fundamentally altered their relationship to South Florida's civic institutions. White Cubans of means, however, were not barred from these institutions and continued to play a role in civic life.

Jim Crow policies slowly worked their way into South Florida by the turn of the century. As noted in the earlier sections of this chapter, the 1885 state constitution created initial Jim Crow policies centered on interracial marriage, segregated schooling, and poll taxes. In the years that followed, segregationist practices were implemented into many facets of everyday life. One of the first examples was the use of segregated railcars on public transportation—a phenomenon occurring throughout the region in the early 1900s. In 1904, the Tampa Electric Company attempted to segregate Black and white passengers.[61] However, the Black community vigorously protested the decision, and the company's owner soon repealed the policy before implementing a modified form in certain sections of the city.[62] In early 1905, a statewide proposal on segregated railcars worked its way through the Florida legislature, with Governor Napoleon Broward signing the bill in May.[63] Using partitions, the bill called for streetcar companies to "furnish equal accommodations in separate cars or divisions of cars for white and colored passengers," with violators being charged with a misdemeanor and either a $25 fine or imprisonment.[64] The proposal was broadly backed by white South Floridians, with one Tampa newspaper asserting that the bill was overdue and "both timely and popular."[65]

From the outset, the bill proved controversial and confusing, especially for Black South Floridians. In Key West, Black residents called for a boycott of the railcars in anticipation of the July 1 start of the law.[66] In Tampa, incidents between white and Black riders—some of them violent—continually occurred in the following years.[67] One of the points of contention involved the law's enforcement. The law called on conductors to be racial arbiters in cases where riders were seated in the wrong section.[68] This presented a number of obvious obstacles in South Florida's multiracial communities. As one Tampa writer observed, this job was especially difficult to determine in certain sections of the city, noting one light-skinned Black woman that routinely confused conductors.[69] This task was made even more difficult in Cuban sections of South Florida. As another Tampa article noted early on, "It is going to be a hard matter in this city for the average conductor to discern the complexion of some of our foreign population. Some of the blackest call themselves white while some of the white looking individuals are really colored."[70]

The writer's observation about Jim Crow enforcement underscored the delicate balance that local officials practiced when policing the cigarmaking sections of Tampa and Key West. In general, Jim Crow laws tended to be more relaxed when segregationist laws intersected with the cigar industry—one of the state's economic drivers. The original 1904 Tampa Electric Company proposal did not apply to rail lines in Ybor City and West Tampa.[71] Even an angered white committee that confronted the company over its later plan to repeal the policy noted that it did not wish to see the policy implemented in either of the Cuban hubs.[72] Nevertheless, confrontations over the railcar law occasionally took place in areas like Ybor City as well.[73]

Even with the trolley law selectively enforced, Cubans of color were still clearly seen as second-class citizens under the state's Jim Crow laws. Moreover, when Cubans of color ventured outside of Cuban enclaves, discrimination and slights became glaringly obvious. The public shame associated with these laws was something that many Black Cubans and interracial couples never forgot. Lydia López, remembering her white Asturian grandfather and her Black Cuban grandmother, recalled their first experience with Jim Crow in Palmetto Beach, just outside of Tampa, when a trolley conductor ordered them to be seated in separate sections: "He says . . . 'What is wrong with me sitting back here? I like to sit in the back, and this is my wife sitting next to me.' And [another passenger serving as a translator] says . . . 'she can sit back there but you have to come to the front.' So, he pulled the string that you pull to get off, and he says, 'Let me off right here on this corner. I will never get on a trolley again.' And he didn't."[74] The story, with echoes to the *Plessy v. Ferguson* (1896) case that served as one of the first building blocks of the broader Jim Crow system, pointed to the ways in which Black Cubans became ensnared within the Southern practices of racial separatism.[75]

THE 1898 TURNING POINT AND CUBAN SEGREGATION

While outside forces such as Jim Crow shaped Cuban American communities in South Florida, there were similar divisions occurring within Cuban communities in Tampa and Key West. As noted in chapter 2, the Cuban independence movement—significantly shaped by Black Cubans—accomplished important work in uniting Cuban émigrés across racial and class lines during the 1890s. The Cuban War of Independence, which produced scores of revolutionary groups and charitable organizations, united wide cross-sections of South Florida's Cuban community. However, the period immediately following the war also exposed cracks in these same coalitions. These changes were accelerated by the Jim Crow system and the decline in radical labor unions. However, these factors alone cannot account for the enormous social and political shift that occurred in Cuban enclaves. These trends also reflected broader racial divisions that became apparent in both South Florida and Cuba during the late 1890s and early 1900s.

Much of this tension sprang from a basic fact: Black Cubans, who made up the majority of the revolutionary army during the Cuban War of Independence, sacrificed greatly and did not receive proportional gains in the early Cuban republic.[76] The few accounts from Black soldiers in the twentieth century underscored the complicated relationship that Black Cubans had with the legacy of the independence movement. Many Black Cubans had participated in the Ten Years' War while enslaved. Remembering the Lucumí people who participated in the war, Esteban Montejo noted that "later, when the war was over, they were returned to work, to slavery. That was why they were cynical about the next war. But they fought anyway."[77] As Ada Ferrer has shown, Ricardo Batrell's 1912 autobiography recounted a similar devotion to Cuba that he hoped would serve as a template to the Cuban republic.[78] In recalling the story of a Black soldier that saved a white colonel, he posited that "here was the human reciprocity that all people, nations, and civilized men fight to achieve. As a young man I lived to breathe that purified air of democracy, and so I will never be able to stand idly by and tolerate injustices that threaten the ideal of civilized humanity."[79] The sacrifice of Black soldiers became minimized over time. On recalling the heroics of the Afro-Cuban Quintín Bandera, Montejo noted that "he had many jobs in the republic, but he was never given a good opportunity. The bust that they made of him was abandoned on the docks for many years. The bust of a patriot. That's why people are still riled up. Because of the lack of respect for the true liberators."[80]

Many Black Cubans recalled 1898 as a dividing line where the interracial cooperation of the war became notably weakened afterward during the US occupation and the early republic. Writing about this period, Batrell asserted that "black and white embraced each other, and so together they celebrated victory; and together they fell under the enemy's steel. But at the end of the war, or as soon as victory was certain, it became necessary to ignore or to obscure the heroism and valor of those with dark skin. For white soldiers, it wasn't possible to present blacks as commanding officers to the privileged white families who visited us."[81]

Montejo similarly remembered that soon after the war and during the US occupation, "not even one percent of the police force were blacks because, the Americans claimed, when a black gets power, when he's educated, it hurts the white race. So then they separated the blacks completely. White Cubans kept quiet, they didn't do a thing."[82] This quotation also pointed to the ways in which Cuban and US racism—while distinct and tied to unique histories—sometimes dovetailed in important ways during this period.[83] While some Black Cubans such as Martín Morúa Delgado found posts in the new Cuban government, these were notable exceptions. Paulina Pedroso, one of the more prominent women leaders of South Florida's Cuban independence movement, experienced a postwar reality that many Black Cubans faced. By the early 1900s, she was in ill health and living in poverty in Cuba. Morúa and others in the Cuban government launched an effort to give her a one-time payment for her sacrifices, but her story reflected how quickly many Black leaders were forgotten in Cuba by the early 1900s.[84] As Serafín Portuondo Linares would later document, the post-1898 period pointed to the ways in which the idealism of the independence era was fractured by "republican reality" and that "racial prejudices were exacerbated" during the early republic.[85]

In South Florida, 1898 also served as a dividing line in Cuban enclaves. Shaped in part by Jim Crow, some of the first major changes in South Florida involved the reorientation of Cuban mutual-aid institutions. Mutual-aid societies were the backbone of many immigrant groups in the United States. On the most basic level, they provided members with health insurance and assistance with burials and other essential services. In many cases, mutual-aid societies also educated young immigrants and hosted concerts, speakers, and union meetings. The two most prominent mutual-aid societies for South Florida Cubans were the Instituto San Carlos in Key West and the Círculo Cubano de Tampa. In the early twentieth century, Black participation in both institutions became less pronounced, with Black members outright barred by the Tampa organization. The reorientation of mutual-aid societies marked one of the first admissions from Cubans that South Florida would no longer be immune to the Jim Crow practices of the American South.

In response to segregationist efforts, some Black Cubans began to organize new groups. Black Cuban groups in South Florida had existed during the nineteenth century as well, but the groups founded in the early 1900s were the product of being forced out of existing multiracial groups. As noted in the opening of the chapter, Tampa's Club Nacional Cubano was originally formed as a multiracial mutual-aid society. However, by the time it was rebranded as El Círculo Cubano at the beginning of the twentieth century, Black Cubans were no longer allowed in the group.[86] Merging two organizations, Black Cubans later founded La Unión Martí-Maceo in 1904.[87] Uniting the ideals and symbolism of José Martí and the multiracial Antonio Maceo, La Unión hoped to represent Black Cubans as equal partners in their communities. The name also spoke to the gulf between the ideals of the independence movement and the reality that followed. Francisco Rodríguez Sr., a Black Cuban in Ybor City, recalled that the end of the Cuban War of Independence marked an important turning point for race relations in Tampa. In regard to white and Black Cubans, he noted that afterward, "each one had to form their group separately," as "the whites did not admit blacks in their company."[88]

Other Cuban mutual-aid societies and schools also started to implement segregationist policies at the turn of the century. In the early 1900s, local Cubans in Key West founded Sociedad Cuba as a mutual-aid society and social club. A report on the club noted that "all males of the Caucasian race of whatever nationality, within the ages of 16 and 50 years of age were eligible for membership."[89] Cuban schools underwent similar shifts. With the passage of Florida's 1885 constitution, integrated schools became barred. The shift to segregated schools did not happen immediately in Cuban communities. In West Tampa, the "Sociedad Patriotica Cespedes de West Tampa" had functioned as a multiracial mutual-aid society and school located in Céspedes Hall during the late 1800s.[90] By 1901, Black students in the area were sent to a segregated school.[91]

The Instituto San Carlos in Key West may have challenged this policy longer than any other Cuban American school, with evidence suggesting the possibility of interracial classrooms in the 1910s.[92] Moreover, the broader facilities were still sometimes used by the city's Black population, including for a 1907 Emancipation Proclamation celebration at the San Carlos.[93] The reports of the San Carlos during this period point to the possibility that the institution followed Jim Crow norms in some instances while challenging them in others. However, by the 1920s and 1930s, it seems likely that some segregationist practices were being used in the San Carlos as well. A later report about the institute noted that "classes are conducted from the primary through the seventh grade" and that "the school is open to children of the white race, without tuition charge."[94] Similarly, when the San Carlos was set to debut its new building in 1924, a Cuban beauty contest explicitly required that participants be white.[95] In Key West, there was no Black Cuban organization on the scale of La Unión Martí-Maceo, but there were reports of an Afro-Cuban Unión Cubana that was at least active during the 1910s.[96] These changes represented a marked shift, considering the San Carlos once proclaimed racial equality, housed an interracial school, and invited the likes of Antonio Maceo and José Martí to lecture in its halls.

A 1910s photograph of the Instituto San Carlos (fig. 8) suggests a great deal about the racial dynamics of Cuban South Florida during this period. The image shows a boys' classroom filled with students, a series of maps, two portraits—one possibly of former General Máximo Gómez—and three men who were likely teachers or administrators at the school. Prominently seated in the front row of the class is a Black student. The image is one of the most significant pieces of evidence to underscore that the Instituto San Carlos defied Jim Crow norms in ways that other institutions in Cuban South Florida did not by the early 1900s.

Beyond that, the image poses more questions than answers. It is difficult to discern how many Black students attended the Instituto San Carlos over the course of its history, and there is a possibility that Black students were few and far between. As noted in chapter 1, one of the earliest Black students at the school during the nineteenth century was Emilio Planas.[97] Planas excelled at the school, later attended Florida's Cookman Institute, and wrote for a variety of publications.[98] While the San Carlos's leadership was historically made up of mostly white Cubans, and elements of anti-Blackness certainly existed in Key West during the independence era, it is instructive to think about Planas in comparison to the anonymous Black student in the 1910s photo. The Key West that Planas inhabited was defined by an interracial independence movement and a Republican Party coalition that brought together Cubans, Bahamians, African Americans, and Anglos. While elements of racism and racial separatism existed in Cuban Key West during the 1870s and 1880s, the political and revolutionary institutions of the island were powerful, if imperfect counterweights. Planas may have similarly found himself as one of the only Black students in some San Carlos classrooms, but the world outside those classrooms would have been decidedly different when compared to that of the unidentified student in the photograph. By the 1910s, elements of exclusion and anti-Blackness were firmly embedded within the social and political spheres of both Key West and Tampa and within the

The Specter of Jim Crow and the Limits of Interracial Democracy • 79

FIGURE 8 *The Instituto San Carlos—founded in 1871, with one of Florida's first interracial schools—combated segregationist practices longer than other Cuban institutions during this period. This photograph of the boys' San Carlos classroom was reportedly taken during the early 1900s. (San Carlos Institute Collection. Image courtesy of the Cuban Heritage Collection, University of Miami Libraries, Coral Gables, Florida.)*

Cuban American community itself. Those elements undoubtedly shaped the experiences of the student in the photograph, and also might explain why other Black Cuban parents would opt to have their children educated elsewhere.

The San Carlos photograph also hints at the limits of the type of interracial organizing the San Carlos school represented. Chapter 2 covered the history of La Resistencia, a union that offered a radical example of interracial organizing at the turn of the century. The 1899 Weight Strike in Tampa represented one of the union's most significant actions. Two photographs—included in chapter 2—captured striking workers and the workers that staffed the union's soup kitchens during the strike.[99] As with any photograph, the images both reveal and distort. In a union that was significantly supported and shaped by women's activism, the photos exclusively depict men and boys. Nevertheless, the images offer a vibrant depiction of the interracial work force that buoyed the union before it was actively repressed by city officials and manufacturers. The images also point to the ways in which the San Carlos and La Resistencia provided two different models of interracial organizing. The former provided openings for Black Cubans but still did so under largely white, male leadership. La Resistencia, conversely, was significantly shaped by Black Cubans and women. As a result, their place in the organization could not be marginalized in the same way.

THE CONTRADICTIONS OF RACIAL DEMOCRACY

During the early twentieth century, events in Cuba continued to shape developments in South Florida. The two regions remained closely linked via trade and migration. Cuba at various moments offered either a mirror or a contrast to the Cuban communities of South Florida. In regard to race relations, there were points of similarity and many points of difference. Following the period of US occupation, the early Cuban republic attempted to implement the ideals of racial democracy that guided the independence movement. Scholars of this period have noted the persistent role of racism in shaping the early republic, while some have also noted how Black Cubans were able to use the aspirational goals of racial democracy to their advantage.[100] By comparison, Jim Crow Florida was a far cry from the multiracial democracy of Key West during the late 1800s. Over time, the chasm between the two regions became more noticeable.

Education was one of the areas where the two regions grew more divergent over time. Just as Black Cubans in Cuba were accessing integrated public schooling at much greater rates in the early 1900s, Black Cubans in South Florida found themselves in a segregated system.[101] In 1909, a rare public debate over the discord between Black and white Cubans in Florida underscored the fundamental tension between Cuba's claim to multiracial democracy while Cuban schools in the United States used segregationist policies. Various officials in Cuba had proposed apportioning funds to émigré schools in South Florida. On the pages of *El Diario de Tampa*, a debate ensued between Eliseo Pérez Díaz of *La Lucha* and José A. López of *La Discusión*.[102] Little can be confirmed about López, but this was likely the same Eliseo Pérez Díaz who worked as Tampa's Cuban consul for decades.[103] In the *Diario*, López argued that it would violate the Cuban constitution for Cubans in Florida to receive the funds, given the segregated nature of their schools. Pérez attempted to insist that failing to fund the schools would hurt all Cubans, Black and white alike. López asserted that the schools violated the constitutional principles of Cuba and argued that students would "be taught from the beginning, that they will not only form a standard completely different from those in Cuban schools, but one that is antagonistic."[104] Pérez, in response, argued that local and federal laws in the US necessitated different systems, that the Black Unión Martí-Maceo and white Círculo Cubano had amiable relations in Tampa, and tellingly quoted Booker T. Washington's 1895 "Atlanta Compromise" speech claiming that the "agitation of questions of social equality is the extremist folly, and that progress in the enjoyment of all the privileges that will come to us must be the result of severe and constant struggle rather than of artificial forcing."[105] While uncommon, other Cubans did occasionally note the dissonance in Cuban support for segregated institutions. In 1918, one Tampa local sharply disagreed with the Círculo Cubano's plea for financial assistance from the Cuban government. Among many reasons for taking this position, the writer noted that the Círculo Cubano was not open to all Cubans, as Cubans of color were "completely excluded."[106]

The founding of the Partido Independiente de Color (PIC), and the 1912 violence that targeted the PIC, only accelerated the racial divisions that became increasingly evident in South Florida. Led by Black military veterans such as Pedro Ivonnet and Evaristo Estenoz, the PIC was founded in 1908 as a means of organizing Black Cubans who were dissatisfied with their treatment in the early Cuban republic. Backlash to the group was swift. In addition to its suppression via the Cuban congress, white Cubans in both Cuba and South Florida depicted the PIC as a racist organization that aspired to undermine the existing government. By 1912, the Cuban government targeted the PIC, resulting in the massacre of many of its members and effectively ending the organization.[107] These events were covered closely in South Florida's Cuban enclaves, with racial tensions sometimes spilling over into Key West and Tampa. In South Florida, this period highlighted the precarious position that Black Cubans were placed in and the limits of racial democracy that became even more constricted in Key West and Tampa.

From its founding in 1908, the PIC was subject to fierce criticism in both Cuba and South Florida. While the organization was often criticized as being devoted solely to the progress of Black Cubans, the PIC's founding documents drew on a much broader set of demands.[108] Their 1908 platform combined aspects of labor reform, civil rights, increased educational access for all Cubans, and greater inclusion of Black officials in Cuban government.[109] The PIC's founders attempted to assuage fears during this early period by noting that "the black race has the right to participate in the government of its country not with the objective of governing anybody, but rather with the aim that we should be well governed."[110] Nevertheless, critics—later including the administration of President José Miguel Gómez—labeled the PIC as a racist organization that was antithetical to Cuban values.[111] Drawing on fears of Black revolt that dated back to the colonial era, critics in Cuba and the United States drew constant comparisons to the Haitian Revolution and other racialized tropes.[112] These characterizations were readily adopted in parts of South Florida. When the PIC was formed in 1908, Tampa's *Diario de Tampa* asserted that "the race of color is going to the elections of November 14th organized against whites" while also suggesting fears of a "Black military republic" and a nation similar to Haiti.[113] Similarly, an analysis from another Tampa newspaper warned that if Black Cubans became a uniform voting bloc in the PIC, "it would rule the republic."[114]

Antagonisms against the PIC soon became more pronounced, with a former Key West émigré playing a central role. Martín Morúa Delgado, who had previously served as a South Florida lector and journalist, led the charge against the PIC as a senator in Cuba. While Morúa had a history of calling for the full inclusion of Black Cubans, he viewed any form of race-based organizing as anti-Cuban and in violation of the Cuban constitution.[115] In 1910, the Cuban congress passed a law sponsored by Morúa that forbade political organizations that were centered on a particular race. Known informally as the Morúa Law, the bill was clearly targeted at the PIC's recent founding.[116] The law delegitimized the PIC and spurred mainstream political parties in Cuba to similarly denounce the organization. The law was fiercely criticized by PIC supporters such as the Afro–Puerto Rican Arturo Schomburg. Referring to Morúa as a Cuban "Judas," Schomburg asserted that Black Cubans were seeking rights that they were historically deprived of and noted that the Morúa Law was comparable to the *Dred Scott v. John F. A. Sandford* (1857) case during the period of US slavery.[117] The PIC's leadership called for a repeal of the Morúa Law as tensions between the organization and the Cuban state grew worse. This would ultimately lead to an armed protest by the PIC in 1912 that soon gave way to the state-sponsored killings of its members that same year. During this conflict, the Cuban state targeted the PIC's remaining members, leading to several incidents of outright massacres that included the killing of "noncombatants."[118]

As was true in Cuba, the anti-PIC paranoia used rumor and racist tropes to cast Black Cubans in Florida as potentially traitorous. During the war, Cubans of color were associated with a variety of plots, with the suspicion among Americans and white Cubans veering into the fanatical. One Florida newspaper noted that the Oriente-based uprising had potentially spread to Havana. The Key West newspaper argued that Black Cubans in the city were acting suspiciously and ordering knives at hardware stores at an alarming rate.[119] Similar claims were made in national outlets as well. The *New York Times* reported on suspicions that thousands of Haitians had arrived in Cuba, "inflaming" Black Cuban rebels.[120] Rumors became so widespread in Key West that Black Cubans organized a public meeting to confront claims that they were helping fund the PIC's army. One member of Unión Cubana, a Black Cuban organization, was pressed to bring financial records to prove he was not funneling money to PIC rebels. In a show of solidarity, an unidentified group of white Cubans attended the meeting to defend the reputation of some of the Cubans in question.[121]

In South Florida, the performative politics of denouncing the PIC were similarly echoed. In Tampa, a mass meeting of white and Black Cubans took place in May 1912 to pronounce their support of President José Miguel Gómez against the PIC.[122] Moreover, the Afro-Cuban Unión Martí-Maceo (fig. 9) publicly declared its support for the Cuban government on various occasions—many assured the city's Cuban consul, Rafael Ybor, that they would be willing to go to Cuba to fight against the PIC.[123] Undoubtedly, many Black Cubans in South Florida supported the Cuban government during the 1912 conflict with the PIC. This was the case in Cuba as well, with many significant Afro-Cuban organizations opposing the PIC and Black Cuban legislators supporting a vision of "racial fraternity."[124] Rebecca J. Scott has similarly noted that while some Cubans of color in Cuba may have sympathized with the broad aims of the PIC, many were likely dissuaded from supporting the group due to their own connections to "multiple cross-racial relationships and alliances in the workplace and in their public lives."[125]

However, there was also a profound pressure on Black Cubans to denounce the PIC in public terms. In Cuba, Black Cubans feared being viewed as promoting "antiwhite racism" in supporting the PIC.[126] The mass meeting in Tampa doubled as a political spectacle that was likely to cast suspicion on Black Cubans who did not show up in support of President Gómez. A separate incident that highlighted such tension involved

FIGURE 9 La Unión Martí-Maceo was founded in 1904 in Ybor City. The group functioned as both a mutual-aid society and a social club for Black Cubans. During the 1912 movement against the Partido Independiente de Color (PIC), the group publicly backed the Cuban government in its war against the PIC, showing the complicated politics of how Black Cubans responded to racial debates. Pictured here is the 1917 Board of Directors. (Tony Pizzo Collection. Image courtesy of University of South Florida Special Collections, University of South Florida Libraries, Tampa, Florida.)

Evaristo Alfonso, identified by the Key West Morning Journal as a "loyal mulatto," and Disdiero Sola, "a colored Cuban."[127] The two men were part of an argument that ended with Alfonso shooting Sola in the foot. As the newspaper noted, "The trouble between the two men is a result of the revolution in Cuba and is said to have been brewing for several days. It seems that Alfonso . . . had taken a stand for the administration in Cuba, and was being severely criticized by several of the colored Cuban colony in this city among whom was Sola."[128] The mention of PIC supporters points to the likelihood that the organization spoke to some of the anxieties and inequities that Black Cubans endured in South Florida. The PIC-led *Previsión* had connections to former émigrés such as Key West's Emilio Planas.[129] The Cuban newspaper also hinted at other connections to Black Cuban Tampans, including a note on a group of organized PIC supporters in Tampa.[130] However, the climate of paranoia and violence toward the PIC also underscored the social pressure of keeping such sympathies private or within the Black Cuban community.[131]

These histories again underscore how a critical feature of the Caribbean South was the ways in which ideas of race, nation, and power were transmitted and actively discussed across the region. Debates over educational access, Black organizing, and US-Cuba relations were occurring both within these communities and across the Florida Straits. These moments also highlight how elements of white supremacy were being deployed simultaneously in both the United States and Cuba. In some cases, these processes produced similarities. Social discrimination, barriers to accessing political power, and anti-Black violence pervaded the region. The subsequent founding of KKK chapters during the 1920s and 1930s in both South Florida and Cuba is perhaps one of the starkest reminders of this commonality.[132] However, there were also important differences in relation to governmental structures and constitutional barriers.

The PIC controversy and the Pérez-López debate on education underscored the delicate and sometimes illusory nature of the early republic's ideals. Near the end of the Cuban War of Independence, Black military leaders were routinely castigated or cast aside in favor of white leaders that would be chosen to lead the new government.[133] Nevertheless, after the war, racial democracy became a founding tenet of the Cuban republic. While flawed in practice, Black Cubans were able to use the aspirational claim to demand a place in Cuban politics and culture. Moreover, this also tempered how white Cubans exercised power. As Alejandro de la Fuente has argued, "Regardless of how racist many Cuban whites were, it was difficult for them to translate their anti-black prejudices into openly discriminatory practices."[134] The strongest proponents of racial equality, such as the PIC, were suppressed by the state, but other Black Cubans found various means of attaining power and legitimacy in the early republic. As a result, Black Cubans had a forceful, if limited, moral and political argument for their place in Cuban society.

In South Florida, white Cubans were not beholden to the same standard. By the beginning of the twentieth century, growing racial antagonisms throughout the American South, where Black Americans were viewed as second-class citizens, defined the region. Under this framework, white Cubans were not beholden to the multiracial ideals of the Cuban republic. Moreover, some of the limits of Cuban multiracial democracy became more pronounced in South Florida. A central premise of Cuba's racial democracy was that the independence movement had taken the racial divisions of the colonial period and turned them into something akin to a raceless society. However, this also placed Black Cubans in a precarious position when attempting to address racial inequality. Under this view, Black claims of racial inequities became viewed as racist accusations meant to divide the Cuban community.[135] Rafael Serra, an Afro-Cuban who was well known for his contributions to the Cuban independence movement in New York City, warned that this view reduced interracial democracy to mere symbolism. In a 1901 letter, he impressed upon Black Cubans the need to cease backing a "degrading and ridiculous patriotism" and instead argue for a system that would give Black Cubans true justice and equality.[136] However, these types of demands were harder to mobilize in Jim Crow Florida, and white Cubans did not approach these new injustices with the same rigor that they had previously approached the independence movement.

For Black Cubans in South Florida, these limits were juxtaposed against a Jim Crow system that began to rapidly diminish Black rights during the early twentieth century. These changes resulted in a tacit but substantial split between white and Black Cubans in Key West and Tampa. While they continued to share workplaces, other spaces such as theaters, schools, hospitals, and other essential services became bifurcated along racial lines. For Black Cubans that participated in the Cuban independence movement, these changes were jarring and a far cry from the united ideals of José Martí and Antonio Maceo. Their children would be born into a South Florida where Jim Crow policies were even more rigid and the Black and white Cuban experience would grow more disconnected.

· 4 ·
"TWO CULTURES AT THE SAME TIME"

Blackness and Whiteness in Cuban South Florida

By the 1920s and 1930s, Cuban children in South Florida were being raised in a region that was fundamentally different from that of their migrant parents. Economically, this period represented the last significant era of Florida's Clear Havana Industry. Labor unions in both cities remained active, but they suffered significant defeats on issues ranging from pay to the use of the lector. The continued decline in union power greatly weakened one of the most important sites of interethnic collaboration. Moreover, the Great Depression and the rise of the mass-produced cigarette led to sharp declines in cigar consumption. While cigarmaking would continue to play an important role in both cities, the industry no longer provided the same degree of security and prosperity that two generations of Cuban Americans had enjoyed. Moreover, the racial disparities that in the early twentieth century had become increasingly clear were cemented by the 1920s. Nearly every facet of daily life was in some way shaped by the Jim Crow system that dominated Florida and the rest of the American South. In addition to the legal structures of Jim Crow that dated back to the 1880s, the rise of vigilante justice and white supremacy groups invaded Cuban South Florida. During the 1920s, Ku Klux Klan (KKK) chapters once again began to appear throughout the United States. The resurgent Klan had a solidified presence in South Florida by the 1920s and was yet another reminder of how far the region had changed, dating back to the multiracial alliances of Key West's Reconstruction period.

As South Florida's Cuban communities became increasingly splintered along racial lines, Black and white Cubans began to develop distinct identities in Key West and Tampa. In the case of the former, many Black Cubans continued to project an image of middle-class respectability in their communities and in organizations like Tampa's La Unión Martí-Maceo. However, they also grew to have much stronger relationships with South Florida's African American communities. Some of this shift was by force, while some of it was the product of concerted choices from both communities. Jim Crow practices brought the two groups together in everyday interactions. Segregated schools, day care facilities, theaters, and hospitals became common sites of collaboration out of sheer necessity. However, over time, Black Cubans—and the younger generation that was often born and raised in the US—began to interact with African Americans in more meaningful ways as they developed friendships, marriages, and collaboration in a wide variety of organizations. These shifts took time. They also required younger Black Cubans to forge a new identity, drawing from their own Cuban heritage as well as from the African American communities that they were raised alongside. This phenomenon led to a different form of "twoness" that placed young Afro-Cubans as actively taking part in both Cuban and African American culture.

White Cubans began to foster a new identity that placed them at fundamental odds with South Florida's Black Cubans. The intensification of Democratic Party rule in South Florida led even more white Cubans to participate in the party. However, doing so also placed them in line with the Party's broader aims during this period to implement hardened racial lines that marginalized Black Floridians throughout the state. Moreover, just as with Black Cubans, segregated institutions brought white Cubans and Anglos closer in a variety of different ways. Schools such as the Instituto San Carlos became less stable as a new generation of white Cubans increasingly attended white public schools that ingratiated them with Key West and Tampa's Anglo communities. White Cubans soon began to articulate a similar "inbetween" position that placed them between Cuban culture and South Florida's dominant Anglo community.[1] While acknowledging their fundamental difference as Cubans and "Latins," they also began to stress the commonalities of shared European ancestry and the common goals sought between Cuban and Anglo communities in the region. In the process, white Cubans often erased or minimized their historic relationships with Black Cubans in the region as they claimed a unique form of whiteness in Key West and Tampa.

BLACK CUBANS: "TWO CULTURES AT THE SAME TIME"

During the 1920s and 1930s, a new generation of young Cubans grew up, with no memories of the nineteenth-century independence era. If the early pressures of Jim Crow during the 1900s were abrupt, by the 1920s they became normalized. For young Cubans, the segregation of social spaces became a central facet of their youth. Movie theaters, tennis courts, pools, and other recreational settings followed strict Jim Crow laws and shaped their social lives. Evelio Grillo, who grew up in Ybor City, recalled that "I always felt strange when I passed the Cuban movie theater. I could not attend it. But some cousins who were light enough to 'pass' attended the movie house weekly."[2] The restrictions were demoralizing for Cubans of color and persisted until the local and national civil rights challenges of the 1950s and 1960s. In West Tampa, Armando Mendez—who attended the neighborhood A. L. Cuesta School in the 1920s—recalled the story of Crecencio Arenas, a Black Cuban youth who "found it necessary to walk more than a mile to school in [the] 1920s, despite living less than a block from the all-white Cuesta school."[3] Residents like Sylvia Griñan experienced considerable difficulty in explaining Jim Crow segregation to her children. She later noted, "When we couldn't sit at the lunch counters to eat and couldn't go to the white theaters, I was constantly lying to my kids so they wouldn't feel inferior."[4]

During the early twentieth century, Black Cubans began to adopt identities that accommodated aspects of their ethnic heritage while also growing closer to African American peers and institutions. As Jim Crow discrimination became entrenched, Black Cubans were pressed into relationships with African Americans. There were definite obstacles in this transition. Black Cubans viewed themselves as fundamentally different from African Americans, with unique histories and cultural characteristics. However, the realities of United States discrimination led to cooperation and personal relationships among the two communities. As Francisco Rodríguez Jr. would later note when thinking about his upbringing in Tampa during this period, "I think the two most prominent influences in my life is the fact that I am a black Latin. That means a whole lot because I lived in two cultures at the same time."[5]

Over time, limited access to schools, hospitals, and other essential services brought African Americans and Cubans of color closer together. This was especially true in regard to education in both Key West and Tampa, where white schools received nearly three times the funding of Black schools.[6] Black Cubans were originally wary of interethnic schools.

During a 1908 meeting of La Union Martí-Maceo, a proposal to support a school that would educate both Black Cubans and African Americans was soundly rejected.[7] However, schools that educated children of both communities became increasingly commonplace. In Ybor City, St. Peter's Claver Elementary School and the Helping Hand Day Nursery were instrumental in bringing together African American and Cuban families. St. Peter's served as a multiethnic institution, dating back to the early 1900s. Similarly, the Helping Hand Day Nursery was founded in 1925 in an effort to provide a respite for working women of color.[8] These institutions spoke to broader networks of female activism revolving around groups like La Unión Martí-Maceo, the Tampa Urban League, and various religious groups. The Tampa Urban League's Helping Hand Day Nursery served as a space where women like Clara Alston and Bernice Palomares built connections between the two communities.[9]

Blanche Armwood Beatty served as one of the most crucial activists that brought African Americans and Black Cubans together in Tampa. Both of her parents were born to early Black Tampa families, and her father, Levin Armwood Jr., became the first Black police officer in the city. Blanche was part of the first graduating class at St. Peter's Claver Elementary School and went on to complete her studies at Spelman Seminary—the forerunner to Spelman College—at the age of sixteen.[10] Upon returning to Tampa, she became associated with nearly every major civic and political organization devoted to Black life in the city. Between her work and charity, she was associated with the Tampa Urban League, the NAACP, the Helping Hand Day Nursery, and the Hillsborough County public school system. As the supervisor of Black schools in Hillsborough County, she played an essential role in founding Booker T. Washington High School, the only public high school available to African Americans and Black Cubans in Tampa. In recognition of her importance to the broader Black community in the city, La Unión Martí-Maceo, which had voted against interethnic schools in 1908, named Armwood an honorary member in 1923 and held a ceremony for her in the club's hall (fig. 10).[11]

In Key West, similar educational networks tied together the city's multiethnic Black community. There, a mix of Cubans of color, African Americans, and Afro-Bahamians united under the few educational institutions available to Black residents of the island. Private religious institutions like the Catholic St. Francis Xavier's School for boys and St. Joseph's School for girls had provided instruction to Black students since the late

FIGURE 10 *Blanche Armwood Beatty was an activist central to the fight for Black education and civil rights in Tampa. In recognition of her efforts, La Unión Martí-Maceo made her an honorary member in 1923 and awarded her this certificate. (Armwood Family Papers. Image courtesy of University of South Florida Special Collections, University of South Florida Libraries, Tampa, Florida.)*

nineteenth century. The Frederick Douglass School, however, provided a public alternative. At Douglass, a true mix of Key West's Black working-class population made up the student body. This can be seen in one of the school's most notable alumni, Theodore "Fats" Navarro. Born to a mother of Bahamian descent and a father of Cuban heritage, the famed jazz trumpeter's family provides a portrait of Key West's multiethnic Black community during the 1920s.[12] In a previous generation, Navarro may have used the status of his father's ethnic background to attend the Instituto San Carlos. However, by the twentieth century, children like Navarro were funneled into institutions like the Douglass School alongside African Americans. Navarro soon gravitated toward African American culture and the emerging bebop scene. After graduating from Douglass, he became a traveling musician and ultimately landed in New

York, playing with the likes of Dexter Gordon and Howard McGhee. While Navarro represents an exceptional case, his story points to the cultural intermingling that resulted from Jim Crow segregation.

Jim Crow laws ultimately fostered fruitful, albeit, complicated relationships between African Americans and Cubans of color. This was true in South Florida and other spaces that linked African Americans and Afro-Cubans during this period.[13] As writers like Grillo have noted, profound differences existed between African Americans and Black Cubans. Religion, customs, and language served as a frequent barrier between the two sides, which frequently viewed each other with suspicion. However, "other realities—such as play, school, work, friendships, love, sex, and marriage—bonded young black Cubans to black Americans."[14] While few records remain from Booker T. Washington High School, the annual *Excelsior* yearbooks and accompanying class rolls point to the intermingling that Grillo outlined. In the 1926 copy of *Excelsior*, class president Edward Morales is listed as dating fellow senior Helen Wilson.[15] Isabel Alyce Noriega, the 1928 associate editor of *Excelsior*, is listed on the senior superlative page alongside George Morris as the school's "Oldest Couple."[16] These types of essential connections persisted in the school's committees, school bands, and parent-teacher associations.

In Key West, women's work and activism was similarly critical in stitching together African Americans, Black Cubans, and Afro-Bahamians. Ellen Sanchez of the Afro-Bahamian Welters family was the daughter of Frank Welters, one of the founders of the prominent Welters Cornet Band. Sanchez continued the family's musical tradition and was a beloved kindergarten and piano teacher in Key West for decades.[17] Among her many initiatives, Sanchez also led the "Island City Choral Singers," which reflected the city's multiethnic Black community—the group included the aforementioned Fats Navarro when he was a child.[18] Another notable example was Grace Palacios. Grace was the daughter of Nelson English, one of the most prominent African Americans in the city, who had previously served as Key West postmaster during the 1880s. Palacios was an educator and active in a wide variety of community efforts ranging from fundraising for the NAACP to Red Cross volunteering.[19] Palacios also played a leadership role in a local women's group named The Terpsichorean Circle.[20]

Palacios was also active in working with the city's Black immigrant community. During the 1930s, Palacios was responsible for teaching naturalization classes to the city's Black population. In 1935, Palacios was awarded a Florida Emergency Relief Administration (FERA) scholarship to undergo additional summer training at Florida A&M College in Tallahassee for her educational work with immigrants.[21] Similarly, in 1940, a representative of the Justice Department's Alien Registration Department arrived in Key West and met with a multiethnic group of residents regarding "intimate subjects connected with naturalization and registration with interested persons."[22] This was likely in response to the recent passage of the 1940 Smith Act, which targeted foreign-born people tied to radical politics.[23] Palacios was one of the meeting's attendees and likely represented the interests of Key West's Black immigrant community. As will be discussed later in this chapter, a significant share of South Florida's Americanization work was done by Anglo women, with much of the funding and labor directed toward the region's white immigrant population. Palacios stood as one of the few examples of Black representation among this movement in the region.

VISIBILITY, DISCRIMINATION, AND POLITICS

During this period, Black Cubans continued to have relationships with white Cubans, but they were often stilted and limited. They continued to labor alongside one another in cigar factories and in labor unions. Both communities also sometimes came together in yearly rituals and special celebrations that became common throughout Cuban South Florida. In both Key West and Tampa, yearly celebrations of the "Grito de Yara" and the "Grito de Baire" were common, with the Cuban government often sending delegations to commemorate the historic role of émigré communities in the independence movement. However, even these occasional moments of union were tinged by Jim Crow realities and the growing distance between the two groups. In Tampa, when the Círculo Cubano asked for representatives from Martí-Maceo, Black Cubans were unsure how to respond. As one member recalled, "Many of them [Martí-Maceo members] didn't want to go. They'd say [to me], 'You go 'cause you're the lightest one and you can go.' The dark ones didn't want to go."[24] A similar dynamic took root in Key West. In 1924, in anticipation of the Grito de Yara celebrations and the debut of the new Instituto San Carlos building, Black Cubans requested that the San Carlos's Board of Directors assist them with providing music for their celebration of the event.[25]

The minutes of the meeting note a cordiality between the two groups but also make clear how both were operating in fundamentally different spheres of Key West society by the 1920s.

Another barrier facing interracial organizing was the rise in vigilante violence. As noted in chapter 2, extralegal violence had been previously used as a means of controlling the labor movement and immigrant organizers during the early 1900s. However, by the 1920s, there was an expansion of racial violence in the region. Part of this rise was attributable to local KKK chapters in South Florida, which targeted residents for a wide variety of reasons. In 1921, a KKK chapter was formed in Key West.[26] Petitioners from the original charter—including members of the "Porter" and "Harris" families—underscored how the group was spearheaded by members that included some of the most influential families on the island.[27] In the greater Tampa area, KKK organizing was also active. In 1923, a motorcade composed of several hundred Klansmen drove through parts of Tampa that included Ybor City and West Tampa.[28] Later in 1923, three separate men—including the Black business owner Andrew Williams and El Pasaje restaurant's Enrique Rosa—were abducted and beaten.[29] All three men were given letters that were signed in Spanish as "Que Que Que," read phonetically as KKK. The letters hinted at the possibility that the attacks were related to prohibition and alleged violators of federal liquor laws.[30] Describing another target of the Klan's ire, one Cuban remembered KKK incursions as also being tied to efforts to suppress labor organizing in Ybor City and other parts of Florida.[31]

However, the most notable act of vigilante violence during this period was tied to the racial politics of South Florida and interracial relationships. Manuel Cabeza was a Key West resident of Canary Island descent, known locally as Isleño. He was a World War I veteran and the owner of a local coffee shop on the island.[32] According to a friend of Cabeza's, he was in a relationship with a local Black woman known colloquially as "Rosita Negra."[33] In 1921, Cabeza was abducted by a group of hooded men who tarred and feathered him because of his relationship with a Black woman.[34] During the attack, Cabeza was able to remove the hoods from several of the men. Days later, Cabeza spotted one of his alleged attackers—Samuel Decker, a manager of a local cigar factory—then shot and killed him on the streets of Key West.[35] Following a shoot-out with local police, Cabeza was arrested and placed in a jail, where he was protected by local Marines. However, later that night, the Marines withdrew and a crowd stormed the jail. Cabeza was beaten, dragged from the back of a car through Key West, and shot multiple times before being publicly hung.[36] The audacity of the murder, for which no one was arrested, spoke to the impunity that many vigilantes operated with during this period. As the writers of the aforementioned "Que Que Que" letters asserted, "If the officers can not [sic] handle you we can and WILL."[37]

In general, public displays of white and Black solidarity were rare by the 1920s and 1930s. Within the Cuban community, Cuban national celebrations and public actions orchestrated by labor unions were occasional sites of interracial activity, but they were far from common. During the late nineteenth century, moments such as the passage of the 1875 Civil Rights Act and the celebration of the US centennial drew significant public gatherings in Key West's interracial community, with white and Black Cubans playing a prominent role.[38] However, these forms of public solidarity were not seen in South Florida by the early twentieth century. In Tampa, January 1 celebrations of Emancipation Day—when the Emancipation Proclamation went into effect—continued to be celebrated during the early and middle twentieth century. In 1915, for instance, Black Tampans held a public parade that ended at the local courthouse.[39] Over time, these celebrations were led by the St. Paul African Methodist Episcopal Church and tended to be more private. The St. Paul celebrations drew on a wide range of regional speakers while also working with members of local institutions such as Booker T. Washington High School.[40] While explicit mentions of Black Cubans do not appear regarding these celebrations, it is likely that some Black Cubans began to attend these types of festivities as the Afro-Cuban and African American communities drew nearer to one another.

Other celebrations also reflected the broader decline in Black political and social power in South Florida. One of the few public acknowledgments of Black contributions to Key West occurred in the 1930s when Nelson English Athletic Field was founded in a predominately Black section of Key West.[41] Named after the influential Black Key West resident who served as assistant postmaster and postmaster during the 1870s and 1880s, the park was in many ways also a celebration of the English family and their many contributions to Key West. Indeed, the previously mentioned Grace Palacios was one of the speakers at the 1934 dedication ceremony.[42] However, even this celebration was a reflection of the era's racial divides. The park was intended for the city's Black residents and was in part led by the New Deal–era Federal Emergency Relief

Administration. Jefferson Browne, a white local who served in various public offices during his life and authored an early history of Key West, played an important role in the park's name. Browne knew the English family, dating back to his childhood, and worked with Nelson English when he was postmaster and English was assistant postmaster. As a result, Browne suggested the name to a FERA administrator and he also played a role in diverting funds for the field's playground.[43] In the glowing letter that recommended the park be named after the English family, Browne recounted his history with the family and their unique role in Key West history. However, the letter also revealed the city's power dynamics in the Jim Crow era. At one point, Browne asserted that "except for the color of their skins, James English and his son Nelson were white men. During the four years that I held the office of Postmaster, I never once had to criticize, correct, admonish or complain of anything about him. His conscientious sense of duty was most remarkable and unusual."[44] While the park celebrated a prominent Black Key West family, it was also a reminder of the absence of Black public officials by the 1930s and the relative lack of political power the city's Black population held at the time.

Voting and local politics became another key barrier for Black South Floridians and a similar issue that splintered Cubans along racial lines. The Democratic Party's stranglehold on state politics already marginalized Black participation in Florida politics. The Republican Party, which was the bastion of Black politics and most Cuban American politics in the late nineteenth century, won few victories in the early twentieth century. Moreover, Florida's poll tax system disenfranchised a wide swath of South Florida's Black and working-class populations. One key way of examining this trend is to look at "qualified voter" records, which were sometimes made public. In 1923, the *Key West Citizen* published a list of the city's qualified voters—a classification that almost certainly would have excluded voters that did not meet requirements such as the poll tax.[45] The list included resident names as well as their race. Broken into six precincts, the voter list first points to the marked residential segregation that had already taken root in Key West by the 1920s. As noted in table 1, Precincts 1 and 6—which contained 891 qualified voters— included only 7 Black voters. Moreover, the voter rolls generally point to the disproportionate disenfranchisement of Black voters. In the 1920 census, Black Monroe County residents made up 22 percent of the overall population.[46] In the 1923 voter rolls, they made up only 6.8 percent of qualified voters in Key West. Conversely, white residents made up 77.7

Table 1. 1923 Qualified Voters in Key West, FL—3,489 Total

	Precinct 1	Precinct 2	Precinct 3	Precinct 4	Precinct 5	Precinct 6
All voters	522	948	403	777	470	369
All white voters	518	924	364	655	422	366
White voters with Spanish surnames	43	87	59	97	200	48
All Black voters	4	24	39	122	48	3
Black voters with Spanish surnames	0	2	5	14	4	1

As this analysis is partly centered on surnames, it offers only a rough approximation of voting rights and Cuban voters. Nevertheless, it offers one way of analyzing the relationship between race, ethnicity, and voting during this period. Source: *Key West Citizen*, November 3, 1923. Florida Keys History Center at the Monroe County Public Library. "Key West Qualified Voters 1923 and 1930" Binder.

percent of Monroe County's population in the 1920 census.[47] In the 1923 list of qualified voters, white voters accounted for 93.1 percent of voters.

The 1923 voter rolls also point to the unique role that Cuban voters would have played in the civic life of Key West. Quantifying the number of Cuban voters is difficult given the limited nature of the published voter data. Using Spanish surnames as a baseline metric presents a number of complications. Women voters and intermarriage, misspellings in names, and the sheer variety of Spanish surnames—both common and obscure—can lead to distortions in either direction when analyzing potential Cuban voters. Moreover, the presence of Spanish immigrants in the city—while less pronounced in Key West when compared to Tampa—presents another obstacle. Nevertheless, the use of Spanish surnames presents one of the only quantifiable means of approximating the influence of Cuban voters on Key West politics. Relative to overall qualified voters, white voters with Spanish surnames represented 15.3 percent of voters in 1923. Black voters with Spanish surnames represented decidedly less influence. Only 26 Black qualified voters with Spanish surnames were counted in 1923, representing 10.8 percent of the city's overall Black voters. As other scholars have noted, Black voters and Spanish-speaking communities in South Florida were less likely to be engaged with local politics due to factors ranging from voter disenfranchisement to low rates of naturalization.[48] Nevertheless, white Cuban voters remained an influential voting bloc, and white Cuban politicians continued to serve in elected roles and via appointments throughout this period. Conversely, Black Cuban voters would have faced the obstacles of voter disenfranchisement and the Democratic Party–controlled system in Florida.

WHITE CUBANS AND BECOMING CUBAN AMERICANS

White Cubans moved along a decidedly different trajectory during the early twentieth century. Politically, they remained an influential voting bloc that continued to exert influence in both immigrant enclaves and county-wide contests. While white Cubans could not replicate their political success during the Reconstruction era—exemplified by Carlos Manuel de Céspedes y Céspedes being elected mayor in 1875—they continued to be courted by major political parties and were able to secure various appointments and elected positions in Key West and Tampa. Socially, they drew nearer to European immigrants and South Florida's Anglo community. These connections were born out of shared educational institutions, intermarriage, business ventures, and local governance. This was especially true in Tampa, where the city's Cuban, Spanish, and Italian residents became collectively known as the city's "Latin" population. While technically inclusive of Black Cubans, the term was often used as a shorthand for the city's white immigrant community, as Black Cubans were rarely included in collaborative efforts. Over time, light-skinned Cubans began to assert a particular definition of Cuban American whiteness that was rooted in integration into US society, collaborations with other white residents, and relationships with Black Cubans that rarely extended beyond the workplace.

For many white Cuban children, their exposure to US integration and South Florida's Anglo community began with education. Even among schools founded by Cubans, a concerted effort began to be made to provide students with the skills to assimilate into American society. The San Carlos Institute in Key West, for instance, began to offer both English- and Spanish-language instruction. As one report on the San Carlos noted, its students "are taught to be good *Cuban Americans*—to become Americanized and yet to maintain their cultural identity as Cubans and Spanish-speaking people."[49] Stronger claims around assimilation were articulated in other institutions, particularly those run by religious groups. The Wolff Mission School in Ybor City and the Ruth Hargrove Institute in Key West were two similar examples. The Hargrove

Institute, where one-third of students were Cuban, noted that "these people bring with them the customs, mental attitudes, and religion of their own country: But when they have come in touch with our home mission schools, they have taken back a vision of a larger life for their own people."[50] Statements such as these must be read critically, as immigrant communities often used religious schools and services according to their own needs.[51] Nevertheless, these types of institutions spoke to the range of interactions that white Cubans had with local Anglo society. In the public schools, similar dynamics could be seen in institutions like Key West's Russell School that boasted student rolls with Anglo American and Cuban children.

The general shift to segregated schools by the early 1900s meant that the interethnic schools of white South Florida led to greater bonds being formed among Anglo and Cuban students. This could be seen in public institutions such as Key West High School. With the possible exception of multiracial students that passed as white, the school was an otherwise white institution during the early twentieth century. The school's *The Conch* yearbooks point to familiarity and friendships between white Cuban Americans and Anglo Americans. This was especially evident in the yearly "Last Will and Testament," where graduating seniors humorously bequeathed "gifts" to other students. In the 1937 edition, Manuel Lopez bestowed to Frank Johnson "my destructive Latin features, and my resemblance to a Spanish Cabellero [sic]."[52] In the 1936 *Conch*, Isidore Rodriguez and Frank Fernandez left to Jack Key their "enviable black, wavy hair . . . being assured of a luxuriant and perpetual growth."[53] These humorous asides certainly indicated difference among the city's Spanish-speaking population—they were exotic "others" with assumed characteristics, and likely faced slights for these differences. Moreover, working-class white Cubans were still more likely to live in immigrant neighborhoods that had smaller Anglo populations. Nevertheless, schools such as Key West High School also reflected the incorporation of white Cubans into South Florida's white institutions as they became peers, friends, and partners with the region's Anglo population.

Connections to the Anglo community were especially common among prominent white Cubans and Spaniards in South Florida. Wealthier Cubans often lived in non-Cuban areas, married into Anglo American families, and joined segregated organizations. Carlos Recio's family serves as one example. Recio was born in Puerto Principe and arrived in Key West in 1872. A man of humble origins, he went on to found a successful grocery business. He was a Mason, an Odd Fellow, and a member of St. Paul's Episcopal Church. Recio and his wife, Emeline, had three daughters: Emelina Teresa, Estella Rebecca, and Herminia. Respectively, they married John Alexander Hayes, Policarp Artman, and Joseph Lancelot Lester.[54] The institutional affiliations and intermarrying trends seen in the Recio family were common in other elite white Cuban and Spanish families. The Havana-born cigar manufacturer Jorge R. Leon married the Alabaman Frances Moragues and was affiliated with the Masons and Elks in Tampa.[55] Martin Caraballo, who was born in Mexico to Cuban parents, moved to Tampa as a toddler. He later became a lawyer in Tampa after attending law school at Washington and Lee University, married Stella B. Deisher, and was a Mason and a Shriner.[56] Many other prominent white Cubans married Cuban or Spanish partners, but the trend of fraternal orders, which for decades had often been segregated, largely held true. Other notable white Cubans such as Rafael Henriquez, Juan Carbonell, Joseph F. Uhrback, and Joseph M. Renedo belonged to organizations such as the Golden Eagles, Elks, Knights of Pythias, Knights of Columbus, Caballeros de la Luz, and the Scottish Rite.[57]

Politics and the Democratic Party continued to be another link that brought together white Cubans and local Anglos. As noted in chapter 3, the poll tax and the all-white party system of the Democratic Party led to widespread disenfranchisement of working-class voters and Black voters specifically. However, many prominent Democratic politicians actively welcomed and encouraged white Cubans and Spaniards to participate in local politics. Democratic leaders found it especially important to form partnerships with prominent members of both groups as a means of forming political and economic ties. Indeed, one of the architects of Tampa's White Municipal Party, D. B. McKay, married into the prominent Spanish Gutierrez family. As one scholar noted regarding McKay's marriage to Aurora Gutierrez, this "broadened his civic and social ties to include part of the Latin community."[58] The Democratic Party was especially active in recruiting Cuban voters and even Cuban candidates. The aforementioned Martin Caraballo was an active member of the Democratic Party, serving as a presidential elector on two occasions.[59] Richard D. Morales, a Havana-born attorney in Tampa, was similarly active in Democratic circles and was at one time a Democratic candidate for a Hillsborough County judgeship.[60] In 1920, Oscar Ayala successfully won a county commissioner seat in Hillsborough County as the Democratic nominee.[61] Similar developments were found in Key West. J. R. Valdez, whose party affiliation was not publicly listed, served as a city council member during the 1910s in the city's Fifth District.[62] While it is unclear if he was of Spanish or Cuban descent, the Key West–born Arthur Gomez ran as a Democratic primary candidate for Monroe County representative in 1918.[63] Gomez later served as a state senator and as a judge in the Eleventh Circuit during the 1930s.[64] While most notable Cubans during this period were affiliated with the Democratic Party, some maintained allegiances to the Republican Party. Andrew L. Lopez of Key West, for instance, served as a US marshall and was affiliated with the Republican Party.[65] Nevertheless, the growing number of prominent white Cubans affiliated with the Democratic Party became another important means of connecting them to Anglo officials throughout South Florida.

Influential white Cubans also provided a means of limiting attacks against other white Cubans in South Florida. Working-class white Cubans were also victims of discrimination and bigotry in the region.[66] However, influential white Cubans served as a check on these types of attacks. In 1915, a resort in the Tampa Bay area posted a "Cubans Not Admitted" sign outside of its establishment. The sign produced an uproar in Tampa, with Cuban consul Rafael Ybor filing a complaint to the State Department, arguing that the sign violated the constitutional rights of Cubans.[67] The manager of the resort reportedly noted that men like Ybor were welcome at the club and that the sign was largely intended for the "lower class, the riff-raff" and as a means of excluding an "objectional element" from the resort.[68] The manager also promised that the sign would not go up again in the future. Pointing to the relationship between white Anglos and Cubans, Ybor later asserted that "such a discrimination, if allowed to go on unchecked, might lead to ill-feeling between the American and Latin races and a prejudice that does not exist and I hope never will exist between the two principal parts of Tampa's white population."[69] A similar incident occurred in 1908, when a performer at the Pathé Theater made offensive remarks regarding Ybor City's residents. After many locals expressed their indignation, the theater's management offered an apology for the comments and assured locals that the performer would no longer be hosted at the venue.[70] Incidents such as these pointed to the ways in which white working-class Cubans—and other white "Latins"—could be discriminated against in institutions and everyday encounters. However, both incidents also underscored the social power that white Cubans continued to hold in the region. This influence was buoyed by prominent white Cubans in Key West and Tampa that were essential to the regional economy and regional politics. As noted in Ybor's remarks, much of this was rooted in a shared concept of whiteness in South Florida.

LATIN WHITENESS AND AMERICANIZATION

In Tampa, white Cubans also grew increasingly close to the city's European immigrants. Analyzing this shift points to the ways in which Cuban whiteness was a process, defined by individual choices made in reaction to a deeply racialized region and a fluid understanding of white identity during this period.[71] During the late nineteenth and early twentieth centuries, an influx of Spanish and Italian immigration diversified traditionally Cuban enclaves such as Ybor City.[72] Combined, these groups made up the core of the city's "Latin" population. All three groups worked in Tampa's cigar factories, and although they had their respective mutual-aid societies, a great deal of camaraderie existed between the Círculo Cubano, L'Unione Italiana, El Centro Español, and the Centro Asturiano. White Cubans offered similar support to L'Unione Italiana and their events were regularly advertised in Ybor City's Cuban newspapers. Black Cubans were almost completely barred from this degree of cooperation. The very concept of "Latin" was sometimes used by Cubans as a means of appealing to whiteness and European roots. While the *Latin* label technically included all Cubans, the term was generally invoked to speak of Tampa's Spanish, Italian, and white Cuban population. The term, rooted in an amorphous concept of peoples springing from the formerly Latin speaking world, inherently privileged Europe.

While white Cubans readily acknowledged their differences to local Anglos, some also used the label's broad nature to speak to a shared European heritage. As previously noted, Oscar Ayala ran as a Democratic Party nominee for a county commissioner seat in Tampa's Hillsborough County in 1920. In the lead-up to both the Democratic primary election and the general election, some of Ayala's opponents tried to demean him as a result of his Latin heritage.[73] These attacks were largely aimed at Hillsborough County voters outside of Tampa. In response, Ayala penned an article in the *Tampa Sunday Tribune* in anticipation of the general election, where he analyzed the concept of the Latin population and their contributions to Tampa. Ayala first noted the contributions of French, Spanish, and Italian people in US history before mentioning the many contributions that Tampa's Latin population had made to the city's economy and the country's World War I effort. He also noted at different points that "all the different branches of the Caucassian [sic] race have made this the greatest republic of history" and that Latin people were "one of the oldest branches of the Caucasian race."[74]

Ayala's framing pointed to one of the more forceful ways that some Cubans attempted to assert a US-based identity rooted in whiteness. During the early twentieth century, it was not uncommon for "in-between" ethnic groups to claim "Caucasian" heritage as a means of trying to acquire the full rights of US citizenship. Notable cases such as *Takao Ozawa v. United States* (1922) and *United States v. Bhagat Singh Thind* (1923) marked two unsuccessful attempts regarding naturalization.[75] Other ethnic groups claimed a similar form of whiteness. The Mexican American–led League of United Latin American Citizens (LULAC) argued in a piece decrying anti-Mexican discrimination that "Latin Americans, or so-called 'Mexicans,' are Caucasian or white."[76] While scholars like Cynthia Orozco have cautioned against understanding LULAC largely through the prism of whiteness, it does point to a type of racial discourse that some people of Latin American descent employed in the US.[77] Ayala similarly attempted to argue for this broad reading of "Caucasians" and white identity. Tellingly, at no point did Ayala make reference to Black Cubans in his analysis of Latin communities. In Ayala's interpretation, Latin Tampa was defined by its ties to Europe and the various waves of European migrants that had shaped the United States. Days after his article was published, Ayala won the county commissioner seat.[78] His campaign spoke to both the real animus that many white Floridians had for Tampa's Latin population while also showing the power that many white Cubans continued to wield during the Jim Crow era.

Ayala's letter was indicative of a broader whitening of Latin Tampa during the 1920s and 1930s. The omission of Black Cubans in depictions of Ybor City were especially common when it came to discussions about economic expansion or tourism. In a 1921 special edition of the *Tampa Sunday Tribune* that was largely dedicated to Ybor City, the city's economic expansion was one of the central points of discussion. The issue announced the newly created Ybor City Businessmen's Association—led by prominent Latin and Anglo businessmen—that was designed to spur additional growth to the "city within a city."[79] Even when discussing Ybor City's cultural institutions, one writer noted and described every major ethnic institution with the exception of La Unión Martí-Maceo.[80] The same writer assured readers that while the city's Latin community was distinct, it was also acclimating to US culture. According to the writer, assimilation via schooling, the English language, and even baseball brought Ybor's Latin community "into the American class of 100 per cent."[81] Going forward, city leaders looked to accentuate the unique nature of Latin culture in a highly curated way that was attractive to investors and tourists. In 1938, the Ybor City Chamber of Commerce led an effort to decorate Ybor City in a way that played up the Latin heritage of the neighborhood during the tourist season. Ben Davis, the Chamber's president, noted that he wished to "make the Latin section of Tampa look Latin."[82] Davis's assertion pointed to the stereotypical way in which many Floridians viewed Cuban, Spanish, and Italian culture. However, events like these and the annual Latin American festival during the 1930s made almost no mention of the neighborhood's Black population. Planning committees for the Latin-American Festival solicited the participation of nearly every major ethnic and civic organization in the city, with the exception of Black organizations.[83] Given the public nature of these events, it is very likely that Black Cubans participated, but they played no visible role in the planning or representation of Latin culture during these celebrations.

A concurrent development in the articulation of Cuban American whiteness was the explicit attempt by Anglo groups and some Cubans to "Americanize" the Cuban community. Efforts around Americanization grew popular throughout the country during World War I and the early 1920s. For some immigrant communities, this became a crucial period where some ethnic groups began to make stronger overtures toward acquiring US citizenship, identifying as American and sometimes claiming whiteness.[84] In the case of Cuban Americans, these efforts came from within the community as well as from outside Anglo-led groups that stressed the importance of assimilation. During the 1920s and 1930s, groups ranging from the Works Progress Administration (WPA) to women's clubs to county public schools played a role in trying to press Cubans to become active, English-speaking citizens in South Florida.[85] In Tampa, one local proponent of Americanization defined it simply as "that training and education which makes a foreign born an American."[86] In practice in South Florida, these efforts largely focused on naturalization, English-language instruction, a basic knowledge of civics, and a patriotism rooted in eschewing more radical strains of politics.

Americanization efforts were often driven by Anglo leaders that proposed a version of Americanization driven by naturalization but also specific US values. In 1924, an Americanization class with sixty students was a collaborative effort between Hillsborough County's board of public instruction and the Círculo Cubano, which housed the class. Bringing together residents from a variety of ethnic groups, the class was largely geared toward guiding foreign-born residents through the naturalization process.[87] In 1935, the WPA began to plan adult education classes to "be conducted in citizenship and Americanization" and a range of other subjects.[88] While Black Cubans were not alluded to in these plans, the committee chair behind the WPA planning noted that classes for Black Tampans would also be made available depending on sufficient interest.[89]

However, other efforts toward Americanization had a more prescriptive view of US identity and values. During a 1921 Fourth of July celebration in Tampa, a YMCA-led event was held with a range of multiethnic speakers that lectured on the importance of the holiday and Americanization efforts. Then mayor Charles Brown was one of the speakers and directed many of his remarks to the city's Latin population, which he repeatedly referred to as the city's "Spanish people." While acknowledging their many contributions, Brown also urged local Latins to "lay hold of the weak ones of your nationality and any others that fail to measure up to American standards."[90] In referring to the violence between striking workers and local police in Chicago in 1886 and labor radicalism more generally, Brown lectured on "what American citizenship means" and warned the crowd that "it does not mean the murdering of the police in the Haymarket of Chicago, or the cheering of the long-haired, white-headed, bewhiskered man who stood on the soap box amid the applause of thousands and said that he favored the dynamiting of every bank, and scattering the money in the streets."[91] In a 1923 article on "Making American Citizens," a Florida writer's remarks similarly noted that the most effective Americanization efforts were those that steered away from tactics that led to "building up class and fostering class hatreds."[92] These types of commentary were a reminder that for many Anglos, Cuban integration into US society was also contingent upon a rejection of labor radicalism and a general acquiescence and loyalty to US government and society.

Other Americanization efforts were led or actively supported by white Cubans. In 1929, a Royal Knights of America chapter was founded by a series of Latin men in Tampa, with the group "primarily dedicated to the Americanization of foreigners" and staking out public positions on other political concerns and candidates.[93] In 1922, a representative from the US Bureau of Naturalization conferred with various leaders from Tampa's ethnic clubs in an effort to spur greater Americanization efforts. The leaders soon wrote a letter of support noting that they backed the effort "to bring about a complete Americanization of the foreign-born element in this community, so that each foreign-born individual may be assimilated into our body politic as an American."[94] The group noted its broad approval of supporting English-language instruction, naturalization efforts, and classes devoted to "the responsibilities of American citizenship and an understanding of American institutions."[95] The letter was signed by the presidents of Círculo Cubano and every other major ethnic institution in Ybor City, with the exception of La Unión Martí-Maceo.

Anglo women's activism was also essential to the work of Americanization in Cuban communities. This was reflective of the broader Americanization movement throughout the United States, which depended on women reformers.[96] In cities like Los Angeles, Anglo women targeted Mexican American women in Americanization programs centered on English and changes to the Mexican American home.[97] In Tampa, groups like the Tampa Woman's Club, the Daughters of the American Revolution, the Woman's Council of the Methodist Episcopal Church, and the Catholic Woman's Club all played varying roles around the project of Americanization. Much of these efforts were centered on education. The Tampa Woman's Club, for instance, promoted Americanization lessons that were taught at the V. M. Ybor School and a variety of other institutions in the city.[98] Similarly, the Tampa Woman's Club and a regional Daughters of the American Revolution chapter planned Flag Day activities and other programs with local Latin children that were heavily focused on instilling a patriotic sensibility among the city's youth.[99] While some of these collaborations occurred in schools like the V. M. Ybor School and West Tampa's Rosa Valdés Settlement, they were even more common in "mission schools" such as the Wolff Mission School. In addition to their work with children, the Wolff Mission also provided a day nursery and English-language instruction for adults that also brought members of the Cuban community to the institution.[100] As one writer noted about these efforts, "The Mission Schools in Ybor City and West Tampa are doing a most invaluable and lasting work moulding little Latins into embryo American citizens. The night schools, the day nurseries, the Foreign Women's and Mothers' Clubs are all most effectively weaving these foreign elements into the very fabric of good citizenship."[101]

Efforts around Americanization and assimilation also fostered meaningful, if limited, collaborations between Anglo and Cuban women. Some of Florida's women's clubs at times made overtures toward working with Cuban women. The Tampa Woman's Club sometimes worked with Cuban women via the Wolff Mission. Referring to one of these groups, one member recalled, "On several occasions we have entertained the Foreign Women by inviting them to our clubs and homes—they usually come in great numbers and are very appreciative and interested. They nearly always immediately plan to return the courtesy by having us visit their clubs."[102] Similarly, the West Tampa Woman's Club held a collaborative event in 1917 with the Havana Woman's Club. The Havana group was formed by Sarah Thurston, a former South Carolina resident, who developed a leadership structure for the Havana club that balanced an even number of Anglo and Cuban women. The collaborative event was centered on a speech from Susana Echemendia de Mederos, a member and delegate from the Cuban club who had previously resided in Tampa. As one writer noted, the event's broader purpose "was in reality a fellowship meeting between the American and Latin women of Tampa, West Tampa and Ybor City."[103] To be sure, Anglo women did not necessarily view Cuban women as equal partners in these endeavors. Women's groups in South Florida were still largely led by Anglo women, and their efforts to collaborate with Cuban women were often blind to the unique needs of working-class people.[104] However, these efforts provided one more avenue that occasionally brought white Cuban and Anglo women together.

PREJUDICE AND HIERARCHY IN CUBAN SOUTH FLORIDA

By the 1930s, white and Black Cubans were only loosely linked to one another. While they continued to share a language, ties to Cuba, and workplaces, both groups grew to have distinct communities with relationships to other ethnic groups. While some of these changes were exacerbated by Jim Crow segregation, it is also important to analyze the role that white Cubans played in hastening this shift and in embracing the ideology of racial separatism. Doing so also helps contextualize racism in other Cuban American enclaves such as New York City during roughly this same period, underscoring how white Cubans enforced racial hierarchies in multiple locations.[105] This task is complicated by the general reluctance among Cubans to remember this facet of Cuban American communities. Even during some of the most consequential moments of racial tension, the historical record is sometimes bare or distorted.

Elements of this growing separatism could be seen in the life of José Ramón Sanfeliz. Sanfeliz was a white Cuban who arrived in Tampa as a young man. He played an active role in independence organizing, serving as president of a group called Los Vengadores de Maceo.[106] He was also the photographer that captured La Resistencia's multiracial work force—reprinted in chapter 2—during the 1899 Weight Strike. In Tampa, he also served as one of the founders of the previously mentioned Club Nacional Cubano, the multiracial precursor to the white Círculo Cubano. In 1935, when remembering how the once-integrated group became an all-white institution as El Círculo Cubano, he asserted that "the negroes were left out," with no further explanation.[107] Sanfeliz's position on the decision to oust Black Cubans was left unclear, but the broader move pointed to the withering multiracial associations within Cuban enclaves.

Decades later, many white Cubans recalled a more harmonious era in South Florida that did not bear the racial animus of much of the American South. As scholars such as Susan Greenbaum have noted, even some researchers have adopted this simplified view of Cuban enclaves.[108] However, the split also reflected older prejudices among white Cubans that were laid bare by the 1920s and 1930s. In addition to the political and educational shifts among white Cubans, cultural practices and personal relationships also point to how white Cubans justified their growing separation from Cubans of color. In the process, white Cubans adopted a hierarchical view of South Florida society in which they imagined themselves as fundamentally separate from their Black counterparts.

Racial differences were especially evident when analyzing personal relationships among Cubans in neighborhoods like Ybor City. One of the more interesting avenues for understanding everyday interactions and community dynamics comes from the Works Progress Administration's Federal Writers' Project (FWP) during the late 1930s. As was true throughout the country, FWP employees in Florida fanned out across the state, recording life histories, songs, and many other pieces that captured the nuances of communities throughout the state. Pieces written by Stetson Kennedy, for instance, combined original writing and interviews to get a sense of communities like Ybor City. In one piece, Kennedy stayed in the home of a Cuban couple anonymized as Pedro and Estrella. The piece detailed various aspects of their lives and family histories while also capturing the dynamics of multiethnic Ybor City. Commenting on one family in the neighborhood, Estrella at one point mentioned, "You may not believe it . . . but that Negro woman is that white-looking kid's mother. They are all colored people in that house—they are very nice people, too. . . . The colored kids, even the white-looking ones, have to go to separate schools."[109] Her comments pointed both to the spaces that white and Black residents sometimes shared, while also highlighting how racial markers led to divergent experiences in 1930s Tampa. Later, when a young woman with a dark complexion walked by, Estrella wondered aloud, "Is she a Negro?" Pedro responded, "No, her mother is Cuban; I don't guess her own mother knows who her father is. She looks like a Puerto Rican—I guess there was some jumping the fence." In the end, Estrella declared, "I sure wouldn't change places with her."[110] While these comments were made in passing, scholars like Tanya Katerí Hernández have noted how the home has been a key site for reproducing aspects of anti-Blackness for families of Latin American descent in the US.[111] Comments like these suggested how white Cubans reaffirmed racialized tropes about Black South Floridians and their place in Tampa society.

In another session with a couple listed as Enrique and Amanda, Kennedy's piece at one point explored dating and the relationships between ethnic groups in Florida. When Amanda discovered that her daughter, Rosa, was dating an Italian, she exhorted, "I don't want no Italian son-in-law in the family."[112] Furthering the point, she wondered, "I don't see why you can't marry a Cuban or an American—anything but an Italian."[113] Rosa assured her that Nicky, the Italian boy, was kind and handsome. She also insisted that she would gladly date an American boy but that this presented difficulties. As Rosa noted, "I do like Americans . . . Sure! But I can't do nothing about it. The only way to get Americans is to be high-toned and live in Hyde Park and I can't do that."[114] For many working-class Cubans in Ybor City and Key West, socioeconomic status was tied to occupations and familial relations—in this context, dating middle-class and wealthy white Americans provided one such pathway to upward mobility.[115] These choices reflected the racial hierarchy that white Cubans internalized by the 1920s and 1930s. In this retelling, Black Cubans and African Americans were nearly always on the margins. Amanda herself noted one Black family that she admired. However, interactions between these groups were sharply limited during this period as a result of both societal restrictions and active choices made by white Cubans.

Forms of anti-Blackness were also common in popular culture in South Florida. This was particularly evident in local theater. The Círculo Cubano and Instituto San Carlos continued to host public events and performances throughout the early twentieth century. Some of the more common performances in South Florida during this period were *teatro bufo*, similar to American minstrelsy. Originating as a caricature-based theater in Spain, teatro bufo eventually became a Cuban style of comedic theater typically featuring performers in blackface. Key West and Ybor City became regular stops for the teatro bufo circuit. In addition to these types of performances, American minstrel shows like A. G. Allen's continued to draw fanfare in South Florida.[116] In examining the collection of plays at the Círculo Cubano, many of the productions included demeaning portrayals of Black characters, where their ancestry or intelligence was called into question. In Mario Sorondo's *La Mujer del Buzo*, the Black Panchito is chided over his African heritage in one of the play's recurring jokes.[117] Similarly, Agustín Rodrígues's *La Loca de la Casa* pits together the white Mondoreño and the Black Monico. In moments of anger, Mondoreño demeans Monico for his ancestry and suggests he is more akin to an animal.[118] This essentialized view of Black Cubans was common and was part of a broader process where Cubans of color were not viewed as fully Cuban. The career of Alberto O'Farrill, a Black Cuban actor on the bufo circuit, speaks to this trend. He arrived in Key West in 1925 on a steamship that also carried fellow Cuban Luis Alfaro. The shipping records marked Alfaro's "Race/Ethnicity" as Cuban, while O'Farrill was labeled as "African." As Antonio López explains, "O'Farrill's identity is both Cuban and excessive to Cuba: He is a 'citizen or subject' of the Cuban nation-state who also belongs to an 'African race,' an 'African people.'"[119]

Context is critical to understanding the significance of teatro bufo in Florida. Some scholars have underscored the subversive nature of the plays during the independence era, noting that while Black characters were stereotyped, the performances also spoke to an embrace of a mixed-race *mestizaje*.[120] This generous reading may have been true during an era defined by battles between Spanish censorship and a multiracial insurrection, but in Jim Crow America, no multiracial alliance combatted racism in a similar manner, and the plays' stereotypes were more likely to reinforce caricatures and slights aimed at Black Cubans.[121] The major institutions that guided interracial cooperation in the nineteenth century—the Cuban Revolutionary Party, labor unions, and mutual-aid societies—were respectively dissolved, weakened, and segregated by the twentieth century. Opportunities for meaningful dialogue between white and Black Cubans narrowed by the twentieth century. As a result, it is important to frame teatro bufo and its related forms within this context.

For Black Cubans raised in the 1920s and 1930s, their interactions with white Cubans were noticeably terse and circumscribed. The distance between the two groups was especially obvious for Cuban children raised in the 1920s and 1930s. Evelio Grillo, an Afro-Cuban raised in Ybor City during this period, noted about his Afro-Cuban mother, "While my mother formed interracial friendships at work, few, if any, such friendships extended to visits in the homes."[122] Recalling his own life, he further asserted that "I don't remember playing with a single white Cuban child. I remember the faces of only three white Cuban men who came to the house, two as music teachers and one as a stout, jolly Sunday boarder whom we called '*Tío Pío.*'"[123] For white Cubans, the diminishing contact with Black Cubans was often linked to the growing relationship with other white ethnic allies. In turn, many white Cubans began to adopt the racial ideology that was dominant in South Florida. As Sylvia Griñan, an Afro-Cuban teacher in Tampa would later note, "When the white Cubans started getting Americanized, they became more like the white Americans in their attitudes toward blacks, including black Cubans."[124]

The 1920s and 1930s proved to be a crucial period in the history of Cuban South Florida. Decades removed from the first large-scale migration of Cubans to Key West, the Cuban communities of Key West and Tampa planted roots and became mainstays of South Florida life and culture. However, with this integration came diverging paths for Black and white Cubans. For Black Cubans, the pressures of Jim Crow led to growing cooperation with African Americans in the region. Even Cuban institutions such as La Unión Martí-Maceo, which at one time viewed itself as separate from the rest of Tampa's Black community, began to draw active connections between the city's multiethnic Black population. In the process, Black Cubans collaborated with African Americans to create shared networks around education, child care, and social life. Conversely, white Cubans continued to be integrated into the broader panoply of white South Florida. Active in local politics and increasingly allied with Anglos and European immigrants, white Cubans continued to be influential in civic and social life in Key West and Tampa. While working-class white Cubans faced obstacles in the workplace and in some social circumstances, their wealthier counterparts led to a broader legitimization of Cubans throughout the region. Going forward, the trajectories of both groups grew more tenuous as the Great Depression, the collapse of the Clear Havana industry, and World War II fundamentally altered Cuban communities throughout Florida. Black and white Cubans largely met these challenges separately in what became a fundamental turning point in Cuban South Florida.

· 5 ·
CUBAN AMERICANS, THE DEPRESSION, AND WORLD WAR II

As part of the United States Army during World War II, Evelio Grillo and his company were making a brief stop in South Africa, in the port city of Durban. The voyage was a reminder of the long and circuitous route that Grillo's life had taken. Born in Jim Crow–era Ybor City to an Afro-Cuban family, Grillo's life straddled the Cuban and African American communities that defined Black life in Tampa. Over time, and with the support of various community members, his ambitions took him farther afield from Ybor City. He finished his secondary education in Washington DC's Dunbar High School before attending Xavier University in New Orleans. After a lifetime of segregated institutions and confronting the many facets of Jim Crow, he found extensions of these systems in the US military and on his stop in South Africa. As the troops were close to landfall, a commanding officer notified him and his company that they were to avoid contact with "native peoples."[1] Reflecting on this moment later, Grillo recalled, "South Africa interested me not at all. I knew that it repressed blacks unmercifully. It seemed ironic to accept its hospitality en route to fight Hitler's racism. The insulting manner in which we were enjoined from contact with black South Africans intensified my disgust and anger."[2]

Grillo's frustration was a reminder of the sizable chasm that defined the experiences of white and Black Cuban Americans during the 1930s and 1940s. Amid the backdrop of the Great Depression and World War II, the divergent trajectories of both groups only grew more pronounced. For Black Cubans, discrimination and the dire economy made community connections to other Black residents essential. As the Grillo case demonstrates, many Black Cubans left South Florida during this period in the search for better opportunities and safer communities. In Grillo's case, this meant traveling to Washington, DC, and later attending Xavier University, a historically Black university in New Orleans. However, for others, it often meant moving farther north, with New York City as a common destination.[3] White Cubans, however, had other options and remained closely tied to important power structures in Key West and Tampa.

Aspects of these shifts began in the 1930s as connections between Cuba and South Florida were redefined and the Great Depression amplified older inequities. In the case of the former, leaders of the Cuban republic began to see South Florida as a means of forging closer collaborations between the Cuban and US governments. In the process, institutions like the Instituto San Carlos shifted from their politicized origins to symbolic institutions that worked with the Cuban state and facilitated specific retellings of the independence era. In addition to these changes, migration in the region slowed, with the exception of the largely white refugee wave during the Cuban administration of Gerardo Machado.[4] With Cuba no longer driving discussions of equality and representation, Cuban Americans looked inward and forged identities in their adopted communities. The realities of the Great Depression presented a series of additional difficulties for Cuban Americans, regardless of race. The declining cigar industry—a product of the Depression and machine-rolled cigarettes—ravaged both Key West and Tampa. In 1934, one Florida publication claimed that as many as 80 percent of Key West's residents were on "relief rolls."[5] As in other cities, federal relief programs and other initiatives grew to be prominent in Tampa and Key West. However, the distribution of services was unequal, with Black South Floridians often unable to secure essential services in both cities.

The World War II era was a reckoning in many ways for both white and Black Cubans. For white Cubans, the sacrifices of service—accomplished both at home and abroad—cemented their status alongside their Anglo and European immigrant neighbors. While Cuban Americans also served in World War I, the contributions of white Cuban Americans to World War II were widely covered in the region. Additionally, those serving were often second- or third-generation Cuban Americans who identified solidly with the United States. For Black Cubans, World War II represented both an opportunity and a harsh realization around the bounds of racial separatism in the United States. Black Cuban Americans served valiantly, but their efforts were glossed over and ignored in South Florida. Experiences like Grillo's were common, and the racism of the war effort served to radicalize some Black Cuban Americans. For many, the war crystallized the importance of working in cross-ethnic alliances around issues of Black civil rights.

CUBAN AMERICA AND CUBA DURING THE EARLY REPUBLIC

The relationship between Cuban Americans and Cuba took on new forms in the early twentieth century. In some ways, connections remained close. Family ties and travel continued to facilitate cultural exchange between the two countries. However, the social and political relationship between Cuba and South Florida changed dramatically as Cuban Americans increasingly identified as US residents between the 1920s and 1940s. In the late nineteenth century, ideological connections between the two regions were constant as discussions over nation, race, and class echoed across Cuban and Cuban American communities. However, by the twentieth century, second- and third-generation Cuban Americans had weaker connections to this type of discourse. The cigar industry and labor radicalism continued to create opportunities for collaboration, but these diminished as the cigar industry gradually declined during the 1930s and 1940s.[6]

One of the key institutions for charting this shift was the Instituto San Carlos in Key West. By the 1920s, the San Carlos had become an institution that was firmly attached to the Cuban state. The Cuban government became owners of the San Carlos building, where they housed a consulate. While the San Carlos would struggle with funding throughout the first half of the 1900s, the Cuban government apportioned some funds for the school. Florida also had a vested interest in the institution, as local funds were apportioned to fund the school's English-language classes. Moreover, the institution became a symbol for demonstrations and celebrations, one that revealed a great deal about Cuba, the United States, and the relationship between the two countries. This was a notably volatile period in Cuban history. From 1933 to 1934 alone, the repressive government of President Gerardo Machado ended, a wide cross-section of Cuban citizens led a social revolution calling for a new republic, the short-lived presidency of Ramón Grau San Martín came and went, and Fulgencio Batista rose to become a dominant force in the Cuban military and in Cuban politics. While Cuban celebrations in Key West often reflected older traditions within the Cuban American community, they should also be analyzed within the vicissitudes of the Cuban republic.

Cuban history, and specific retellings of that history, became embedded within Key West society over time. The most public presentations of Cuban identity in Key West were centered on Cuban holidays and memorials whose celebrations dated back to the nineteenth century.[7] During the 1930s and 1940s, these events continued to be held regularly and sometimes celebrated widely throughout the city. The calendar included commemorations ranging from José Martí's birthday to the "Grito de Baire," which signaled the beginning of the Cuban War of Independence in 1895.[8] The celebrations also pointed to widespread collaborations between a variety of Cuban, Cuban American, and US groups.[9] However, the biggest celebration was the annual commemoration of the 1868 "Grito de Yara" on October 10, which had been celebrated in South Florida for decades. Aside from its obvious importance in beginning the Cuban wars of independence, the Key West Yara celebrations carried additional meaning as the Ten Years' War triggered the first significant Cuban American community in the island city. The celebrations, often spread out over two days, sometimes led to the closure of local city offices, with the main day of celebrations being announced as a holiday.[10] In 1934, for instance, the program included a memorial march that began at the Instituto San Carlos, a series of concerts and dances, baseball games between Tampan and Key West teams, a nighttime "Electrical Parade," and other events.[11] Examining the program reveals that the participants included a wide range of local politicians, Cuban American leaders, representatives from the Depression-era Federal Emergency Relief Administration, local fraternal organizations, and a contingent of Cuban officials.

However, the celebrations of the 1930s and 1940s were less about aspirational ideals—as they were in the nineteenth century—and more about depicting a sanitized history of Cuban South Florida and US-Cuba relations. In the process, discussions over race, democracy, and imperialism were shelved in favor of a harmonious depiction of Cuban and Cuban American history. This was especially true after 1934, when Fulgencio Batista began a prolonged period of indirect and direct rule in Cuba. Batista's ascent was aided by US officials that backed him and his efforts to temper the more radical elements of the 1933 revolution.[12] Batista would similarly go on to use connections with old émigré centers to legitimize his place within Cuban history and to foster close relations with the United States. This was the case with the proposal for the Parque Amigos José Martí in Tampa that was founded as a collaboration between South Florida and Cuban officials, with Batista serving as an honorary chairman.[13]

The varied and sometimes contradictory symbols of Cuban celebrations in South Florida could be seen during the Grito de Yara celebrations of the 1930s and 1940s. The uses of José Martí were one way to examine this shift. A José Martí statue at Bayview Park (fig. 11), added in the 1930s as a collaboration between Cuban and Key West officials, became a permanent fixture of Cuban celebrations in the city. However, the symbol was folded into a broader set of people and ideas that promoted a selective reading of Martí and his ideals. It was common during the Yara events to have a procession that moved from the memorials devoted to Cuban veterans of independence and the USS *Maine* to the Martí statue.[14] Indeed, the Maine became a common symbol in Cuban American events, including stops to the city's Maine memorial as well as a "naval station float" that recreated the Maine "correct to the minutest detail."[15] As noted before, the explosion and sinking of the USS *Maine* became the impetus for US involvement in the Cuban War of Independence, a worry Martí famously expressed in his "Nuestra América" essay when thinking about US influence in Latin America.[16] However, given the strong presence of the US military in Key West and the relationship between Batista and the US government, military officials and symbols became a common presence in celebrations like the Grito de Yara events.

The Grito de Yara celebrations became a means of drawing Cuban Americans closer to Anglo South Florida while also creating harmonious narratives around Cuba-US relations. In the case of local relations, part of this was embedded in the leadership structure of the events themselves. For instance, in the planning of the 1932 celebrations, Key West Mayor William H. Malone was named chairman of the executive committee.[17] The incorporation of groups like the American Legion, Girl and Boy Scouts, the Key West National Guards, and other local groups was common. Moreover, these collaborations were meant to underscore the idea that the former Cuban refugees of the nineteenth century had become Americanized Cuban Americans. As one writer noted about the celebration, "This little Island City, haven for refugees during the revolution in the closing days of the last century . . . has a population made up in large part of Cuban American naturalized citizens, native born citizens, but

FIGURE 11 *The José Martí statue at Bayview Park—along with the Instituto San Carlos on Duval Street—became public sites that were commonly used during Cuban celebrations in Key West during the 1930s and 1940s. Just as with the Instituto San Carlos, the statue was used to stress the importance of Cuban American history in the city while also promoting US-Cuba relations. (Image courtesy of Florida Keys History Center, Monroe County Public Library, Key West, Florida.)*

still having a warm place in their hearts for Cuban history and events that led to their emancipation."[18] Ideas such as these cemented Cuban Americans in civic history and pointed to their old roots in the city. At the same time, these celebrations were used to show ties between Cuba and the United States. In addition to aforementioned efforts to commemorate Cuban and US veterans of the Cuban War of Independence, there were many collaborations between the two governments for these events. In planning the Cuba-centric aspects of the celebrations, organizers often reached out directly to the Cuban government, including the office of the president in 1934.[19] As one report noted, "Elaborate plans that will bring Cuba and the United States closer together have been laid by the committee in earlier meetings."[20] This included the regular participation of Cuban officials in events as well as the occasional presence of Cuban gunboats.[21]

When these types of events included Black Cubans, they sometimes underscored contradictions within Cuban and Cuban American communities and their memories of the past. In 1933 a group of representatives from the Cuban government visited Tampa, in part due to a new Pan American Airways route between Tampa and Havana.[22] While in Tampa, the representatives were hosted by various members of the Cuban American community. A Círculo Cubano event included a representative from the Afro-Cuban La Unión Martí-Maceo, who provided remarks alongside leaders of other Cuban American organizations.[23] However, the more revealing event was at a reception held at La Unión Martí-Maceo for the visitors. While it is unclear if other local white Cubans attended, the Cuban representatives were joined by Cuban consul Jorge Trelles and members of the Legionarios de Martí group. A member of the local Spanish-speaking press noted that the president of Martí-Maceo, Juan Casellas, provided remarks that welcomed the guests while also "letting them know the feelings of the members of the society they preside over."[24]

While the note on Casellas's speech was vague, the white speakers at the event pointed to the complicated racial dimensions at play. The aforementioned Trelles reportedly spoke of the "good relations that have always existed between Cubans of the two races," while one of the guests, Pablo Lavin, spoke of the importance of the history of interracial solidarity while quoting from Martí.[25] The Trelles quotation would have been complicated by the twentieth-century history in both Cuba and Cuban America. In the case of Cuba, the visit was taking place mere months after Gerardo Machado fled the country. Black Cubans were far from a monolith in regard to their views of the *Machadato*. Machado received support from some of the more prominent Afro-Cuban societies in Cuba and also appointed several Black Cubans to governmental posts.[26] These relationships sometimes extended into émigré centers, as when the Machado administration donated books to the Martí-Maceo library in Tampa.[27] However, the Black working class was still largely marginalized during the Machado era and a younger generation of Black Cubans organized within labor circles and the Communist Party during the 1930s while also criticizing other Black Cubans that supported Machado.[28] Nevertheless, anti-Blackness was still highly visible in the post-Machado landscape. During the same month that Trelles spoke in Tampa of the "good relations" between Black and white Cubans, an Afro-Cuban organization's offices were bombed in Cuba—one of several similar attacks during this period.[29] Months before, a "Ku Klux Klan Kubano" group was founded in Cuba with many of the same white supremacist aims of the US group.[30] In the Cuban American context, Trelles was speaking at an institution that existed primarily because of a split that saw white Cubans purge Black Cubans from an older, multiracial organization in Tampa. The Trelles and Lavin speeches were telling, as they revealed an approach that many white Cubans in the US would continue to use: a framing that invoked the independence era as a means of pointing to an interracial past while obfuscating or avoiding the present-day realities of Black Cubans.

Given the selective memory of Cuban history in South Florida, Black Cuban heroes were rarely part of the region's rituals and celebrations. Occasional invocations of Antonio Maceo, the most famous Afro-Cuban from the independence era, were some of the only mentions to notable Black Cubans. During the 1930s, the Instituto San Carlos reportedly flew their Cuban flags at half-mast to commemorate the day of his death, but other mentions to Maceo were sparse.[31] It is unsurprising that some Black Cuban youth had little exposure to Black Cuban history in South Florida. As the aforementioned Evelio Grillo noted about his own childhood in Ybor City, Maceo was the only Black Cuban he learned about and "there were no photographs in my home of historically significant Cuban blacks."[32] In many ways, writing Black Cubans into the history of Cuban South Florida would have subverted and complicated popular depictions of both communities. Invoking Martí in a manner that included his criticisms of Jim Crow and the United States, or of Maceo's visit to the Instituto San Carlos that promoted a multiracial insurrection, would have acknowledged the significant changes that had taken place in Cuban American communities. Moreover, they would have served as stark contrasts to the segregated practices that were routine in Key West and Tampa.

To add to these issues, working-class and Black migrants from the Caribbean would have faced additional hurdles due to changes in the immigration system during this period. While the introduction of the quota system in 1924 marked a significant shift in US immigration policy, Roger Daniels has noted that earlier moments in the 1900s revealed a "piecemeal immigration restriction."[33] From 1903 to 1917, the "head tax" for entering migrants was raised multiple times, naturalization moved from local to federal control, the naturalization of anarchists was barred, and a long-debated literacy test was approved.[34] The targeting of labor radicals in particular became an important means of limiting the types of activism that South Florida had thrived on during earlier periods.[35] Later, the 1924 Johnson-Reed Act and its accompanying quota system sharply limited or barred migration from certain global regions. While the Western hemisphere was technically separate from this system, migrants from English Caribbean nations—such as the Bahamas—faced additional hurdles. As Lara Putnam has noted, countries deemed to be "non-self governing" were placed under similar quotas, resulting in a "nearly total ban on immigrant visas for British Caribbeans."[36] While Cuban and other Caribbean migrants continued to be among the larger immigrant groups in the region, immigrants made up a much smaller share of the overall population by 1940.[37]

A brief influx of new migrants occurred during the administration of Cuban president Gerardo Machado. Originally elected in 1924, Machado increasingly relied on intimidation, violence, and other authoritarian tactics to stay in power.[38] In the wake of the global Great Depression, Machado grew only more repressive, violating constitutional rights and using secret police to silence the growing anti-Machado chorus in Cuba. At the height of the crisis in 1932 and 1933, refugees fleeing the island often found their way to South Florida, with Key West, Tampa, and the growing hub of Miami being common destinations.[39]

The Cuban refugees of the Machado era generally received favorable treatment in South Florida. Part of this was due to their class status and the ways they were perceived in the region. A local news account noted about a group of refugees in Key West that "most of them speak English and several of them are said to belong to prominent families in the Island Republic."[40] Indeed, profiles of refugees from the Machado era often noted their professions and backgrounds: lawyers, an electrical engineer, police officers, University of Havana students, the children of a former police chief in Havana.[41] Critical to their integration into cities like Key West were locals, including well-known Cuban Americans that vouched for them. In a typical case, when one group of refugees was being held by local authorities, a "number of prominent" people that included Justice of the Peace Rogelio Gómez advocated on their behalf and led to their release.[42] Similarly, when Jorge Pérez de Alderate did not petition as a refugee and was set to be deported back to Cuba, a group of Cubans in Key West successfully argued that he would face immediate danger due to his anti-Machado sentiments and brought him back to the city.[43]

Conversely, reports of Black Cubans entering South Florida during the 1930s and 1940s were less frequent, with additional scrutiny being used in some cases. In one notable case, the famed Afro-Cuban boxer Eligio Sardiñas Montalvo, better known as "Kid Chocolate," was deported from Key West in 1933 over an immigration dispute.[44] Other anecdotes point to new Black Cuban migrants that simply felt unwelcome in South Florida. Christina D. Abreu, for instance, has pointed to the social and linguistic challenges musician Arsenio Rodríguez faced during a brief stay in Tampa—a stay that he would later recount in a song titled "Pasó en Tampa."[45] After 1924, many Cubans—including Black Cubans—entered the US via South Florida, sometimes overstaying tourist visas.[46] However, this did not mean that they stayed in South Florida. While Black Cubans did not have the same limitations that migrants from the British Caribbean had, they still arrived in a region that was increasingly hostile to Black residents. As a result, new migrants and even multigenerational Black Cuban families looked further north for opportunities. The pressures of the Great Depression only hastened these choices.

RESOURCES AND RELIEF IN SEGREGATED SOUTH FLORIDA

The Clear Havana industry in Key West and Tampa, a central feature of both economies for decades, was under considerable strain during the Depression. This shift was especially stark in Tampa. In 1929, the Tampa cigar industry produced just over 500 million cigars, bringing in $2,640,438 in revenue. By 1933, 292,285,000 cigars were produced, generating $1,818,385 in revenue.[47] In addition to declining production, other potential threats lingered for cigar makers and manufacturers. Changing rules about tourists bringing cigars from Cuba into the United States, proposed changes to how cigars were taxed, the relocation of iconic factories to different parts of the United States, and the changing nature of the cigar industry itself led to marked shifts in working-class South Florida.[48] In a typical article of the era, one Tampa writer wrote of the inherent challenges of "factories in other portions of the country . . . putting their product on the market at prices that are prohibitory to made-in-Tampa cigars—due to the employment of machines and much lower wage scale."[49] As jobs grew scarce, organizations like the Cigar Makers' International Union tried to help unemployed cigar makers gain employment or benefits via federal unemployment programs.[50] The scarcity of employment exacerbated existing inequalities in the cigar factory system. Dating back to the nineteenth century, Black workers and women rarely ascended to the more privileged, higher-paying positions in the cigar factory. It is telling that when Evelio Grillo and Francisco Rodríguez Sr. remembered this period of Ybor City, both remembered the Afro-Cuban lector Facundo Acción.[51] Grillo remembered him as the sole Afro-Cuban lector in Tampa and considered him "without question, the black Cuban community's recognized leading intellectual."[52]

Aside from the cigar industry, the Depression also limited access to essential services for working-class and Black South Floridians. One example was seen in Key West's Mercedes Hospital, a charity hospital originally created by twenty-six Cuban women and run for decades by María Valdés de Gutsens.[53] Gutsens was a widely admired Cuban American who provided essential medical services to impoverished Key West residents and whose work was awarded a Carlos Manuel de Céspedes medal by the Cuban government.[54] The hospital also routinely took in Black patients.[55] It was precisely institutions like this that struggled during the Depression. Gutsens and the hospital were long accustomed to depending on a creative combination of private donations and city funds to keep the hospital afloat, but the economic downturn added considerable difficulties to the charity hospital. By the late 1930s, Gutsens was pleading with local officials for additional donations to keep the hospital running.[56] When Gutsens passed away in 1941, the loss of her leadership coupled with the hospital's economic troubles led to the closure of the facility in 1943.[57]

With charitable and cultural institutions struggling to continue and the cigar industry faltering, the role of the federal government and New Deal initiatives became essential in Tampa and Key West. In the early years of the Depression, the Federal Emergency Relief Administration (FERA) was an active agency in both cities. In Key West, the recently created FERA became one of the most influential institutions in the city due to the town's precarious economic state. In 1934, the Key West city council and county commissioners "declared themselves in a state of emergency beyond their control and petitioned the governor to take over all their legal powers."[58] FERA was soon charged with revitalizing the Key West economy, employing thousands of residents in a voluntary work corps to tackle a wide range of projects.[59] These projects included trash pickup, repairs to city hall and the county courthouse, water main repairs, and other infrastructure projects.[60] While not as visible, FERA was similarly active in Tampa. FERA conducted studies on Ybor City and unemployed cigar makers, sponsored adult education programs, and also took part in recreational groups such as the Tampa FERA Orchestra.[61]

Federal relief could not escape the strictures of the Jim Crow system firmly in place in South Florida by the 1930s. To be sure, FERA officials sometimes had biases that applied to all Cubans. When Julius F. Stone Jr. was appointed as emergency relief administrator of Florida, he conducted an interview with the *New York Times* on FERA's proposed Key West overhaul. Promoting a program with the cry of "Help to All Who Help

Themselves," he analyzed the unique demographics of the city, asking "where in America can a Latin population be transplanted so that it will not still be on relief and its economic plight not be aggravated by social difficulties?" and asserting that "experiences in Tampa have shown that large groups of Latin people are not easily assimilable into the Florida population."[62] While these biases were telling, white Cuban institutions still became embedded within FERA's work. In Tampa, FERA's adult education classes were held in Ybor City and West Tampa in facilities like the V. M. Ybor School and West Tampa Junior High.[63] When FERA offered a series of aviation classes in Spanish, they were given at the local Cuban Club and taught by a local Cuban resident, Captain Guillermo Martull.[64]

Black South Floridians were also aided by federal funds, but these efforts were often uneven. In Key West, the Frederick Douglass School was in urgent need of a new building, as the existing structure suffered from "cramped quarters" and "poor lighting."[65] A new school was planned, with half of the costs coming from a sale of the original building to the US Navy and the other half coming from the New Deal's Federal Works Agency (FWA).[66] However, there were delays in the project, leading the Navy to move into the old building before the new school had been completed, leaving Black students without a school in the interim. A white high school being concurrently built in Key West was funded entirely by the FWA without similar delays.[67] Aspects of segregation in federal aid also appeared in recreational programs. Given the Cuban heritage of both Key West and Tampa, baseball drew faithful supporters in both cities. In Key West, FERA sponsored a Black baseball league that regularly played at Nelson English Park and seemed to include Black Cuban players.[68] Although playing in segregated leagues, baseball proved to be one of the spaces that could occasionally blur Jim Crow norms. While uncommon, Black and white teams would sometimes play one another in exhibitions. One writer later recalled a 1936 Key West game between the Coconuts ("the best colored nine here at the time") and the Acevedo Stars ("the best white club in the city").[69] The game was played at Navy Field, where the Key West crowd was still segregated into Black and white seating areas.[70] Cuban ballplayers were almost certainly on both teams, serving as a stark contrast to the integrated baseball teams ninety miles away in Cuba.

The multiethnic Black populations of Key West and Tampa continued to look to one another to weather the Depression. In Tampa, schools, churches, and La Unión Martí-Maceo continued to be common points of contact across the Black community. The Afro-Cuban mutual-aid society continued to host events designed for Tampa's Black community and became a mainstay of Black celebrations in the city.[71] Part of this shift was out of necessity, as many Afro-Cubans left Tampa during this period and appealing to the broader Black community became important for the financial well-being of the institution.[72] Similarly, Martí-Maceo paired with the local Urban League in a youth group sponsored by the Works Progress Administration (WPA) during the Depression.[73] During Tampa's jubilee celebrations in 1937, a largely segregated day of events was planned throughout the city.[74] The day's events for Black Tampans, which included an event at Martí-Maceo, included dances and a celebratory barbecue for Black residents and their descendants, who had lived in the city for fifty years.[75] In Key West, churches, schools, and public spaces such as Nelson English Park continued to be common sites of collaboration. The park in particular became a site of recreation as well as organizing, hosting Black celebrations as well as meetings among Black workers.[76] Moreover, groups like the Island City Civic League lobbied for Black Key West residents in other ways. Grace Palacios and St. Elmo Greaux were two notable members of the Black Key West group.[77] Palacios was a long-time activist in the city who also administered WPA-funded adult education classes to Black residents, while the Afro-Bahamian Greaux was a local school principal.[78] The Island City Civic League lobbied relief agencies and the local government for projects ranging from playgrounds to sanitation services to a Black hospital.[79] Reflecting the racial turmoil of the era, the League also requested an investigation into the killing of George Charles Hepburn while he was in police custody in 1943.[80]

White Cubans, meanwhile, continued to exert political influence in South Florida. This was especially true in Key West during the 1930s and 1940s and continued a broader trend of Cuban Americans in power in previous decades.[81] White Cuban Americans regularly occupied posts in the justice and policing systems as well as other essential agencies in Monroe County. Enrique Esquinaldo Jr., who was involved in the Democratic Party, served as justice of the peace and later replaced fellow Cuban American Juan Francisco Fleitas as election commissioner in the city.[82] Similarly, Maximo Valdez served as a county commissioner in Monroe County, while Juan Carbonell Jr. briefly became Key West mayor in 1945, a position not occupied by a Cuban American since Carlos Manuel de Céspedes y Céspedes during the 1870s.[83] Rogelio Gómez and Raul Carbonell also served as justices of the peace, with Gómez later serving as a county judge.[84] The police department was also regularly staffed with white Cuban Americans, such as captain of night police Alberto Camero and patrol officer Elmer del Pino.[85] The police department in Key West was not an all-white institution. It was common to have at least one Black police officer on the force, including a "José Valdez" from 1945 to 1946.[86] Nevertheless, as a result of these appointments and positions, white Cuban Americans were regularly charged with enforcing many of the most basic aspects of the Jim Crow system that regularly targeted Black residents. During the early 1940s, for instance, arrests for vagrancy regularly targeted working-class and Black residents in particular.[87] These power dynamics did not go unnoticed by locals and likely led to the perception of a growing chasm between white and Black residents in the city. In 1943, the previously mentioned del Pino was witness to a dispute between two Black residents. When del Pino approached one of them, the man reportedly said to del Pino, "What you want, white man? No white man's going to arrest me."[88] The brief aside pointed to the increasing number of ways that white Cuban Americans became associated with local institutions of power and whiteness in the region.

WORLD WAR II, SACRIFICE, AND VISIBILITY

As with cities across the United States, the events of Pearl Harbor and the subsequent US declaration of war had far-reaching implications in Tampa and Key West. The two cities, which at times could feel removed from the rest of the country, became pulled into national efforts to mobilize for war, reorient their respective economies, and grapple with aspects of ethnic and national identity. For many Cuban Americans, the war cemented their identities within the United States, albeit in different ways for Black and white Cubans. For white Cubans, the war often became one more way of proving their loyalty to the nation and identifying fully as US citizens of Cuban descent. This was accomplished via naturalization, supporting domestic war efforts, and wartime service. Black Cubans attempted many of the same methods, but with differing results. Black Cubans similarly proved invaluable to the domestic economy and the broader war effort. However, for Black South Floridians that stayed in Key West and Tampa, their efforts were not as visible or celebrated as those of white South Floridians. For Black Cubans sent to war, the Jim Crow strictures of the US military became some of the strongest memories of military service. For returning servicepeople, these experiences often led to redoubled efforts to fight for equality back home.

Early on in the war effort, demonstrating loyalty became a key theme in South Florida's immigrant communities. In January 1942, a typical article declared that "Ybor City Gets in the War, Heart and Soul." Quoting the Spanish American Frank de la Grana throughout, the secretary of the Ybor City Chamber of Commerce reminded readers of Latin participation in World War I and argued that Cuban, Spanish, and Italian migrants had grown close to their adopted homes over time. The writer of the article similarly assured readers that "Ybor City is still the colorful old world community with all the traditions and charm of other days. But its heart today is American."[89] Cuban mutual-aid societies soon backed wartime programs and supported a wide variety of Americanization efforts. In Tampa, the Afro-Cuban Unión Martí-Maceo similarly joined in efforts to support the war and encouraged local community members to buy defense bonds.[90] In some ways, proving loyalty was even more urgent to Spanish and Italian Americans in Tampa, given the fascist movements taking root in both European countries. Anti-fascist organizing—which included Cubans and other people of Latin American descent—had older roots in places like Tampa and New York City during the 1930s.[91] By the 1940s, the war effort amplified some of these calls. In 1942, Spanish Americans voted in favor of a resolution that "repudiated Franco's present leanings and . . . reaffirmed their adherence to the democratic principles of the Allied Nations."[92] A writer commenting on this and other developments in the city's Latin community asserted that "we are pleased that the members of the Tampa Latin Clubs have taken a decided stand and join with them in an earnest wish for the survival of democratic liberty and freedom in their fatherlands."[93] Mutual-aid societies and organizations such as the Ybor City Chamber of Commerce were similarly tied to naturalization efforts during the war, with many Cubans making up lists of newly naturalized citizens.[94]

Within days of Pearl Harbor, Cuban Americans and other South Floridians became involved in the war in a variety of ways. In the weeks and months that followed, reports of local enlistees became regular features of local newspapers.[95] Cuban Americans were sometimes singled out as a way of encouraging other locals to enlist. When Charles Gonzalez Mendoza enlisted in the Navy, a member of the local recruiting office reminded others that "if you see Charley on the streets in civvies, just remember this is war and the size uniform that would fit him, fits hundreds of thousands built just like him."[96] The same article reminded Spanish-speakers that the Navy had "better than average opportunities offered" for bilingual soldiers.[97] This was similarly stressed when Cuban American Luis Norcisa Jr. did not meet a height requirement but was allowed to enlist "because of his excellent command of both the England [sic] and Spanish language."[98] Women were also encouraged to join the war effort in many ways. Two days after Pearl Harbor, local women in Key West were urged to report to the local "Home Defense office" if they "ever had any office training."[99] Later in the war, groups such as Women Accepted for Voluntary Emergency Services (WAVES), Semper Paratus Always Ready (SPARS), and the Women's Auxiliary Army Corps (WAAC) also recruited women in South Florida.[100]

While not as recognized or heralded, similar efforts were made to recruit Black South Floridians. Domestically, some programs worked to train Black Americans as workers in wartime industries. In Key West, NAACP chaplain Joseph Suarez worked to recruit Black youth to a training program in a Daytona Beach "War Defense Training Center."[101] One of the original recruits was listed as "Julian Carrero."[102] This was likely Julian Carrera, who was born into an Afro-Cuban and Afro-Bahamian family and ultimately served in the US Army during World War II.[103] Suarez similarly worked to recruit Black women into WAAC.[104] In Tampa, WAAC officials recruited Black women in Tampa, holding recruiting drives along Central Avenue, a key site of Black Tampan life.[105] In addition to local Black enlistment, many Black soldiers were also stationed at nearby MacDill Air Force Base.[106] While pointing to the varied roles that Black Americans played in the war effort, the larger presence of Black soldiers also reflected Jim Crow segregation in the region. In 1944, for instance, a local defense council representative was forced to point out that there were "no swimming pool or beach bathing facilities" that Black soldiers could use in Tampa.[107]

As the war went on, the efforts of white Cuban Americans became catalogued by the local press in a way that publicly documented their sacrifices at every stage of the conflict. Told alongside the stories of other largely white ethnic groups, the narratives became a public testament to Cuban American service and sacrifice. Wrapped in imagery of patriotism, these accounts continued to imbue Cuban Americans into the power structures and dominant narratives of the region. Early on, this occurred via stories of enlistment and lives upended by the war. This was seen in a profile of Blas Sánchez, the son of a cigar factory reader, who went from head bartender of the famed La Concha hotel to an airplane mechanic.[108] As the war dragged on, narratives of white Cuban Americans also covered uncertainty, fear, and loss. Such was the case when Clara Suarez was widowed after James Leonard Coleman was killed in action or when Ernest Ogden—son of Rachel Sánchez—died in Germany during the latter stages of the war.[109] These accounts often pointed to the local and personal dimensions of the war. This was the case when Purple Heart recipient Marcos Mesa Jr.'s letter to his parents was quoted in the *Key West Citizen* or when the same newspaper catalogued Cleveland Henriquez's capture and eventual release as a Japanese prisoner of war.[110]

Local Afro-Caribbean soldiers that served in the war received notably different treatment, both at home and abroad. The local press would sometimes document the role of Black soldiers, but this was often obscured by the dominant narratives of non-Black servicepeople. As a result, references to Afro-Caribbean soldiers tended to be sparse. As an example, when a local newspaper catalogued six Key West teenagers who had joined the US Navy, there was a brief mention of a Black recruit named "Jose Camacho Ellis."[111] This was likely José (Joseph) Ellis, who was Afro-Bahamian and raised in an Afro-Cuban and Afro-Bahamian home.[112] Reflecting the segregated roles Black troops were often assigned to, the other five recruits were sent to Jacksonville while Camacho Ellis was sent to a "Navy Construction Regiment" in Virginia.[113] Once in the service, these divergent experiences often grew more pronounced. As Evelio Grillo recalled early on while aboard the USS *Santa Paula*, "We were to fight the opening battle in the primary war for black US troops in World War II: The war against segregation within the United States Army!"[114] This echoed the experiences of other Afro-Caribbean soldiers during the war and spoke to older practices of segregation within the US military.[115] Different aspects of this also applied to Mexican Americans, many of whom remembered various forms of discrimination during the war while also reflecting on legacies of discrimination in their home towns.[116] Aboard the ship, Grillo recalled segregated meals, unequal recreational spaces, fresh water being reserved for white soldiers, and a series of other indignities that led Grillo and other Black soldiers to write a petition sent to a commanding officer on the ship.[117] Grillo's account also pointed to the ways in which Black Cubans continued to find common cause alongside African Americans and other Black soldiers. A similar experience could be seen in the service of Norberto González, an

Afro-Cuban who had recently migrated to New York, who first passed into a white regiment before requesting a transfer to a Black regiment where he felt more comfortable.[118]

The war's conclusion and aftermath were similarly experienced in different ways for white and Black Cubans. For white Cubans, their status as veterans was used as a means of upward mobility and broader acceptance into US society. In the immediate aftermath, some white Cubans served as the public face of the veteran community upon their arrival. Yngacio Carbonell, for instance, became a leader in the local Red Cross, reminding the public about the role of the institution in supporting soldiers abroad.[119] The war also allowed white Cubans greater flexibility and options for crafting futures outside of Cuban American enclaves. Echoes of this story could be seen in the World War II experiences of Sergio Poyo, the descendant of José Dolores Poyo, the well-known editor and supporter of Cuban independence in Key West. Although born and raised in Cuba, Sergio Poyo was in the United States when Pearl Harbor occurred. Soon after, he enlisted in the US Army. As historian and relative Gerald Poyo would note about his service, "As with other Latinos, the military experience and willingness to give his life for the United States influenced his identity transition. He proudly adopted nationalist World War II narratives and fiercely identified with the values of that American generation."[120] In recalling how his postwar career took him from Indiana to New Jersey and then to South America, Gerald Poyo noted that "his light skin, fluent English, and lack of an accent allowed him, when convenient, to avoid being identified as 'Hispanic' and 'pass' as an American."[121]

For Black Cubans, the postwar period only highlighted the ongoing struggles that all Black Americans faced. As writers of the *Pittsburgh Courier* originally articulated, many Black servicepeople during World War II adopted the idea of fighting the "Double V": freedom abroad and freedom at home from racial prejudice.[122] For some Black Cubans, this mission was clear before they formally entered into the service. Francisco Rodríguez Jr. was a young teacher in Tampa when the war commenced and he joined the US Marine Corps. Recalling the pervasive racism in the education system at the time, Rodríguez Jr. later recalled: "I swore then that I would go to the service and if the Lord would send me back I was going to fight with every nerve and sinew in my body to do something about that condition."[123] Indeed, Rodríguez Jr. would spend his postwar years as a Florida-based NAACP lawyer, working on issues such as educational inequality, police brutality, and discriminatory policies in public transportation.[124] Similarly, Evelio Grillo spent much of his later life in Oakland as a community organizer working with African Americans and Mexican Americans.[125]

CUBAN IDENTITY AND DIVERGENT PATHS

By the 1930s and 1940s, Cuban Americans had forged an enduring and multilayered history in South Florida. At the conclusion of World War II, Cubans had significantly shaped the region for nearly eighty years. Born out of the tumult of Cuban independence, Cuban Americans went on to endure the long and arduous path to independence, the rise and collapse of its signature industry, two world wars, and the creation of countless cultural and political institutions in the region. In the process, Cuban American identity became a complex and fractured idea. In the 1930s, Gerardo Castellanos penned an overview of Key West's importance within Cuban history. In one of the closing chapters, Castellanos turned his attention to present-day Key West and noted how knowledge of Cuban history and identity were fraying in the city. While he acknowledged there were still some Cubans who carried these broader traditions and histories with them, he also lamented a larger group, who "imitate with their exotic father or mother, not speaking Spanish, scorning their ancestors and looking for relationships and futures among the locals . . . though they sometimes hold two Spanish-Cuban surnames, branches to magnificent patriots of days past, [they] do not know a word of Spanish, nor one episode of Cuban history."[126]

In addition to the broader process of Americanization that Castellanos outlined, race played a crucial role in how Cuban Americans continued to identify with their Cuban heritage. For white Cuban Americans, this was the byproduct of decades of relationships with the "locals" Castellanos referred to: multigenerational Anglos and recent immigrants from Spain and Italy. Their changing relationship to Cuban identity was also a byproduct of the sheer opportunities afforded to them as they navigated American life in Florida cities that widely recognized their role in the early histories of Key West and Tampa. In the coming decades, the preservation of institutions such as the Instituto San Carlos and the Círculo Cubano as well as the revitalization of historic Ybor City would continue to serve as a reminder of their foundational role in the region. For Black Cubans, different ties to Cuban identity were often the product of years of segregation and fading relationships with white Cubans. While an older generation was hesitant to collaborate with African Americans, younger Black Cubans in South Florida increasingly viewed these relationships as essential to social and political life in the region.

Nevertheless, the remaining Black Cuban community persisted and went on to continue La Unión Martí-Maceo. Moreover, as some Black Cubans grew older, some returned to Tampa after decades of having been away from the city during the Jim Crow era and rejoined the organization.[127] The older generation of Black Cubans also began to retell their stories and assert the fact that they, too, were foundational to the creation of Cuban South Florida. In 1978, Francisco Rodríguez Sr. was interviewed as he was entering his ninetieth year of life. The interview was led by two English speakers, with the previously mentioned Francisco Rodríguez Jr. serving as intermediary and translator for the session. After recounting the history of Black Cubans in Tampa and in the cigar industry, Rodríguez Sr. broke from the format, spoke in English, and addressed his remarks to the two interviewers: "I worked for more than 60 years in the cigar factory. All of my family were raised here. This is the youngest one of my children. And I've sustained them, I've [kept] them, with my work in the cigar factory. All the time."[128] Indeed, Black Cubans helped sustain families and traditions that were central to the history of Cuban South Florida. As the tape rolled on, alongside his World War II veteran son, Rodríguez's life story became a reminder of the rich history of Cuban American communities, their successes and struggles, and the history of a region that became fundamentally altered by prejudice and the color line.

EPILOGUE
Memory and Historic Cuban America

Few suspected it then, but the Cuban American story in South Florida would be substantively rewritten by a budding revolutionary visiting Tampa in 1955. Following his release from prison after a previous attempt to overthrow the government of Fulgencio Batista, Fidel Castro was once again organizing against the sitting Cuban government. Castro soon found himself in the United States, visiting historic Cuban American enclaves to rally support for his cause. Castro received a lukewarm welcome in Tampa. Originally booked to speak at the historic L'Unione Italiana, the club's leadership discussed the proposed visit and ultimately informed Castro that he would need to find another location due to the inherently political nature of his event.[1] Tampa's other Latin clubs soon followed suit. The president of the Círculo Cubano, Armando Dortas, noted that in addition to barring political speeches in the venue, "we want to keep harmony among the members."[2] While there were some Castro supporters among Tampa's Afro-Cuban population, the leadership of La Unión Martí-Maceo not only declined Castro's request to use their hall, but also refused a request from Castro to borrow a Cuban flag.[3] Undeterred, Castro booked the event at a Congress of Industrial Organizations hall in Ybor City. Railing against the Batista government, Castro spoke for ninety minutes to a crowd of several hundred, with one reporter also noting a number of empty seats.[4]

By 1959, South Florida would once again be reshaped by events reverberating from Cuba. Castro's July 26 Movement was ultimately victorious, spurring thousands of Cuban exiles to flee the island. After Castro's public overtures toward Marxism-Leninism and the Soviet Union, US-Cuba relations became one of the most contentious sites of Cold War conflict. Over time, Cuban exiles became parts of broader political discourse in both nations—innocent migrants fleeing Communism from the vantage point of the United States and a purge of undesirables according to the Cuban state. To be sure, this wave of Cuban migration was decidedly different from the original exile communities of the nineteenth century. To begin, Key West and Tampa were no longer the center of Cuban American migration. While Key West in particular would prove crucial as a first stop for exiles during the post-1959 migratory waves, Miami became the center of Cuban America during the early years of the Cuban Revolution. Moreover, the initial migrant waves to South Florida were a far cry from the working-class communities that founded Cuban American enclaves in Key West and Ybor City. While subsequent exile waves would come from broader socioeconomic backgrounds, initial waves to South Florida were often drawn from wealthy and upper-middle-class society in Cuba. Moreover, the early waves were overwhelmingly composed of white Cubans, a fact that would remain true until the 1980 Mariel boatlift and subsequent waves.

In the decades that followed 1959, Cuban Tampa and Key West underwent significant changes. Some of these shifts were a part of broader changes that were occurring in cities throughout the United States. Suburbanization, urban renewal, and the broader South Florida move toward tourism all had significant influence on Cuban American enclaves. Along the way, particular aspects of Cuban American history were highlighted while others were obscured. The 1965 destruction of La Unión Martí-Maceo's Ybor City building was the most visible aspect of the latter development. Over the years, Black Cubans and other community members have gradually begun to reincorporate Black Cuban history into the region, often with considerable difficulty. Other changes in Cuban South Florida were tied to events in Cuba. While Tampa and Key West did not occupy center stage in the post-1959 period, the ramifications of the Cuban Revolution were plainly evident in the historic Cuban American enclaves following Castro's ascent. The symbols of the older Cuban American communities of Ybor City and Key West often became reclaimed by newer exiles looking for inspiration and legitimacy in the symbols of the region's original Cuban exiles. In the process, the narratives of the original Cuban American communities of South Florida were tested, debated, and reformed amid the Cuban Revolution and the broader socioeconomic changes taking place in South Florida.

THE REVOLUTION AND CITIES REMADE

Unsurprisingly, the legacy of José Martí would become one of the earliest ideological battlegrounds in post-1959 Tampa. During his 1950s visits to South Florida, Castro was in many ways attempting to retrace Martí's steps and reclaim the mantle of the poet's unfinished revolution. Following the Cuban Revolution, the newly opened Parque Amigos José Martí in Tampa became a key site of contested history with older Cuban Americans and recent Cuban exiles also claiming Martí in their fight against Castro and Marxism. As early as 1960, anti-Castro protestors and local supporters of the July 26 Movement held contrasting ceremonies at the site and sometimes clashed with one another.[5] By 1961, these events sometimes took a violent turn. In addition to a confrontation that led to several arrests at a November event, a December event at José Martí park was temporarily halted due to a bomb threat.[6] At the latter event, José Miró Cardona, the Cuban politician turned leader of the US Cuban Revolutionary Council, assured attendees that "soon all the bells will be ringing freedom in Cuba and we will go back to the island."[7] Miró's vision would prove elusive.

During the 1960s, the Cuban American enclaves of Tampa would change in other ways. Suburbanization and white flight left many formerly dense neighborhoods vulnerable to wholesale changes and urban renewal projects. For Ybor City, this meant the closure or demolition of homes and previously important institutions. Following the creation of an "Urban Renewal Office" in the early 1960s, the city of Tampa attempted to "rehabilitate, clear and redevelop slum areas."[8] Many of the razed areas in and around Ybor City included blocks inhabited by Black families. As part of this process in 1965, La Unión Martí-Maceo's building was demolished. Club members later recalled being overcome with emotion at the site, with one member saving a brick to keep as a memento of the building.[9] The city's four other significant Latin clubs—Círculo Cubano, Centro Asturiano, Centro Español, and L'Unione Italiana—were all spared, with the Cuban and Spanish clubs applying for National Register of Historic Places status in the 1970s and 1980s.[10] In conjunction with the largely abandoned cigar industry, the legacy of urban renewal in the city was largely one of displacement for communities of color in the area.

Key West's Cuban community experienced a similar degree of rupture following the Cuban Revolution. Given the Instituto San Carlos's connection to the Cuban government, the consequences of the revolution were acute in the oldest Cuban American institution in South Florida. With the Cuban embargo in place by the early 1960s, the Cuban consulate within the San Carlos closed. By 1973, over a century after instruction began in one of the few interracial schools in the US South, the San Carlos school also closed.[11] Following years of struggling to fund the institute, the Cuban Revolution led to a gradual hollowing-out of the building and its programs. In the meantime, Key West would continue to play an essential, albeit transient, role in the history of Cuban exiles in the wake of the Cuban Revolution. In one of the largest refugee waves of the post-Castro era, over 120,000 Cubans fled the island and arrived in the United States during the six-month Mariel boatlift in 1980. In a break with emigration policy, the Castro administration briefly allowed certain Cubans to leave the island from the Port of Mariel after a group of dissidents stormed the Peruvian embassy in Havana requesting the right to leave the country. The Cuban government's begrudging announcement triggered a massive rush by Cuban Americans to send ships to bring the refugees to the United States. The US government crafted policies to provide refuge and documented status to the Cuban refugees. In the meantime, Cubans attempting to leave dealt with being accosted by Cuban officials and locals who targeted the budding exiles as traitors. Tomas Calle, an Afro-Cuban Mariel refugee, remembered Cuban officials asking, "What are you going to do in the United States? . . . Don't you know they do not like blacks there?"[12]

For many Cubans, Key West became a temporary refuge before being reunited with family or settling in different parts of the United States. During the Mariel boatlift, Cubans often landed in Key West before being sent to processing centers in other cities. The migrant wave overwhelmed the small island city and produced emotional stories that communicated the rupture and tumult of the period.[13] Similar acts of desperation occurred during the Balsero Crisis of the 1990s. After the fall of the Soviet Union triggered an economic collapse in Cuba, thousands of Cubans took to makeshift rafts in an attempt to flee the island and land in Key West. As it had been for well over a century, the southernmost point of the United States continued to symbolize refuge and hope for a new generation of Cuban exiles.

(RE)PRESENTING HISTORIC CUBAN AMERICA

While Cuban American populations remained relatively small in Tampa and Key West in the post-1959 period, elements of their early histories would be commemorated in revealing ways throughout the late twentieth and early twenty-first centuries. Backed by historic preservation efforts, community activism, and political groups, these efforts recounted particular visions of Cuban American history that were inevitably shaped by the distant and recent past. Many of these efforts were intended as correctives to the selective retelling of certain aspects of Cuban American history. For visitors of contemporary Key West and Tampa, it became possible to move through historical spaces and markers without a full understanding of the region's historical diversity or that Jim Crow norms were commonplace in South Florida. In the process, the attempts at retelling history in public became ways of understanding competing interpretations of the region's original Cuban American community.

Some of the efforts to tell a more complete story of Cuban South Florida came from Afro-Cubans associated with La Unión Martí-Maceo. After their building was demolished in 1965, they moved to a different structure, on 7th Avenue and 13th Street, where the group has continued to operate until the present day. While membership remained small, the organization was revitalized by older members who migrated back to Tampa after prolonged periods away from South Florida.[14] Members such as Juan Mallea and Ricardo Menendez, who would go on to take leadership roles in the organization, had both been gone for decades before returning amid a broader period of attempting to catalog and preserve the history of La Unión Martí-Maceo.[15] In addition to the returning community members, Afro-Cubans with long ties to the city would continue to shape the institution. This was true of Sylvia Griñan, a long-time educator and member of the Grillo family, who remained in the organization and communicated about the historic importance of the city's Black Cuban community.[16] In addition to club events, Martí-Maceo members also looked to chronicle histories of Black Cubans in other ways. During the 1980s, they donated their club records to the University of South Florida, spurring partnerships with faculty members such as Susan Greenbaum and Gary Mormino that would chronicle the Afro-Cuban experience in oral histories and published works.

Moreover, there were occasional moments of reckoning as some Martí-Maceo members attempted to address the segregation that made

La Unión Martí-Maceo necessary to begin with. In 1999, Belinda Casellas-Allen—a Martí-Maceo member who would become president—recognized the "Dosal" surname when she saw a mention of Círculo Cubano member Paul Dosal in the local newspaper. After leafing through family records and consulting with Dosal, she was able to confirm that they shared the same great-grandfather.[17] While the two families shared an ancestor, race led to two fundamentally different experiences in South Florida. Casellas-Allen recalled that when she would walk by the Cuban Club as a child, "my grandmother, she would pull me hard and say, 'Don't even look.' . . . All I knew is I couldn't go in that place."[18] The reunion was part of broader efforts to collaborate between Círculo Cubano and La Unión Martí-Maceo, including a 2001 picnic between the two groups and the Club Civico Cubano.[19] The historic tensions between the groups could still be seen in some ways, but this served as another example of Martí-Maceo members attempting to think about the role of reckoning and reconciliation.

Incorporating the life and legacy of Antonio Maceo became another way of counteracting simplified narratives of Tampa history. As the most significant Cuban of color associated with the Cuban wars of independence, Maceo was a widely revered figure in the region whose name and legacy lived on well after his passing. Nancy Raquel Mirabal and Christina D. Abreu have shown how similar debates over memory and race were underscored in an attempt to memorialize Maceo in New York City.[20] In the 1990s, Afro-Cubans and other locals used the coming centennial of his death as a way to think about how Cuban history was preserved in Tampa. Remember Maceo, Maceo's great-niece and a Tampa resident, asserted in 1996 that "Tampa is a city that is part of Cuban history, and the history of Cuba without Maceo isn't history."[21] In anticipation of the centennial, a group of locals organized the Comite Busto Antonio Maceo, which was formed to fund and build a bronze bust of Maceo that would be placed within the Parque Amigos José Martí. One of the groups courted for support was the local Tampa Bay Area Cuban Exile Council.[22] The local anti-Castro group was a reminder of how recent exiles continued to engage with broader histories in the region. One of the Comite's organizers, Carlos Gonzalez, noted that there were many locals in the city interested in supporting the effort. Nevertheless, in response to local "grumblings" about Maceo being placed alongside Martí, Gonzalez remarked that "people are saying this is Martí's park, but Martí didn't fight the war by himself. . . . It may have to do with the fact that Maceo was black. Maybe someone doesn't want a black hero."[23] By June of 1996, Tete Pujol's statue was unveiled at the park, with a ceremony and dinner planned. In the lead-up to the ceremony, Remember Maceo noted that "what I am interested in is that the Cuban youth of Tampa and America learn the history of their ancestors and great patriots of the past."[24]

In Key West, the city's most iconic Cuban symbol grew to be an amalgam of the original history of the community and the post–Cuban Revolution exiles. During the 1970s and 1980s, the Instituto San Carlos became a largely forgotten relic of the city's original Cuban American community. Without dedicated funding from the Cuban government, the institute's major programs and initiatives ceased, and club artifacts were lost or damaged. In a sign of the institution's general degradation, a tourist in 1981 was injured when a piece of the building's façade crashed down upon the sidewalk.[25] It was at this point that a newer generation of Cuban Americans proved instrumental in saving the Instituto San Carlos. By 1985, a San Carlos Rescue Committee and statewide Hispanic Commission brought together Cuban Americans from Miami and Key West to raise funds to restore the San Carlos. One of the project leaders, Rafael Peñalver Jr., was a Miami lawyer who recalled learning of the San Carlos when he was growing up in Cuba.[26] For the next several years, Peñalver and his collaborators raised millions of dollars between state funding and private donations. The funds covered an ambitious restoration that included architects, artists, electricians, and a variety of other craftspeople that worked to restore the building to many of its original 1924 details. The institute symbolically reopened in 1992, a century after José Martí would have first visited the previous San Carlos building in anticipation of the final war of Cuban independence.

The San Carlos restoration spoke to the ways in which recent exiles imbued the older histories of Cuban America with their own histories. In turning the San Carlos into a heritage site and museum, San Carlos leaders added a series of artifacts and exhibitions that spoke to a broader history of Cuban exiles. One of the earliest additions was a commissioned statue of Félix Varela, the Catholic priest and abolitionist who lived in exile in New York City during the early and mid-1800s.[27] Over time, the museum also grew to have exhibits and symbols of more recent waves, including actual rafts that were used by Cuban exiles to reach Key

West. Told side by side, the history of distinct groups of Cuban exiles has also sometimes obscured the class differences among different waves. As noted in this text, the original Cuban American community crafted a legacy of working-class militancy that led many Cuban Americans to associate with anarchism and socialism. The politics of newer exiles were decidedly different. In restoring the San Carlos, organizers worked with a wide range of groups. This included the Cuban American National Foundation, one of the more active and conservative Cuban American institutions, under the leadership of entrepreneur Jorge Mas Canosa.[28]

The broader, unified vision of Cuban American history in spaces like the San Carlos made it harder to incorporate aspects of difference, rupture, and tension that also defined Cuban American history at different moments. Similar dynamics have been true in Ybor City. Many of the more iconic Ybor structures, such as cigar factories, have often been preserved but repurposed as office space or entertainment spaces. As a result, the difficult legacies of Jim Crow, racial separatism, and Black Cuban influence have been harder to track in some of the more notable Cuban American spaces in South Florida.

Nevertheless, smaller efforts have attempted to address a more inclusive vision of South Florida's turn-of-the-century history. In Ybor City, figures such as Paulina Pedroso and Antonio Maceo have been included in broader mural projects that attempt to recreate the area's history.[29] In Key West, the legacy of James Dean pointed to a more direct attempt at racial reckoning. As noted in chapters 1 and 3, Dean was one of the last publicly elected Black officials in Key West during the late nineteenth century. He was removed from office under charges of "malfeasance" for providing marriage licenses to couples—including Cubans—that allegedly violated the state's interracial marriage laws. Over a century later, local attorney Calvin J. Allen began a quest to educate the public on Dean's legacy and posthumously restore his seat.[30] Allen argued that the malfeasance charge was unfounded, that Dean's removal did not follow proper procedure, and that the case also obscured the more complicated racial heritages of Key West's multiethnic, multiracial populations at the time. In 2002—113 years after Dean was removed from office—Allen's campaign was successful, with local officials and then governor Jeb Bush posthumously reinstating Dean.[31] As part of the process, a portrait of James Dean was placed in the local courthouse.[32]

Over a decade later, a similar reckoning occurred with the legacy of Manuel Cabeza, the man of Canary Island descent who had been lynched for having an interracial relationship in 1921 Key West. As noted in chapter 4, Cabeza's murder was one of the more brazen acts of violence that occurred during the Jim Crow era in Key West. In the aftermath, the World War I veteran's gravesite was "neglected for nearly a century."[33] In 2019, city officials held a memorial service for Cabeza's life, which included a new military headstone and a series of speakers.[34] With Cabeza's niece in attendance, one of the speakers was City Commissioner Clayton Lopez, who himself is of Cuban and African American descent. Another city commissioner, Sam Kaufman, remarked to Cabeza's niece that "today is a day of redemption for us. . . . Not only for your family but it is for our entire community."[35]

Redemption, of course, would require more than a ceremony. Cabeza's story, like so many in this text, was part of broader histories of segregation and rupture. The consequences of this racial separatism have echoed throughout the region in the decades that have followed. The recent attempts at telling a more complete picture of South Florida's history—while noteworthy and important—are but fragments to this broader retelling. For Cuban Americans, this history is foundational to understanding the nearly two-century history of Cuban communities in the United States. While this history is often told from the vantage point of Miami, it was in Key West and Tampa that Cuban Americans gained a foothold in the region. From these outposts, Cuban exiles articulated a distinct vision of Cuban independence and created communities and diasporic ties that have persisted across generations.

The story of race in these communities is equally foundational. While Cuban Americans in South Florida reflected the tensions and inequalities born out of the Cuban colonial era, they were still able to initially build communities that defied the racial norms of both Cuba and the US during the late nineteenth century. The example of early Key West in particular points to an interracial community that modeled many of the aspirations of Reconstruction and the Cuban independence movement, even as it wrestled with aspects of racism that lingered within the Cuban community. This moment, however, was fleeting. The earliest inklings of the Jim Crow system and persistent racial tensions in Cuba would creep into both Key West and Tampa by the late nineteenth century. Sometimes imposed and sometimes reflective of older prejudices among Cubans, these forms of racial separatism would lead to a significant break in the Cuban American community along racial lines. Both white and Black Cubans would go on to build rich legacies in the region, but they did so largely apart from one another. For a descendant like former Martí-Maceo president Belinda Casellas-Allen, the task of attempting to reconcile racial divisions within Cuban American Tampa more than a century after the community was split apart proved daunting but necessary. As Casellas-Allen would contemplatively note about the divisions among older generations, reconciliation, and the work ahead, "We've lost too many years."[36]

NOTES

INTRODUCTION

1. *Tampa Sunday Tribune*, October 21, 1956, 14C; Tom O'Connor, "Cuban Patriot Jose Marti's House in Ybor City Begins to Fall as Mayor Swings Ax," *Tampa Sunday Tribune*, October 28, 1956, 10A.

2. *Tampa Tribune*, February 25, 1960, 1D; *Tampa Tribune*, February 1, 1962, 1C; Chuck Schwanitz, "Marti Park Gets First Ybor Plaques," *Tampa Times*, February 1, 1962, 2A.

3. Pro- and anti-Castro forces used the park and Martí's legacy as a means of debating the Cuban Revolution. A series of confrontations—including one bomb threat—took place in the years immediately following Castro's ascent. See Frank Bayle, "Air of Mystery Hangs over Marti Dedication," *Tampa Times*, February 29, 1960, 4; *Tampa Tribune*, November 28, 1960, 14; *Tampa Tribune*, November 27, 1961, 1A, 1B; *Tampa Tribune*, November 28, 1961, 1B; Jerry Wallace, "Anti-Castro Rally Told Cubans Soon to Be Free Again," *The Tampa Tribune*, 1B.

4. The José Martí statue and the informational plaque were created in 1960 and 1961. The Antonio Maceo bust was added in 1996 to commemorate the centennial of Maceo's death. For more on the efforts behind the Maceo bust, see Tania Spencer, "Statue Unveiling Ceremony Memorializes Cuban War Hero," East Hillsborough, *Tampa Tribune*, June 9, 1996, 8.

5. For more on Paulina Pedroso and her life, see Josefina Toledo Benedit, *La Madre Negra de Martí* (Havana: Casa Editorial Verde Olivo, 2009).

6. Juan Pérez Rolo was among the first pupils of the Instituto San Carlos school and later chronicled some of its early history. See Juan Pérez Rolo, *Mis Recuerdos* (Key West: circa 1920s), 12–13, 41–56. University of Florida Digital Collections, https://ufdc.ufl.edu/UF00089813/00001/1j.

7. The Instituto San Carlos is currently run as a nonprofit cultural center and museum. See https://www.institutosancarlos.org.

8. "Las fiestas del 10 de oct.," *Florida* (Key West), July 26, 1924, 1; unless part of a translated work, Spanish-language sources in this text have been translated by the writer.

9. Evelio Grillo, *Black Cuban, Black American: A Memoir* (Houston, TX: Arte Público Press, 2000), 7.

10. Gerald E. Poyo, *"With All, and for the Good of All": The Emergence of Popular Nationalism in the Cuban Communities of the United States, 1848–1898* (Durham, NC: Duke University Press, 1989); Gerald E. Poyo, *José D. Poyo, Key West and Cuban Independence* (Gainesville: University Press of Florida, 2014); Consuelo E. Stebbins, *City of Intrigue, Nest of Revolution: A Documentary History of Key West in the Nineteenth Century* (Gainesville: University Press of Florida, 2007);

C. Neale Ronning, *José Martí and the Emigré Colony in Key West: Leadership and State Formation* (New York City: Preager, 1990).

11. For broader works on the cigar communities, see Loy Glenn Westfall, *Key West: Cigar City, U.S.A.* (Key West: Willis & Co., 1997); Loy Glenn Westfall, *Tampa Bay: Cradle of Cuban Liberty* (Key West: Key West Cigar City USA, 2000).

12. Durward Long, "'La Resistencia': Tampa's Immigrant Labor Union," *Labor History* 6, no. 3 (1965): 193–213; Gary R. Mormino and George E. Pozzetta, *The Immigrant World of Ybor City: Italians and Their Latin Neighbors in Tampa, 1885–1985* (Urbana: University of Illinois Press, 1987); Sarah McNamara, *Ybor City: Crucible of the Latina South* (Chapel Hill: University of North Carolina Press, 2023).

13. Lisandro Pérez's recent text on Cuban New York City and Dalia Antonia Caraballo Muller's book on Cuban communities in Mexico speak to some of these connections. Caraballo Muller in particular considers how the Cuban community in Veracruz had notable similarities and differences when compared to Key West. See Dalia Antonia Muller, *Cuba Émigrés and Independence in the Nineteenth-Century Gulf World* (Chapel Hill: University of North Carolina Press, 2017); Lisandro Pérez, *Sugar, Cigars, and Revolution: The Making of Cuban New York* (New York: New York University Press, 2018).

14. Susan D. Greenbaum, *More than Black: Afro-Cubans in Tampa* (Gainesville: University Press of Florida, 2002); Nancy Raquel Mirabal, "Telling Silences and Making Community: Afro-Cubans and African Americans in Ybor City and Tampa, 1899–1915," in *Between Race and Empire: African-Americans and Cubans before the Cuban Revolution*, ed. Lisa Brock and Digna Castañeda Fuertes (Philadelphia: Temple University Press, 1998), 49–69; Winston James, "From a Class for Itself to a Race on Its Own: The Strange Case of Afro-Cuban Radicalism and Afro-Cubans in Florida, 1870–1940," in *Holding Aloft the Banner of Ethiopia: Caribbean Radicalism in Early Twentieth-Century America* (New York: Verso, 1999), 232–257.

15. Nancy A. Hewitt, *Southern Discomfort: Women's Activism in Tampa, Florida, 1880s–1920s* (Urbana: University of Illinois Press, 2001).

16. Gerald E. Poyo and Paul Ortiz have been some of the only scholars to write about Key West's Cuban community during Reconstruction, the former in the context of the early independence era and local politics and the latter in relation to a broader work on interracial and interethnic organizing between African American and Latinx communities. See Gerald E. Poyo, "Cuban Revolutionaries and Monroe County Reconstruction Politics, 1868–1876," *The Florida Historical Quarterly* 55, no. 4 (April 1977): 407–422; Paul Ortiz, "Global Visions of Reconstruction: The Cuban Solidarity Movement, 1860s to 1890s," in *An African American and Latinx History of the United States* (Boston: Beacon Press, 2018), 71–94.

17. José Martí, "With All, for the Good of All," in *José Martí Reader: Writings on the Americas*, trans. Elinor Randall, Mary Todd, and Carmen González Díaz, ed. Deborah Shnookal and Mirta Muñiz (Melbourne: Ocean Press, 1999), 135.

18. James, *Holding Aloft the Banner of Ethiopia*, 250–252.

19. The three authors look at different periods and themes, but all of them closely examine how race shaped these communities. Just as I do in this text, they also consider the relationships Cubans built with other Caribbean migrants and African Americans. See Jesse E. Hoffnung-Garskof, *Racial Migrations: New York City and the Revolutionary Politics of the Spanish Caribbean, 1850–1902* (Princeton:

Princeton University Press, 2019); Nancy Raquel Mirabal, *Suspect Freedoms: The Racial and Sexual Politics of Cubanidad in New York, 1823–1957* (New York: New York University Press, 2017); Christina D. Abreu, *Rhythms of Race: Cuban Musicians and the Making of Latino New York City and Miami, 1940–1960* (Chapel Hill: The University of North Carolina Press, 2015).

20. See Frank Andre Guridy, *Forging Diaspora: Afro-Cubans and African Americans in a World of Empire and Jim Crow* (Chapel Hill: University of North Carolina Press, 2010).

21. Miriam Jiménez Román and Juan Flores, "Introduction," in *The Afro-Latin@ Reader: History and Culture in the United States*, ed. Miriam Jiménez Román and Juan Flores (Durham, NC: Duke University Press, 2010), 2.

22. Tanya Katerí Hernández, *Racial Innocence: Unmasking Latino Anti-Black Bias and the Struggle for Equality* (Boston: Beacon Press, 2022).

23. Hernández, *Racial Innocence*, 12.

24. See Muller, *Cuban Émigrés and Independence in the Nineteenth-Century Gulf World* (Chapel Hill: University of North Carolina Press, 2017), 6–8; Guridy, *Forging Diaspora*, 7–13.

25. As Felipe Fernández-Armesto has noted, an Anglicized view of US history has often obscured the nation's more complicated origins that are exemplified by locations such as Florida. The area's unique ties to Spanish colonialism and the broader Spanish-speaking world have shaped Florida for centuries. While Fernández-Armesto was emphasizing the region's links to "Hispanic" culture, Florida's connections to the Caribbean—both Spanish-speaking and non-Spanish-speaking—have been just as evident for centuries. See Felipe Fernández-Armesto, "The Fountain of Youth: The First Colonies in What Was to Be the United States, c. 1505–1763," in *Our America: A Hispanic History of the United States* (New York City: W. W. Norton & Company, 2014), 3–34.

26. Guridy, *Forging Diaspora*, 10.

27. Julio Capó Jr., for instance, has written about Miami's relationship to Caribbean migrants and LGBTQ communities in the early twentieth century. See Julio Capó Jr., *Welcome to Fairyland: Queer Miami Before 1940* (Chapel Hill: University of North Carolina Press, 2017).

28. See Patricia Silver, *Sunbelt Diaspora: Race, Class, and Latino Politics in Puerto Rican Orlando* (Austin: University of Texas Press, 2020).

29. In their analysis of "Afro-Latin@s in Movement," Rivera-Rideau, Jones, and Paschel have stressed the histories of "constant exchange of ideas about race and nation among political elites, as well as among Afro-Latino and Afro-Latin American citizens who sought to challenge hegemonic nationalist projects." They have further noted the importance of a transnational approach by asserting that "the perpetual movement of people, politics, and culture undermines the separation of the study of Afro-Latin America from that of Afro-Latinos in the United States." Petra R. Rivera-Rideau, Jennifer A. Jones, and Tianna S. Paschel, *Afro-Latin@s in Movement: Critical Approaches to Blackness and Transnationalism in the Americas* (New York: Palgrave Macmillan, 2016), 3–4.

30. Francisco Rodriguez Jr., interview by Otis Anthony, May 30, 1978, 1, University of South Florida Special Collections, Department of Anthropology African Americans in Florida Project, Box 11, Folder "Interviews—Transcripts—Rodriguez, Francisco [Jr.] 5/30/1978."

31. Ernesto Chávez, *The U.S. War with Mexico: A Brief History with Documents* (Boston: Bedford / St. Martin's, 2008), 26.

32. See Laura E. Gómez, "How a Fragile Claim to Whiteness Shaped Mexican Americans' Relations with Indians and African Americans," in *Manifest Destinies: The Making of the Mexican American Race* (New York: New York University Press, 2007), 81–115.

33. Glenn A. Chambers, *From the Banana Zones to the Big Easy: West Indian and Central American Immigration to New Orleans, 1910–1940* (Baton Rouge: Louisiana State University Press, 2019), 133–134.

34. As Chambers noted in regard to New Orleans, "work and education were the primary vehicles by which Latin Americans transitioned into whiteness." See Chambers, *From the Banana Zones*, 132.

CHAPTER 1: MULTIRACIAL DEMOCRACY AND RADICAL RECONSTRUCTION

1. Tom Chaffin, *Fatal Glory: Narciso López and the First Clandestine U.S. War against Cuba* (Charlottesville: University Press of Virginia, 1996), 39–40.

2. For more on López's political alliances and his final expeditions, see Tom Chaffin, "'Sons of Washington': Narciso López, Filibustering, and U.S. Nationalism, 1848–1851," *Journal of the Early Republic* 15, no. 1 (Spring 1995): 79–108, https://doi.org/10.2307/3124384.

3. Ada Ferrer, *Cuba: An American History* (New York: Scribner, 2021), 112.

4. For additional details on this filibuster, see Chaffin, *Fatal Glory*, 126–139.

5. Chaffin, *Fatal Glory*, 215–216.

6. Diego Vicente Tejera, "Education in Democratic Societies," in *A Century of Cuban Writers in Florida: Selected Prose and Poetry*, trans. Carolina Hospital, ed. Carolina Hospital and Jorge Cantera (Sarasota: Pineapple Press, 1996), 53.

7. For more on the beginning of the Ten Years' War and the insurrection's debates over race and enslavement, see Ferrer, *Cuba*, 129–132.

8. Candelaria Figueredo, *La Abanderada de 1868, Candelaria Figueredo (Hija de Perucho)* (Havana: Comisión Patriótica "Pro Himno Nacional" a la Mujer Cubana, 1929), 31.

9. Juan Pérez Rolo, *Mis Recuerdos* (Key West: circa 1920s), 9. University of Florida Digital Collections, https://ufdc.ufl.edu/UF00089813/00001/1j.

10. While the clear majority of the exile communities were in the United States and parts of the Caribbean, there were also others in the greater Gulf of Mexico region. See Dalia Antonia Muller, *Cuban Émigrés and Independence in the Nineteenth-Century Gulf World* (Chapel Hill: University of North Carolina Press, 2017).

11. Lisandro Pérez, *Sugar, Cigars, and Revolution: The Making of Cuban New York* (New York: New York University Press, 2018), 103, 132, 137.

12. See Joan Casanovas, *Bread, or Bullets! Urban Labor and Spanish Colonialism in Cuba, 1850–1898* (Pittsburgh, PA: University of Pittsburgh Press, 1998), 79–84.

13. Joan Casanovas has noted that during the various conflicts within insurgent circles during the Ten Years' War, exiled Cuban workers articulated a vision of a free Cuba that was more inclusive and increasingly "clashed with the more conservative wing, the Aldamistas." See Casanovas, *Bread, or Bullets!*, 10, 111–113.

14. Jean Stubbs, *Tobacco on the Periphery: A Case Study in Cuban Labour History, 1860–1958* (Cambridge: Cambridge University Press, 1985), 69.

15. Stubbs, *Tobacco on the Periphery*, 69.

16. "La Union de Tabaqueros," *The Tobacco Leaf*, November 8, 1879, 2. University of South Florida Digital Commons, https://digitalcommons.usf.edu/tobacco_leaf/1086; Pérez Rolo, *Mis Recuerdos*, 29.

17. For more on the history of the lector, see Araceli Tinajero, *El Lector: A History of the Cigar Factory Reader*, trans. Judith E. Grasberg (Austin: University of Texas Press, 2010).

18. José Rivero Muñiz, "La Lectura en las Tabaquerías: Monografía Histórica," *Revista de la Biblioteca Nacional José Martí* 2, no. 4 (October–December 1951): 215–216. Oficina del Historiador de la Ciudad de La Habana—Colecciones Digitales, https://repositoriodigital.ohc.cu/s/repositoriodigital/item/37259.

19. See appendix of Susan S. Nelson, *The Transformation of Key West: The Cigar Workers of Cuba and the Built Environment, 1869–1930* (Boston University, December 1996), 40–46, Florida Keys History Center at the Monroe County Public Library, Box Industries: Banks, Crawfishing/Lobstering, Film, Cigar Making; *El Yara* in particular was one of the more notable separatist publications in Key West. For more on the newspaper and its editor, José Dolores Poyo, see Gerald E. Poyo, *Exile and Revolution: José D. Poyo, Key West, and Cuban Independence* (Gainesville: University Press of Florida, 2014).

20. Casanovas, *Bread, or Bullets!*, 85.

21. "Key West," *New York Times*, January 11, 1874, 3.

22. The 1885 Key West census mentioned here and throughout this chapter is a digitized version compiled by Professor Consuelo Stebbins that has been provided to the author. For a hard copy of this census, see 1885 Key West Census, Florida Keys History Center at the Monroe County Public Library.

23. *Stemmer* and *stripper* were used interchangeably to describe this particular position. In the 1885 Key West census, over 90 percent of tobacco stemmers were women. See 1885 Key West Census, Florida Keys History Center at the Monroe County Public Library.

24. During the 1890s, many issues of *Revista de Cayo Hueso* catalogued the fundraising and charity work of Cuban women in Key West and other exile centers. See *Revista de Cayo Hueso*, University of Florida Digital Collections, accessed September 23, 2020, https://ufdc.ufl.edu/AA00046724/00008/allvolumes.

25. See Antonio Rafael de la Cova, "Cuban Exiles in Key West during the Ten Years' War, 1868–1878," *Florida Historical Quarterly* 89, no. 3 (Winter 2011): 298.

26. Teófilo Domínguez, *Figuras y Figuritas: Ensayos Biográficos* (Tampa: Lafayette Street, 1899), 29, 34, 43, 51. Internet Archive, https://archive.org/details/figurasyfigurita00domi.

27. Martín Morúa Delgado, "Cuba and the Colored Race," in *A Century of Cuban Writers in Florida: Selected Prose and Poetry*, trans. María Elena Valdés, ed. Carolina Hospital and Jorge Cantera (Sarasota: Pineapple Press, 1996), 66.

28. Oilda Hevia Lanier, *El Directorio Central de Las Sociedades Negras de Cuba (1886–1894)* (Havana: Editorial de Ciencias Sociales, 1996), 39.

29. Diego Vicente Tejera, "Blancos y Negros," in *Enseñanzas y Profecías* (Havana: La Prueba, 1916), 65–87.

30. Tejera, "Education in Democratic Societies," 51.
31. Tejera, "Education in Democratic Societies," 51.
32. Antonio Diaz y Carrasco, "Como y cuando se fundó 'San Carlos,'" *Revista de Cayo Hueso*, May 19, 1897, 7.
33. Domínguez, *Figuras y Figuritas*, 15; Hospital and Cantera, *A Century of Cuban Writers in Florida*, ed. Carolina Hospital and Jorge Cantera (Sarasota: Pineapple Press, 1996), 43.
34. Teófilo Domínguez, "Emilio Planas," *Revista de Cayo Hueso*, July 10, 1898, 19.
35. Pérez Rolo, *Mis Recuerdos*, 42–44.
36. Diaz y Carrasco, "Como y cuando se fundó 'San Carlos,'" *Revista de Cayo Hueso*, May 19, 1897, 7.
37. For more on this visit, see José L. Franco, *Antonio Maceo: Apuntes para una historia de su vida*, vol. 1 (Havana: Editorial de Ciencias Sociales, Instituto Cubano del Libro, 1975), 288–289.
38. To commemorate the one-year anniversary of Maceo's death, the bulk of the December 12 edition of Key West's *Revista de Cayo Hueso* was dedicated to Maceo and his broader importance in the history of Cuban independence. See *Revista de Cayo Hueso*, December 12, 1897.
39. *El Yara*, October 31, 1885.
40. *El Yara*, October 31, 1885.
41. Eric Foner, *Freedom's Lawmakers: A Directory of Black Officeholders during Reconstruction* (New York: Oxford University Press, 1993), 136, 147.
42. W. E. B. Du Bois, *Black Reconstruction in America: An Essay toward a History of the Part which Black Folk Played in the Attempt to Reconstruct Democracy in America, 1860–1880* (New York: Oxford University Press, 2007), 171; Paul Ortiz, *Emancipation Betrayed: The Hidden History of Black Organizing and White Violence in Florida from Reconstruction to the Bloody Election of 1920* (Berkeley: University of California Press, 2005), 11.
43. Foner, *Freedom's Lawmakers*, 30, 77–78, 84, 147, 173, 186; Jerrell H. Shofner, *Nor Is It Over Yet: Florida in the Era of Reconstruction, 1863–1877* (Gainesville: University Presses of Florida, 1974), 91–92, 214, 227–228.
44. "A Queer Town," *New York Times*, January 2, 1874, 3.
45. For a broad overview of Key West's Black community during the nineteenth century, see Sharon Wells, *Forgotten Legacy: Blacks in Nineteenth Century Key West* (Key West: Historic Key West Preservation Board, 1982).
46. For more on the increasing migration of Bahamians to Key West in the late nineteenth century, see Howard Johnson, *The Bahamas from Slavery to Servitude, 1783–1933* (Gainesville: University Press of Florida, 1996), 151–154; Gail Saunders, *Race and Class in the Colonial Bahamas, 1880–1960* (Gainesville: University Press of Florida, 2016), 90–91.
47. Jeanne E. English, "English Family Research," 3, Florida Keys History Center at the Monroe County Public Library, Biographical Files D-E, "English Nelson / English James Nelson."
48. English, "English Family Research," 3; Canter Brown Jr., *Florida's Black Public Officials, 1867–1924* (Tuscaloosa: University of Alabama Press, 1998), 173.
49. Wells, *Forgotten Legacy*, 6; *Key West Citizen*, February 9, 1996, clipping, Florida Keys History Center at the Monroe County Public Library, Biographical Files GA-GE, "Gabriel Robert."

50. "Key West—People," *Good Templars' Watchword*, March 12, 1879, clipping, Florida Keys History Center at the Monroe County Public Library, Box 1 African-American History, Folder Slave Trade—Letters and Transcriptions; Jefferson B. Browne, *Key West: The Old and the New* (St. Augustine: The Record Company Printers and Publishers, 1912), 22.

51. "Hon J. Willis Menard," *New York Globe*, June 2, 1883, 1; Bess Beatty, "John Willis Menard: A Progressive Black in Post-Civil War Florida," *Florida Historical Quarterly* 59, no. 2 (October 1980): 123–143.

52. *Weekly Floridian*, July 4, 1882, clipping, Florida Keys History Center at the Monroe County Public Library, Box 1 African-American History, Folder Black History File no. 2.

53. For more on the connections between Menard's life and the Caribbean, see Tim Watson, "The Caribbean Career of John Willis Menard," *Journal of Caribbean History* 50, no. 2 (2016): 171–188.

54. Jerrell H. Shofner, "Florida," in *The Black Press in the South, 1865–1979*, ed. Henry Lewis Suggs (Westport: Greenwood Press, 1983), 93; Beatty, "John Lewis Menard," 135.

55. This is particularly true in his poems "Stanzas on Cuba" and "Free Cuba." See John Willis Menard, *Lays in Summer Lands* (Tampa, FL: University of Tampa Press, 2002), 9, 49.

56. James Weldon Johnson, *The Autobiography of an Ex-Colored Man* (New York: Dover Publications, 1995), 31.

57. Johnson, *Autobiography*, 33.

58. Paul Ortiz, *An African American and Latinx History of the United States* (Boston: Beacon Press, 2018), 74–79.

59. "A Question of Citizenship," *Key of the Gulf*, July 1, 1876, 1.

60. For more on Cuban political activity during this period, see Gerald E. Poyo, "Cuban Revolutionaries and Monroe County Reconstruction Politics, 1868–1876," *Florida Historical Quarterly* 55, no. 4 (April 1977): 407–422.

61. *Key West Dispatch*, quoted in *Nassau Guardian*, May 20, 1876, 2.

62. Figueroa is listed alongside other Black representatives in Canter Brown Jr.'s research on Black elected officials in Florida. While mentions of Figueroa are sparse in the historical record, a "Jose J. Fiqueroa" was listed as being an alderman in Walter C. Maloney's 1876 text on Key West, although no mention was made of his race. However, there is a record of a José Figueroa's death that identifies him as a Black Cuban who passed away in Key West in 1887 at the age of sixty-two. See Canter Brown Jr., *Florida's Black Public Officials, 1867–1924* (Tuscaloosa: University of Alabama Press, 1998), 172–173; Canter Brown Jr. to Tom Hambright, April 7, 1995, Florida Keys History Center at the Monroe County Public Library, Box 1 African American History, Folder Black History File no. 2; Walter C. Maloney, *A Sketch of the History of Key West, Florida* (Newark: Advertiser Printing House, 1876), 76. Library of Congress, https://www.loc.gov/item/01021587; entry for "Jose Figueroa," July 14, 1887, Florida Deaths, 1877–1939, FamilySearch.org.

63. Pérez Rolo, *Mis Recuerdos*, 28–29.

64. "Total Population—Foreign Born," 1870. SocialExplorer.com (based on data from US Census Bureau; accessed August 12, 2020).

65. The overwhelming majority of this group would have been from the Bahamas. Key West's Caribbean population was almost exclusively Cuban or Bahamian.

66. "Total Population—Foreign Born—Cuba," 1870. SocialExplorer.com (based on data from US Census Bureau; accessed August 12, 2020); "Total Population—Foreign Born—West Indies," 1870. SocialExplorer.com (based on data from US Census Bureau; accessed August 12, 2020).

67. "Total Population—Foreign Born," 1880. SocialExplorer.com (based on data from US Census Bureau; accessed August 12, 2020).

68. "Total Population—Colored," 1880. SocialExplorer.com (based on data from US Census Bureau; accessed August 12, 2020).

69. Robert B. Elliott, "Robert B. Elliott on Civil Rights (1874)," in *Voices of Freedom: A Documentary History*, 4th ed., vol. 1, ed. Eric Foner (New York: W. W. Norton & Company, 2014), 329.

70. *Key West Dispatch*, quoted in "Celebration of the Civil Rights Bill," *Nassau Guardian*, April 3, 1875, 2.

71. *Key West Dispatch*, quoted in "Celebration," 2.

72. *Nassau Guardian*, October 13, 1875, 2.

73. *Key West Dispatch*, quoted in *Nassau Guardian*, October 27, 1875, 2.

74. A July 5, 1875, celebration in Vicksburg, Mississippi, that included many Black participants was broken up by a "white mob" that attacked and killed some of the participants. See David W. Blight, *Race and Reunion: The Civil War in American Memory* (Cambridge: Belknap Press of Harvard University Press, 2001), 134.

75. Shofner, *Nor Is It Over Yet*, 92.

76. "One Hundredth Anniversary of American Independence!," *Key of the Gulf*, July 8, 1876, 2.

77. Shofner, *Nor Is It Over Yet*, 213–214, 340.

78. *Key of the Gulf*, November 11, 1882, 2.

79. A "C. Borrego" was listed as one of the members of the executive committee. Carlos Borrego was an active member of Key West's Cuban community and played a role in *Sociedad El Progreso*. See "Republican Mass Meeting," *Key of the Gulf*, May 13, 1876, 2; Gerald E. Poyo, *"With All, and for the Good of All": The Emergence of Popular Nationalism in the Cuban Communities of the United States, 1848–1898* (Durham, NC: Duke University Press, 1989), 82.

80. One local observer recalled this election as the "the most bitter election ever held in Monroe county." See Browne, *Key West*, 131–132.

81. Ironically, Carlos Manuel de Céspedes y Céspedes found himself on the other end of political ire during the 1882 election. By this time, Céspedes was working in the city's customs house alongside Wicker. See *Key of the Gulf*, November 4, 1882, 2.

82. *Key of the Gulf*, October 14, 1882, 2.

83. "Cubans True to Themselves," *Key of the Gulf*, November 11, 1882, 3.

84. *Key West Dispatch*, quoted in "San Carlos Theatre," *Nassau Guardian*, October 27, 1875, 2.

85. *Key West Democrat*, November 1, 1880, 3; "Republican Mass Meeting," *Key of the Gulf*, May 13, 1876, 2.

86. In a description of the theater, one local publication referred to it as "the best building of its kind in Key West." See *Key West Dispatch* quoted in "San Carlos Theatre," *Nassau Guardian*, October 27, 1875, 2.

87. De la Cova, "Cuban Exiles," 298.

88. 1885 Key West Census, Florida Keys History Center at the Monroe County Public Library.
89. 1885 Key West Census.
90. 1885 Key West Census; Poyo, *With All*, 82.
91. See Gary R. Mormino and George E. Pozzetta, *The Immigrant World of Ybor City: Italians and Their Latin Neighbors in Tampa, 1885–1985* (Urbana: University of Illinois Press, 1987).
92. 1885 Key West Census, Florida Keys History Center at the Monroe County Public Library; the 1885 census included an individual's place of birth as well as the birthplace of the individual's parents. Given that nearly all Cuban and Bahamian residents were first- or second-generation immigrants, this task was fairly straightforward. Identifying African Americans is a bit more nuanced. Nevertheless, I have counted "likely African Americans" here as individuals identified in the census as Black or "mulatto" whose heritage is within the United States. These individuals were born in or had parents from Florida, Georgia, South Carolina, and Virginia.
93. 1885 Key West Census.
94. Howard Johnson, "Bahamian Labor Migration to Florida in the Late Nineteenth and Early Twentieth Centuries," *International Migration Review* 22, no. 1 (Spring 1988): 85–87.
95. Jerrell Shofner, for instance, noted that some violent incidents between 1873–1874 may have been motivated by competition over work. Paul Ortiz has also pointed to William Artrell's negative comments about African American parishioners. See Shofner, *Nor Is It Over Yet*, 236; Ortiz, *Emancipation Betrayed*, 96–97.
96. "Gabriel Blows the Trumpet," *Key West Dispatch*, March 22, 1879, 3.
97. Wells, *Forgotten Legacy*, 42.
98. "Church Directory," *Key of the Gulf*, August 23, 1879, 1.
99. "Key West—People," *Good Templars' Watchword*, March 12, 1879, clipping, Florida Keys History Center at the Monroe County Public Library, Box 1 African-American History, Folder Slave Trade—Letters and Transcriptions; *Key West Democrat*, September 15, 1883, 2; "The National Capital," *New York Globe*, December 1, 1883, 1.
100. "Key West," *Key of the Gulf*, January 8, 1876, 1.
101. Wells, *Forgotten Legacy*, 42.
102. This is referenced in a report by an Episcopal bishop when he visited Key West and was met by a Cuban delegation. See *The Episcopal Register*, quoted in "Florida," *Nassau Guardian*, April 1, 1876, 2.
103. "Church Directory," *Key of the Gulf*, August 23, 1879, 1.
104. "Tribute of Respect," *Key of the Gulf*, November 11, 1882, 2; *Key West Democrat*, April 29, 1882, 3.
105. Jesse E. Hoffnung-Garskof, *Racial Migrations: New York City and the Revolutionary Politics of the Spanish Caribbean, 1850–1902* (Princeton, NJ: Princeton University Press, 2019), 74.
106. Pérez Rolo, *Mis Recuerdos*, 29.
107. *Key West Dispatch*, February 22, 1879, 1.
108. As David Fahey has noted, the International Order of Good Templars (IOGT) offered membership to African Americans, although he did note that "the controversy over the rights of blacks culminated in the great schism that divided

the international organization from 1876 to 1887." Fahey has also contextualized Artrell within these broader debates. For more on the IOGT, race, and Artrell's work with the IOGT, see David M. Fahey, *Temperance and Racism: John Bull, Johnny Reb, and the Good Templars* (Lexington: University Press of Kentucky, 1996), 6, 78, 120–123; *Key of the Gulf*, April 29, 1882, 3; *Key West Democrat*, April 29, 1882, 2.

109. "A Question of Citizenship," *Key of the Gulf*, July 1, 1876, 1.

110. *Key West Democrat*, April 29, 1882, 2.

111. *Key of the Gulf*, quoted in *Key West Democrat*, September 1, 1883, 2.

112. *Key West Democrat*, September 1, 1883, 2.

113. *Key West Democrat*, September 1, 1883, 2.

114. Poyo, "Cuban Revolutionaries," 419.

115. "Grand Democratic Rally and Torchlight Procession, Friday Night," *Key West Democrat*, November 1, 1880, 2.

116. "Grand Democratic Rally," 2.

117. *Key West Democrat*, September 1, 1883, 2; *Key West Democrat*, September 15, 1883, 3.

118. *Key West Democrat*, September 1, 1883, 2.

119. Ferrer surmised these as being seen in "old but changing anxieties about black power, in misgivings about black mobilization, in racialized assumptions about civilization and politics." See Ada Ferrer, *Insurgent Cuba: Race, Nation, and Revolution, 1868–1898* (Chapel Hill: University of North Carolina Press, 1999), 197–198.

120. *Key West Democrat*, November 1, 1880, 3; *Key West Democrat*, August 18, 1883, 2, 3; *Key West Democrat*, September 15, 1883, 2.

121. *Key West Democrat*, September 15, 1883, 2, 3.

122. Foner, *Freedom's Lawmakers*, xiii.

123. L. W. Livingston, "Peculiarities of Key West," *New York Age*, November 3, 1888, clipping, 1, Florida Keys History Center at the Monroe County Public Library, Box 1 African-American History, Folder Black History File no. 2.

124. At the time, "Conch" was the informal name given to white Bahamians. Over time, and in the present day, the term has come to signify any Key West resident, regardless of ethnicity.

125. Livingston, "Peculiarities of Key West."

126. L. W. Livingston, "Freest Town in the South," *New York Age*, December 1, 1888, clipping, Florida Keys History Center at the Monroe County Public Library, Box 1 African-American History, Folder Black History File no. 2.

127. Livingston, "Freest Town in the South"; Paul Ortiz used Livingston's writing in a chapter that drew connections between African American activism and the Cuban independence movement. See Paul Ortiz, *An African American and Latinx History of the United States* (Boston: Beacon Press, 2018), 86–90.

128. Livingston, "Freest Town in the South."

CHAPTER 2: LIBERTY AND LABOR IN CUBAN SOUTH FLORIDA

1. In 1978, Rodríguez was interviewed for a series on the history of Black life in Florida. See Francisco Rodríguez Sr., interview by Fred Beaton and Otis Anthony, August 11, 1978, University of South Florida Special Collections, African Americans in Florida Project, https://digitalcommons.usf.edu/otis_anthony_ohp/55.

2. Francisco Rodríguez Sr., interview.

3. Francisco Rodríguez Sr., interview.

4. Nancy A. Hewitt, *Southern Discomfort: Women's Activism in Tampa, Florida, 1880s–1920s* (Urbana: University of Illinois Press, 2001), 119–120.

5. Diego Vicente Tejera, "Blancos y Negros," in *Enseñanzas y Profecias* (Havana: La Prueba, 1916), 67.

6. Francisco Rodríguez Sr., interview.

7. Teófilo Domínguez, *Figuras y Figuritas: Ensayos Biográficos* (Tampa: Lafayette Street, 1899), 15, 34, 50–51. Internet Archive, https://archive.org/details/figurasyfigurita00domi; for more on Serra and Black Cuban New York, see Jesse Hoffnung-Garskof, *Racial Migrations: New York City and the Revolutionary Politics of the Spanish Caribbean* (Princeton: Princeton University Press, 2019).

8. Domínguez, *Figuras y Figuritas*, 15.

9. Domínguez, *Figuras y Figuritas*, 51.

10. Domínguez, *Figuras y Figuritas*, 62.

11. Domínguez, *Figuras y Figuritas*, 43.

12. Domínguez, *Figuras y Figuritas*, 53.

13. Jesse Hoffnung-Garskoff, in his analysis of Caribbean New York City, used Domínguez's book to emphasize the text's focus on "self-making" among Black Cubans. See Hoffnung-Garskof, *Racial Migrations*, 12.

14. Domínguez, *Figuras y Figuritas*, 29, 34, 43, 51.

15. Esteban Borrero Echeverria, "Maceo Ha Muerto," *Revista de Cayo Hueso*, December 12, 1897, 11.

16. S. F., "Juan Gualberto Gomez," *Revista de Cayo Hueso*, June 12, 1898, 6; Carlos Moner y Bonilla, "Velada en honor de Juan Gualberto Gomez," *Revista de Cayo Hueso*, August 28, 1898, 13.

17. *Revista de Cayo Hueso*, November 28, 1897, 17.

18. José Miró, *Muerte del General Maceo* (Key West: El Yara, 1897).

19. John E. Lewis to *Wisconsin Weekly Advocate*, December 30, 1899, in *Smoked Yankees and the Struggle for Empire: Letters from Negro Soldiers 1898–1902*, ed. Willard B. Gatewood Jr. (Urbana: University of Illinois Press, 1971), 234.

20. "Club 'Discipulas de Marti,'" *Revista de Cayo Hueso*, September 26, 1897, 14; C. P., "El Club 'Emilio Nuñez,'" *Revista de Cayo Hueso*, December 12, 1897, 19.

21. *Tampa Morning Tribune*, September 30, 1896, 1.

22. "Club 'Mariana Grajales de Maceo,'" *Revista de Cayo Hueso*, June 23, 1898, 9.

23. "Club 'Mariana Grajales de Maceo,'" *Revista de Cayo Hueso*, June 23, 1898, 9.

24. Hewitt, *Southern Discomfort*, 74.

25. Wenceslao Gálvez y Delmonte, *Tampa: Impressions of an Emigrant*, trans. Noel M. Smith (Gainesville: University Press of Florida, 2020), 82–84; *Morning Tribune* (Tampa), May 15, 1897, 1.

26. Josefina Toledo Benedit, *La Madre Negra de Martí* (Casa Editorial Verde Olivo: Havana), 2009, 11, 33; entry for "Paulina Pedroso," March 16, 1905, Florida, Key West Passenger Lists, 1898–1945, NARA Microfilm Publication T940, FamilySearch.org.

27. Entry for "Ruperto Pedroso" and "Paulina Hernandez," December 25, 1886, Florida, County Marriages, 1830–1957, FamilySearch.org.

28. Octavio de la Suaree, "Reliquias Historicas," *El Avance Criollo*, March 17, 1955, clipping, University of South Florida Special Collections, Tony Pizzo Collection, Box 173, Folder Pizzo—Photographs—Pedroso, Paulina.

29. Toledo Benedit, *La Madre Negra de Martí*, 94.

30. "One of Cuba's Heroines," *Tampa Morning Tribune*, June 15, 1913, 27; Rodríguez Sr., interview.

31. Many Black Cubans took umbrage with suggestions that they should be indebted to white leadership. As Ada Ferrer has noted, Rafael Serra "and other activists did not deny white leadership. Rather, they suggested that black Cubans' debt to that leadership had been paid in the course of the war. The war had not indebted them; it had entitled them." See Ada Ferrer, *Insurgent Cuba: Race, Nation, and Revolution, 1868–1898* (Chapel Hill: University of North Carolina Press, 1999), 135.

32. Lillian Guerra, *The Myth of José Martí: Conflicting Nationalisms in Early Twentieth-Century Cuba* (Chapel Hill: University of North Carolina Press, 2005), 27, 37–38.

33. Carmen E. Lamas, "The Black *Lector* and Martín Morúa Delgado's *Sofía* (1891) and *La Familia Unzúazu* (1901)," *Latino Studies* 13, no. 1 (2015): 117, https://doi:10.1057/lst.2014.73.

34. Ferrer, *Insurgent Cuba*, 132–133.

35. José Martí was central to this vision. As Ada Ferrer has noted about Martí's view on race in a future Cuban republic, "Martí posited powerful images of a nation premised on racial unity: a new kind of republic that would not be white or Black, but simply Cuban." See Ada Ferrer, *Cuba: An American History* (New York: Scribner, 2021), 143.

36. Lisandro Pérez, *Sugar, Cigars, and Revolution: The Making of Cuban New York* (New York: New York University Press, 2018), 14.

37. For an overview of his early visits to Tampa and Key West, see Gerald E. Poyo, *"With All, and for the Good of All": The Emergence of Popular Nationalism in the Cuban Communities of the United States, 1848–1898* (Durham, NC: Duke University Press, 1989), 98–100.

38. José Martí, "With All, for the Good of All," in *José Martí Reader: Writings on the Americas*, trans. Elinor Randall, Mary Todd, and Carmen González Díaz, ed. Deborah Shnookal and Mirta Muñiz (Melbourne: Ocean Press, 1999), 133.

39. See Hoffnung-Garskof, *Racial Migrations*, 134.

40. Martí, "With All," 140–141.

41. José Martí, "My Race," in *José Martí: Selected Writings*, ed. and trans. Esther Allen (New York: Penguin Books, 2002), 319.

42. Martí, "My Race," 320.

43. See Hoffnung-Garskof, *Racial Migrations*, 175.

44. Danielle Pilar Clealand, *The Power of Race in Cuba: Racial Ideology and Black Consciousness during the Revolution* (New York: Oxford University Press, 2017), 56.

45. Carolina Hospital and Jorge Cantera, "Diego Vicente Tejera," in *A Century of Cuban Writers in Florida*, ed. Carolina Hospital and Jorge Cantera (Sarasota: Pineapple Press, 1996), 43.

46. Tejera, "Blancos y Negros," 68.

47. Tejera, "Blancos y Negros," 70–73.

48. Tejera, "Blancos y Negros," 75.
49. Tejera, "Blancos y Negros," 76.
50. Tejera, "Blancos y Negros," 77.
51. Tejera, "Blancos y Negros," 77.
52. Guerra, *Myth of José Martí*, 40.
53. Tejera, "Blancos y Negros," 87.
54. Martí, "My Race," 320.
55. Manuel de la Cruz, *La Revolución Cubana y la raza de color: Apuntes y datos* (Key West: La Propaganda, 1895), 18.
56. De la Cruz, *La Revolución Cubana*, 11.
57. De la Cruz, *La Revolución Cubana*, 16–17, 20.
58. Domínguez, *Figuras y Figuritas*, 13–15.
59. Pérez, *Sugar, Cigars, and Revolution*, 305–307; Hoffnung-Garskof, *Racial Migrations*, 220–223.
60. Rafael Serra, "Carta Abierta," in *Para Blancos y Negros: Ensayos Políticos, Sociales y Económicos* (Havana: El Score, 1907), 93. Hathitrust Digital Library, https://hdl.handle.net/2027/coo.31924020422501.
61. Serra, "Carta Abierta," 93.
62. Jean Stubbs, *Tobacco on the Periphery: A Case Study of Cuban Labour History, 1860–1958* (Cambridge: Cambridge University Press, 1985), 57.
63. For an overview, see Jean Stubbs, "Militancy and the Growth of the Unions" and "Early Reformism and Anarcho-Syndicalism," in *Tobacco on the Periphery: A Case Study of Cuban Labour History, 1860–1958* (Cambridge: Cambridge University Press, 1985), 85–107; Frank Fernández, *Cuban Anarchism: The History of a Movement*, trans. Charles Bufe (Tucson: See Sharp Press, 2001), 17–18.
64. Joan Casanovas, *Bread, or Bullets!: Urban Labor and Spanish Colonialism in Cuba, 1850–1898* (Pittsburgh, PA: University of Pittsburgh Press, 1998), 166.
65. Both ships were owned by the Plant Steamship Company. For more on the company's history and its relation to Cuban South Florida, see Arsenio M. Sanchez, "The Olivette and Mascotte of the Plant Steamship Line," *Sunland Tribune* 20, article 7 (1994). University of South Florida Digital Commons, https://digitalcommons.usf.edu/sunlandtribune/vol20/iss1/7.
66. Evan Matthew Daniel, "Cuban Cigar Makers in Havana, Key West, and Ybor City, 1850s–1890s: A Single Universe?," in *In Defiance of Boundaries: Anarchism in Latin American History*, ed. Geoffroy de Laforcade and Kirwin Shaffer (Gainesville: University Press of Florida, 2015), 27–28.
67. Fernández, *Cuban Anarchism*, 17, 19.
68. Galleani and Malatesta also visited Tampa. See George E. Pozzetta, "An Immigrant Library: The Tampa Italian Club Collection," *Ex Libris* 1, no. 4 (Spring 1978): 10–12.
69. Pozzetta, "Immigrant Library," 12.
70. "La Union de Tabaqueros," *Tobacco Leaf*, November 8, 1879, 2. University of South Florida Digital Commons, https://digitalcommons.usf.edu/tobacco_leaf/1086.
71. Casanovas, *Bread, or Bullets!*, 166.
72. Fernández, *Cuban Anarchism*, 21.
73. Fernández, *Cuban Anarchism*, 19.
74. "Cigarmakers' Strikes," *United States Tobacco Journal*, August 8, 1885,

clipping, University of South Florida Special Collections, Arsenio Sanchez Papers, Box 5, Folder Sanchez Cigar Industry—Strikes.

75. Fernández, *Cuban Anarchism*, 22.

76. Martín Morúa Delgado, "¡Viva el socialismo!," in *Obras Completas*, vol. 3 (Havana: Publicaciones de la Comision Nacional del Centenario de Don Martin Morua Delgado, 1957), 131.

77. Martín Morúa Delgado, "El taller y la patria," in *Obras Completas*, vol. 3 (Havana: Publicaciones de la Comision Nacional del Centenario de Don Martin Morua Delgado, 1957), 132–134.

78. Domínguez, *Figuras y Figuritas*, 29; Fernández, *Cuban Anarchism*, 20, 27.

79. C. Neale Ronning, *Jose Marti and the Emigre Colony in Key West: Leadership and State Formation* (New York: Praeger, Publishers, 1990), 30; Gerald E. Poyo, *"With All, and for the Good of All": The Emergence of Popular Nationalism in the Cuban Communities of the United States, 1848–1898* (Durham, NC: Duke University Press, 1989), 92; in a founding announcement of the Tampa Liga, "Guillermo Sorando" was listed as a founding officer. See "Of the Liga Obrera de Trabajadores de Tampa," *Weekly Tribune* (Tampa), April 5, 1900, 3.

80. Poyo, *"With All,"* 81, 92.

81. Fernández, *Cuban Anarchism*, 25.

82. Poyo, *"With All, and for the Good of All"*, 74.

83. "Key West Is Wild," *Florida Times-Union*, January 3, 1894, clipping, Florida Keys History Center at the Monroe County Public Library, Florida Times-Union 1888–1895 Binder; "Contract Laborers at Key West," *New York Times*, January 19, 1894, 8; "To Be Sent Back to Cuba," *New York Times*, January 29, 1894, 9.

84. José Martí, "To Cuba!," in *José Martí: Selected Writings*, ed. and trans. Esther Allen (New York: Penguin Books, 2002), 322.

85. Martí, "To Cuba!," 327.

86. Fernández, *Cuban Anarchism*, 34; Daniel, "Cuban Cigar Makers," 44.

87. Fernández, *Cuban Anarchism*, 30–31.

88. Gálvez y Delmonte, *Tampa*, 89.

89. Eusebio Hernández y Pérez, *El Período Revolucionario de 1879 a 1895* (Havana: Revista de la Facultad de Letras y Ciencias, 1914), 55. Digital Library of the Caribbean, http://ufdc.ufl.edu/AA00063390/00001.

90. Domínguez, *Figuras y Figuritas*, 28–29.

91. Poyo, *"With All,"* 74.

92. *Brooklyn Blue Label Bulletin*, reprinted in "Cuban Cigar Making," *Cigar Makers' Official Journal*, August 1898, 8.

93. *Brooklyn Blue Label Bulletin*, 8.

94. "Resistencia to the Front," *Tampa Morning Tribune*, November 10, 1900, 2.

95. Nancy Hewitt has also noted how the reporter writing about this event "viewed the racial composition of the queen and her court as unusual and potentially threatening to Anglo sensibilities." See Hewitt, *Southern Discomfort*, 99.

96. "Labor Day Exercises," *Tampa Morning Tribune*, September 5, 1899, 5.

97. "Labor Day Exercises," 5; "Clearwater Press," quoted in "Press Hits Hard," *Tampa Morning Tribune*, April 17, 1900, 2.

98. "Resistencia to the Front," 2.

99. "Resistencia to the Front," 2.

100. "The International Issues an Address," *Tampa Morning Tribune*, November 27, 1900, 1; "Sympathetic Strike Called Off; Unions Go to Work Monday," *Tampa Morning Tribune*, December 2, 1900, 1.

101. "The International Issues an Address," 1.

102. "Is Liberty Dead?," *Cigar Makers' Official Journal*, November 1900, 13.

103. "Business Men Are Called," *Tampa Morning Tribune*, November 15, 1900, 1.

104. As Robert Ingalls noted about the general strategies of the CMIU and the AFL, "by focusing on immediate economic demands and rejecting political action, the AFL and the CMIU appeared to accept the existing order in return for a bigger piece of the pie." See Robert P. Ingalls, *Urban Vigilantes in the New South: Tampa, 1882–1936* (Knoxville: University of Tennessee Press, 1988), 62.

105. "Sympathetic Strike Called Off; Unions Go to Work Monday," *Tampa Morning Tribune*, December 2, 1900, 1.

106. "Resistencia on Its Last Legs; Large Secession from Ranks," *Tampa Weekly Tribune*, August 22, 1901, 1.

107. "How Padilla Made Escape," *Tampa Weekly Tribune*, August 15, 1901, 6.

108. "Resistencia Works Bold Bluff: Proclamation of 'Business Men,'" *Morning Tribune* (Tampa), August 23, 1901, 8; Hewitt, *Southern Discomfort*, 128–129.

109. "Two More Strike Leaders Missed," *Tampa Weekly Tribune*, August 29, 1901, 8.

110. One writer noted the crowd was composed of "Americans, Cubans, Spaniards and Italians." See "Resistencias Now Voting upon Eleven Articles of Agreement," *Tampa Weekly Tribune*, November 22, 1900, 7.

111. "To American Women," *Morning Tribune* (Tampa), August 29, 1901, 1.

112. "Resistencia Works Bold Bluff: Proclamation of 'Business Men,'" *Morning Tribune* (Tampa), August 23, 1901, 8.

113. "Only Luz Left," *Morning Tribune* (Tampa), September 12, 1901, 4.

114. *Jacksonville Metropolis*, quoted in "To American Women," 1.

115. For an overview of the cigar industry, vigilante violence, and the local Citizens' Committee during this period of Tampa's history, see Robert P. Ingalls, "'Pro Bono Publico': The Citizens' Committee of 1901," in *Urban Vigilantes in the New South: Tampa, 1882–1936* (Knoxville: University of Tennessee Press, 1988), 55–86.

116. Ingalls, "'Pro Bono Publico,'" 75.

117. Ingalls, "'Pro Bono Publico,'" 79.

118. Ingalls, "'Pro Bono Publico,'" 80–81.

119. "Favor the Strikers," *Tampa Weekly Tribune*, August 15, 1901, 1.

120. Armando Mendez, *Ciudad de Cigars: West Tampa* (Tampa: Florida Historical Society, 1994), 93.

121. Mendez, *Ciudad de Cigars*, 93.

122. "People Protest," *Morning Tribune* (Tampa), November 15, 1902, 1, 4.

123. Winston James, *Holding Aloft the Banner of Ethiopia: Caribbean Radicalism in Early Twentieth-Century America* (New York: Verso, 1999), 254–255.

124. One Tampa report on a mass meeting noted that he "accused the leaders of Resistencia of doing all they could to impede rather than facilitate a settlement of the strike." See "Happy Workers in Rousing Rally," *Morning Tribune* (Tampa), November 2, 1901, 1.

CHAPTER 3: THE SPECTER OF JIM CROW AND THE LIMITS OF INTERRACIAL DEMOCRACY

Sections of this chapter first appeared in the *Journal of American Ethnic History*. See Andrew Gomez, "Jim Crow and the Caribbean South: Cubans and Race in South Florida, 1885–1930s," *Journal of American Ethnic History* 36, no. 4 (Summer 2017): 25–48.

1. "700 New Cases 'Spif' Yesterday and 7 Deaths; Will Open Hospital," *Tampa Morning Tribune*, October 15, 1918, 5.

2. "Cuban Hospital Has Been Closed," *Tampa Daily Times*, November 7, 1918, 5.

3. "Cigar Factories Get New Order," *Tampa Daily Times*, October 19, 1918, 1.

4. "Epidemic Working toward Peak; 22 Deaths and 1,022 New Cases," *Tampa Morning Tribune*, October 22, 1918, 5.

5. See Nancy K. Bristow, "'The Whole World Seems Upside-Down': Patients, Families, and Communities Confront the Epidemic," in *American Pandemic: The Lost Worlds of the 1918 Influenza Epidemic* (Oxford: Oxford University Press, 2012), 40–81.

6. Gary R. Mormino and George E. Pozzetta, *The Immigrant World of Ybor City: Italians and Their Latin Neighbors in Tampa, 1885–1985* (Urbana: University of Illinois Press, 1987), 184.

7. "'Flu' Situation Is Better Here," *Tampa Daily Times*, October 25, 1918, 5; "Encouraging Reports in Epidemic Put Tampa in Convalescent Class," *Tampa Morning Tribune*, October 26, 1918, 5.

8. The Clara Frye Hospital was Tampa's first Black hospital, founded in 1908. See Nancy A. Hewitt, *Southern Discomfort: Women's Activism in Tampa, Florida, 1880s–1920s* (Urbana: University of Illinois Press, 2001), 157–158.

9. For more on racial divides in Cuban Ybor City, see Susan D. Greenbaum, *More Than Black: Afro-Cubans in Tampa* (Gainesville: University Press of Florida, 2002); Nancy A. Hewitt, *Southern Discomfort*; Winston James, "From a Class for Itself to a Race on Its Own: The Strange Case of Afro-Cuban Radicalism and Afro-Cubans in Florida, 1870–1940," in *Holding Aloft the Banner of Ethiopia: Caribbean Radicalism in Early Twentieth-Century America* (New York: Verso, 1999), 232–257.

10. For more on voting and the Democratic Party in Florida during this period, see Robert Cassanello, "The Right to Vote and the Long Nineteenth Century in Florida," *Florida Historical Quarterly* 95, no. 2 (Fall 2016): 194–220.

11. Aline Helg, *Our Rightful Share: The Afro-Cuban Struggle for Equality, 1886–1912* (Chapel Hill: University of North Carolina Press, 1995), 20.

12. A. H. King, *Constitution of the State of Florida, Adopted by the Convention of 1885, Together with An Analytical Index* (Jacksonville: Dacosta Printing and Publishing House, 1887), 30, 34. Hathitrust Digital Library, https://hdl.handle.net/2027/hvd.hl43la.

13. Referred to in the 1885 constitution as a "capitation tax." King, *Constitution of the State of Florida*, 23, 26.

14. Cassanello, "Right to Vote," 215–216.

15. Edward C. Williamson, *Florida Politics in the Gilded Age, 1877–1893* (Gainesville: University Presses of Florida, 1976), 142.

16. For an overview of Florida's Jim Crow policies and legislation, see Pauli Murray, *States' Laws on Race and Color* (Athens: University of Georgia Press, 1997), 77–88.

17. Lafayette Lowe to Governor of Florida, Florida Keys History Center at the Monroe County Public Library, Biographical Files D-E, "Dean James."

18. Lafayette Lowe to Governor of Florida.

19. The *Florida Sentinel*, reprinted in "Judge Dean's Removal," *New York Age*, August 17, 1889, 2, clipping, Florida Keys History Center at the Monroe County Public Library, Box 1 African-American History, Folder Black History File no. 2.

20. In a chapter on María Valdés de Gutsens, Consuelo Stebbins quoted Dean on this subject within a broader contextualization of race relations in late-nineteenth century Key West. See Consuelo E. Stebbins, "María Valdés de Gutsens, 1860–1941: The Soul of Key West's Mercedes Hospital," in *The Varieties of Women's Experiences: Portraits of Southern Women in the Post-Civil War Century*, ed. Larry Eugene Rivers and Canter Brown Jr. (Gainesville: University Press of Florida, 2009), 107.

21. Michaela Valdes to Manuel Delgado, May 18, 1889, Florida Keys History Center at the Monroe County Public Library, Biographical Files D-E, "Dean James."

22. Michaela Valdes to Manuel Delgado, May 18, 1889.

23. This was likely José de C. Palomino, a Cuban activist in Florida that supported workers' rights. Palomino's race has not been mentioned by other scholars. As a result, it is unclear if this note reflects Palomino's identity or the writer's perception of his identity (listed in the *Florida Times-Union* article as a "colored Cuban"). For more on Palomino, see Gerald E. Poyo, *"With All, and for the Good of All": The Emergence of Popular Nationalism in the Cuban Communities of the United States, 1848–1898* (Durham, NC: Duke University Press, 1989), 87.

24. "A Big Protest," *Florida Times-Union*, August 7, 1889, clipping, Florida Keys History Center at the Monroe County Public Library, Florida Times Union 1888–1895 Binder.

25. "A Big Protest."

26. As noted in chapter 1, the white leadership of the Republican Party in Florida often marginalized Black voices during Reconstruction. Similar trends were seen in Key West after Reconstruction. In 1889, for instance, local Black politicians in the city took umbrage with the appointment of Republican John F. Horr as Collector of Customs. See "All around Fair Florida," *Florida Times-Union*, July 30, 1889, clipping, Florida Keys History Center at the Monroe County Public Library, Florida Times Union 1888–1895 Binder.

27. "Monroe Not in Trim for 1892," *Florida Sentinel*, November 14, 1890, 4, clipping, Florida Keys History Center at the Monroe County Public Library, Box 1 African-American History, Folder African-American—Heritage Articles; "Key West Politics," *Florida Times-Union*, April 6, 1892, clipping, Florida Keys History Center at the Monroe County Public Library, Florida Times Union 1888–1895 Binder.

28. *Daily Equator-Democrat*, June 7, 1889, 4.

29. The *Florida Sentinel*, reprinted in "Judge Dean's Removal," *New York Age*, August 17, 1889, 2, clipping, Florida Keys History Center at the Monroe County Public Library, Box 1 African-American History, Folder Black History File no. 2.

30. "Strikes and Politics," *Florida Times-Union*, August 20, 1889, clipping, Florida Keys History Center at the Monroe County Public Library, Florida Times

Union 1888–1895 Binder; Jefferson B. Browne, *Key West: The Old and the New* (St. Augustine: Record Company Printers and Publishers, 1912), 69.

31. *Daily Gulf Pennant*, June 21, 1893, 1, clipping, Florida Keys History Center at the Monroe County Public Library, Biographical Files D-E, "Delono Angel Judge."

32. "Grand Democratic Rally and Torchlight Procession, Friday Night," *Key West Democrat*, November 1, 1880, 2.

33. Gerald E. Poyo, "Cuban Revolutionaries and Monroe County Reconstruction Politics, 1868–1876," *Florida Historical Quarterly* 55, no. 4 (April 1977): 418–419.

34. A reverend from St. Peter's Episcopal Church was also reportedly arrested for officiating the marriage. See "A Serious Case," *Florida Times-Union*, November 20, 1899, clipping, Florida Keys History Center at the Monroe County Public Library, Florida Times Union 1896, 1897, 1899 Binder; "Key West," *Florida Times-Union*, November 23, 1899, clipping, Florida Keys History Center at the Monroe County Public Library, *Florida Times Union* 1896, 1897, 1899 Binder.

35. *Florida Times-Union*, November 28, 1893, clipping, Florida Keys History Center at the Monroe County Public Library, Florida Times Union 1888–1895 Binder.

36. "Black School Is Burned," *Florida Times-Union*, February 21, 1894, clipping, Florida Keys History Center at the Monroe County Public Library, Florida Times Union 1888–1895 Binder.

37. See Paul Ortiz, *Emancipation Betrayed: The Hidden History of Black Organizing and White Violence in Florida from Reconstruction to the Bloody Election of 1920* (Berkeley: University of California Press, 2005), 79; Thomas F. Fleischmann, "Black Miamians in The Miami Metropolis, 1896–1900," *Tequesta: The Journal of the Historical Association of Southern Florida* 52, no. 1 (1992): 22.

38. "Race War Threatened," *New York Times*, June 25, 1897, 1.

39. "Race War Threatened"; *Florida Times-Union*, June 26, 1897, clipping, Florida Keys History Center at the Monroe County Public Library. Florida Times Union 1896, 1897, 1899 Binder; "Key West Fears a Riot," *New York Times*, June 26, 1897, 1; *Key West Herald* and *Key West Advertiser*, reprinted in *Miami Metropolis*, July 2, 1897, 8.

40. "A Negro Hanged for Assault," *New York Times*, September 24, 1897, 4.

41. *Florida Times-Union*, November 11, 1899, clipping, Florida Keys History Center at the Monroe County Public Library, Florida Times Union 1896, 1897, 1899 Binder; *Florida Times-Union*, January 24, 1902, clipping, Florida Keys History Center at the Monroe County Public Library. Florida Times Union 1900–1905 Binder.

42. James M. Denham and Canter Brown, Jr., "Black Sheriffs of Post–Civil War Florida," *Sheriff's Star*, September–October 1998, 15.

43. "Political Plums," *Tampa Morning Tribune*, November 3, 1898, 1.

44. Denham and Brown, "Black Sheriffs," 15; *Key West Citizen*, February 9, 1996, clipping, Florida Keys History Center at the Monroe County Public Library, Biographical Files GA-GE, "Gabriel Robert."

45. Hewitt, *Southern Discomfort*, 30.

46. Thomas K. Spencer to Whom It May Concern, May 27, 1895, University of South Florida Special Collections, Armwood Family Papers, Box 3, Folder "Miscellaneous: Correspondence—Letters—1877, 1895 General Family Papers."

47. "Key West's Municipal Muss," *Florida Times-Union*, September 26, 1889,

clipping, Florida Keys History Center at the Monroe County Public Library, Florida Times Union 1888–1895 Binder.

48. *Florida Times-Union*, October 6, 1892, clipping, Florida Keys History Center at the Monroe County Public Library, Florida Times Union 1888–1895 Binder; José G. Pompez was one of the founders of the Cuban Revolutionary Party in Key West. While his racial heritage is unclear, his son was Alejandro (Alex) Pompez—a leading figure in the history of Black baseball in the US and someone who was identified as Black. Little can be confirmed about Alejandro's mother, Loretta Pérez Pompez. See "Fundadores del P.R.C. en Key West," *Revista de Cayo Hueso*, February 27, 1898, 10; Adrian Burgos Jr., "Making Cuban Stars: Alejandro Pompez and Latinos in Black Baseball," in *Playing America's Game: Baseball, Latinos, and the Color Line* (Berkeley: University of California Press, 2007), 111–140.

49. Armando Mendez, "Fernando Figueredo: A Cuban Hero Who Was Mayor of West Tampa," *La Gaceta*, December 20, 1996, clipping, University of South Florida Special Collections, Armando Mendez Papers, Box 4, Folder Fernando Figueredo.

50. "Key West Commissioners," *Florida Times-Union*, June 10, 1890, 2, clipping, Florida Keys History Center at the Monroe County Public Library, Florida Times Union 1888–1895 Binder; "Monroe County Politics," *Florida Times-Union*, July 15, 1890, clipping, Florida Keys History Center at the Monroe County Public Library, Florida Times Union 1888–1895 Binder.

51. "Banqueted by Cubanos," *Florida Times-Union*, November 1, 1890, clipping, Florida Keys History Center at the Monroe County Public Library, Florida Times Union 1888–1895 Binder; *Daily Gulf-Pennant* reprinted in "That Key West Letter," *Florida Times-Union*, October 18, 1892, clipping, Florida Keys History Center at the Monroe County Public Library, Florida Times Union 1888–1895 Binder; "Call at Key West," *Florida Times-Union*, November 5, 1892, clipping, Florida Keys History Center at the Monroe County Public Library. Florida Times Union 1888–1895 Binder.

52. "Florida Laws," *Weekly Floridian* (Tallahassee), June 4, 1889, 3; Williamson, *Florida Politics in the Gilded Age*, 160.

53. "Monroe County Politics," *Florida Times-Union*, July 15, 1890, clipping, Florida Keys History Center at the Monroe County Public Library, Florida Times Union 1888–1895 Binder.

54. "Monroe County Politics."

55. For an overview of this history, see Steven F. Lawson, "The Rise and Fall of the White Primary," in *Black Ballots: Voting Rights in the South, 1944–1969* (New York: Columbia University Press, 1976), 23–54.

56. Lawson, "Rise and Fall," 30.

57. As Pam Iorio has noted, this change meant "black voters were relegated to the Republican Party, whose impact on Florida politics was inconsequential." See Pam Iorio, "Colorless Primaries: Tampa's White Municipal Party," *Florida Historical Quarterly* 79, no. 3 (Winter 2001), 297.

58. Cassanello, "Right to Vote," 216.

59. "Pay Your Poll Tax," *Tampa Morning Tribune*, March 8, 1896, 4.

60. Iorio, "Colorless Primaries," 297–318.

61. For more on this policy and early confrontations over it, see University of South Florida Special Collections, Department of Anthropology African Americans in Florida Project, Box 13, Folder "News Clips—Jim Crow—Trolley Cars."

62. "Color Line on Trolley Cars," *Morning Tribune*, June 16, 1904, 1; "Color-Line Is Lifted," *Morning Tribune*, June 21, 1904, 1; "Color Line Is Now in Force," *Morning Tribune*, July 20, 1904, 1.

63. "Jim Crow Bill Has Arrived," *Tampa Morning Tribune*, April 7, 1905, 1; "'Jim Crow' Bill Is Passed," *Tampa Morning Tribune*, April 22, 1905, 1; *Tampa Morning Tribune*, May 23, 1905, 1.

64. "Here's the 'Jim Crow' Bill," *Tampa Morning Tribune*, April 23, 1905, 9.

65. "The Legislative Lay-Out, Seen through a Bright Woman's Eyes," *Tampa Morning Tribune*, April 16, 1905, 10.

66. "Key West News Notes," *Florida Times-Union*, June 24, 1905, clipping, Florida Keys History Center at the Monroe County Public Library, Florida Times Union 1900–1905 Binder.

67. "A 'Jim Crow' Case," *Tampa Morning Tribune*, November 26, 1907, 12; "Negro Objects to White Man on Seats for Blacks," *Tampa Morning Tribune*, December 27, 1909, 10; "Life of a Street Car Man Is Not a Bed of Flowers," *Tampa Tribune*, March 27, 1910, 10.

68. An older statute also gave conductors policing power when they witnessed someone breaking a state law. See Murray, *States' Laws*, 85.

69. "Life of a Street Car Man," 10.

70. *Tampa Morning Tribune*, May 18, 1905, 4.

71. "Color Line on Trolley Cars," *Morning Tribune*, June 16, 1904, 1.

72. "Committee of Citizens Urge Color Line on Street Car," *Morning Tribune*, July 16, 1904, 1.

73. "Chased a Jim Crow," *Tampa Morning Tribune*, November 5, 1905, 2.

74. Lydia López Allen, interview by Susan Greenbaum, July 9, 1994, 19, University of South Florida Special Collections, USF Department of Anthropology African Americans in Florida Project, Box 9, Folder Interviews—Transcripts—Allen, Lydia Lopez, 7/9/1994.

75. Rebecca J. Scott has also pointed to the other ways in which Cuban history intersected with the Homer Plessy case. Scott argued that the case, and the subsequent activism opposed to segregationist policies in Louisiana, should be framed within a "larger Gulf of Mexico" that included Cuban exiles such as Ramón Pagés, for whom "the struggle in Cuba was of a piece with the struggle for equal rights in Louisiana." See Rebecca J. Scott, "The Atlantic World and the Road to 'Plessy v. Ferguson,'" *Journal of American History* 94, no. 3 (December 2007): 731–732, https://doi.org/10.2307/25095133.

76. Helg, *Our Rightful Share*, 119–120, 127–128.

77. Miguel Barnet, *Biography of a Runaway Slave*, trans. W. Nick Hill (Evanston, IL: Curbstone Books, 2016), 126.

78. Ada Ferrer, *Insurgent Cuba: Race, Nation, and Revolution, 1868–1898* (Chapel Hill: University of North Carolina Press, 1999), 159–162.

79. Ricardo Batrell, *A Black Soldier's Story: The Narrative of Ricardo Batrell and the Cuban War of Independence*, trans. Mark A. Sanders (Minneapolis: University of Minnesota Press, 2010), 29.

80. Barnet, *Biography of a Runaway Slave*, 138.

81. Batrell, *Black Soldier's Story*, 141.

82. Barnet, *Biography of a Runaway Slave*, 165.

83. Ada Ferrer has similarly argued that the appointment of prominent officials within Cuba was already being slanted in ways that disenfranchised Black Cubans before the US intervention. After US intervention, Ferrer notes that nationalist leaders stressed "refinement, civility, and whiteness" in an effort to portray the nation in a specific way. See Ferrer, *Insurgent Cuba*, 186–187, 191.

84. Josefina Toledo Benedit, *La Madre Negra de Martí* (Havana: Casa Editorial Verde Olivo), 2009, 111–116.

85. Serafín Portuondo Linares, *Los independientes de color: Historia del Partido Independiente de Color*, 2nd ed. (Havana: Editorial Caminos, 2002), xxviii.

86. See "Jose Ramon Sanfeliz," 1935, 7, University of North Carolina at Chapel Hill, Louis Round Wilson Special Collections Library, Southern Historical Collection, Federal Writers' Project Papers no. 3709. Wilson Library Special Collections Digital Exhibitions and Collections, https://dc.lib.unc.edu/cdm/ref/collection/03709/id/886.

87. Hewitt, *Southern Discomfort*, 119.

88. Francisco Rodríguez Sr., interview by Fred Beaton and Otis Anthony, August 11, 1978, University of South Florida Special Collections, African Americans in Florida Project. University of South Florida Digital Commons, https://digitalcommons.usf.edu/otis_anthony_ohp/55.

89. Key West Writers Program, "Sociedad Cuba Inc.," in *Key West* (Key West: circa 1930s), 227, University of Florida, P. K. Yonge Library of Florida History. University of Florida Digital Collections, https://ufdc.ufl.edu/AA00090265/00001/images/228.

90. Armando Mendez, *Ciudad de Cigars: West Tampa* (Tampa: Florida Historical Society, 1994), 79.

91. Mendez, *Ciudad de Cigars*, 80.

92. This is seen in a photograph of a boys' classroom where a Black student is seated in the front row. In archival records, there are conflicting dates for the photograph. Two prints of the image can be found at the University of Miami's Cuban Heritage Collection. One standalone print—reprinted in this book—has a handwritten 1917 date on the back, while a late-twentieth-century pamphlet from the Instituto San Carlos includes the image and lists a 1912 date. See University of Miami Libraries, Cuban Heritage Collection, San Carlos Institute Collection, Unnumbered Box, San Carlos Institute binder; Instituto San Carlos, "San Carlos Institute: Restoration Project," 8, University of Miami Libraries, Cuban Heritage Collection, San Carlos Institute Collection, Box 1.

93. "Key West News Notes of General Interest," *Florida Times-Union*, January 8, 1907, 1, clipping, Florida Keys History Center at the Monroe County Public Library, Florida Times Union 1906–1908 Binder.

94. Key West Writers Program, "San Carlos Institute," in *Key West* (Key West: circa 1930s), 237, University of Florida, P. K. Yonge Library of Florida History. University of Florida Digital Collections, https://ufdc.ufl.edu/AA00090265/00001/images/238.

95. "Las fiestas del 10 de oct.," *Florida* (Key West), July 26, 1924, 1.

96. "Union Cubana Held Meeting Sunday," *Key West Morning Journal*, June 11, 1912, 1.

97. Teófilo Domínguez, "Emilio Planas," *Revista de Cayo Hueso*, July 10, 1898, 19.

98. Domínguez, "Emilio Planas," 19–20.

99. The images are a part of José Ramón Sanfeliz's Ybor City photo album. See University of South Florida Special Collections, Tony Pizzo Collection, Box 205, Folders "Jose R. San Feliz Album—22" and "Jose R. San Feliz Album—23."

100. For scholars like Aline Helg, this period underscored how white Cubans in power and foreign interests "used a racial ideology together with a myth of racial equality to subordinate and repress Afro-Cubans." In her text, a central case study is the massacre of many Black leaders and supporters of the Partido Independiente de Color in 1912. As she noted, this event "damages forever the myth of Cuban racial equality." Alejandro de la Fuente has acknowledged the role of racism in Cuban society during this period but has also noted that "the rhetorical exaltation of racial inclusiveness as the very essence of nationhood has made racially defined exclusion considerably more difficult, creating in the process significant opportunities for appropriation and manipulation of dominant racial ideologies by those below while limiting the political options of the elites." Rebecca J. Scott similarly noted about the early republic in Cuba that "a practiced eye could easily detect the element of hypocrisy in the Cuban system. But a practiced eye could also see that these formal guarantees created a space for alliance, negotiation, voting, military service, office-holding, union organizing, and education." See Helg, *Our Right Share*, 2–3, 226; Alejandro de la Fuente, *A Nation for All: Race, Inequality, and Politics in Twentieth Century Cuba* (Chapel Hill: University of North Carolina Press, 2001), 8; Rebecca J. Scott, *Degrees of Freedom: Louisiana and Cuba After Slavery* (Cambridge: Belknap Press of Harvard University Press, 2005), 256.

101. As Alejandro de la Fuente has noted, considerable gains were made in regard to Black Cubans accessing public schooling in Cuba, even as segregation in private schools was a persistent issue. See de la Fuente, *Nation for All*, 139–143.

102. "Habla el Sr. José A. López," *Diario de Tampa*, May 29, 1909, 1.

103. See *Herencia: The Anthology of Hispanic Literature of the United States*, ed. Nicolás Kanellos (Oxford: Oxford University Press, 2002), 458.

104. "Habla el Sr. José A. López," *Diario de Tampa*, May 29, 1909, 1.

105. "Carta Abierta," *Diario de Tampa*, June 2, 1909, 1; in addition to Washington's fame at the time, some Cubans also would have been directly familiar with his work. As Frank Andre Guridy has noted, Booker T. Washington recruited Black Cubans to be part of the Tuskegee Institute following the US military intervention in Cuba in 1898. See Frank Andre Guridy, *Forging Diaspora: Afro-Cubans and African Americans in a World of Empire and Jim Crow* (Chapel Hill: University of North Carolina Press, 2010), 27–28.

106. The document does not have a clear author but was likely penned by José Ramón Avellanal. See "Círculo Cubano (Solicitaciones en Cuba)," University of South Florida Special Collections, José Ramón Avellanal Collection, Box 3, Folder 12.

107. See Helg, *Our Rightful Share*, 193–226.

108. For an analysis of this platform, see Linares, *Los Independientes de Color*, 37–52.

109. El Partido Independiente de Color, "The Independent Party of Color," in *The Cuba Reader: History, Culture, Politics*, trans. Aviva Chomsky, ed. Aviva Chomsky, Barry Carr, and Pamela Maria Smorkaloff (Durham, NC: Duke University Press, 2003), 164.

110. El Partido Independiente de Color, "Independent Party of Color," 165.

111. As Rebecca J. Scott noted, the Gómez administration was also calculated in attempting to frame the PIC's goals around the concept of a "race war." See Scott, *Degrees of Freedom*, 242.

112. Helg, *Our Rightful Share*, 162–163.

113. "¿Una República negra?," *Diario de Tampa*, September 22, 1908, 1.

114. "Out of Cuban Racial Troubles May Grow Political Party of Powerful Influence," *Tampa Morning Tribune*, January 31, 1910, 1.

115. "Gomez Pardons Former Official," *Tampa Morning Tribune*, February 21, 1910, 4; Helg, *Our Rightful Share*, 40–41.

116. For more on the law and its context, see Portuondo Linares, "La Enmienda Morúa," in *Los Independientes de Color*, 77–87.

117. Arthur A. Schomburg, "General Evaristo Estenoz," *The Crisis* 4, no. 3, (July 1912): 143. Hathitrust Digital Library, https://hdl.handle.net/2027/hvd.32044009723073.

118. Helg, *Our Rightful Share*, 221–225; Scott, *Degrees of Freedom*, 243.

119. "President Gomez Wants Martial Law Established in His Country," *Key West Morning Journal*, June 5, 1912, 1.

120. "Haitian Negroes and Cuban Rebels," *New York Times*, May 22, 1912, 1.

121. "Union Cubana Held Meeting Sunday," *Key West Morning Journal*, June 11, 1912, 1.

122. "Cuban Colony Joins in Support of Government," *Tampa Daily Times*, May 28, 1912, 5.

123. "Cuban Trouble Is Soon to Be Ended," *Tampa Morning Tribune*, May 23, 1912, 12; "Cuban Negroes Here Offer Government Aid," *Tampa Daily Times*, June 12, 1912, 5; "Cuba Offered Aid by Tampa Negroes," *Tampa Weekly Tribune*, June 13, 1912, 10; "Marti-Maceo Society Calls on Consul Ybor," *Tampa Morning Tribune*, November 20, 1912, 9.

124. Alejandro de la Fuente, "Myths of Racial Democracy: Cuba, 1900–1912," *Latin American Research Review* 34, no. 3 (1999): 66–67; de la Fuente, *Nation for All*, 77; for more on the response by Black Cuban organizations that opposed the PIC in Cuba see Melina Pappademos, *Black Political Activism and the Cuban Republic* (Chapel Hill: The University of North Carolina Press, 2011), 58.

125. Scott, *Degrees of Freedom*, 229.

126. Helg, *Our Rightful Share*, 185–186.

127. "Murmers [sic] of Revolution Have Reached Key West," *The Key West Morning Journal*, June 13, 1912, 1.

128. "Murmers [sic] of Revolution," 1.

129. For a translated version of a Planas article in *Previsión*, see "Jonatás [Emilio Planas], 'Welcome,' Previsión (Havana, Cuba: Oct. 20, 1909" in *Voices of the Race: Black Newspapers in Latin America, 1870–1960* ed. and trans. Paulina Laura Alberto, George Reid Andrews, and Jesse Hoffnung-Garskof (Cambridge: Cambridge University Press, 2022), 233–235.

130. A thank-you to Professor Jesse Hoffnung-Garskof, who provided the author with digitized copies of *Previsión*. One 1908 article documented the construction of La Unión Martí-Maceo's building and the role of women within the organization. Another 1908 article mentions, and seemingly quotes from, an organized group of PIC supporters in Tampa. See "'Previsión' en Tampa," *Previsión*, December 7, 1908, 6; "Se acentúa el entusiasmo," *Previsión*, October 1908, 4.

131. As Nancy Raquel Mirabal has noted in her analysis of Tampa, Black Cubans rarely discussed racial strife in public or in their own institutional records. As a result, analyzing and reading "silences" is critical to understanding South Florida's racial dynamics. See Nancy Raquel Mirabal, "Telling Silences and Making Community: Afro-Cubans and African-Americans in Ybor City and Tampa, 1899–1915," in *Between Race and Empire: African-Americans and Cubans before the Cuban Revolution*, ed. Lisa Brock and Digna Castañeda Fuertes (Philadelphia: Temple University Press, 1998), 49–69.

132. In Cuba, these were chapters of the Ku Klux Klan Kubano (KKKK). See de la Fuente, *Nation for All*, 92, 204–205, 207.

133. Ferrer, *Insurgent Cuba*, 173–182; Scott, *Degrees of Freedom*, 152.

134. De la Fuente, "Myths of Racial Democracy," 67.

135. Helg, *Our Rightful Share*, 105–106.

136. Rafael Serra, "Carta Abierta," in *Para Blancos y Negros: Ensayos Políticos, Sociales y Económicos* (Havana: El Score, 1907), 92. Hathitrust Digital Library, https://hdl.handle.net/2027/coo.31924020422501.

CHAPTER 4: "TWO CULTURES AT THE SAME TIME"

Sections of this chapter first appeared in the *Journal of American Ethnic History*. See Andrew Gomez, "Jim Crow and the Caribbean South: Cubans and Race in South Florida, 1885–1930s," *Journal of American Ethnic History* 36:4 (Summer 2017): 25–48.

1. The concept of "inbetween peoples" has been used by James R. Barrett and David Roediger to describe the racialization of some immigrants during this period. See James R. Barrett and David Roediger, "Inbetween Peoples: Race, Nationality and the 'New Immigrant' Working Class," *Journal of American Ethnic History* 16 no. 3 (Spring 1997): 3–44.

2. Evelio Grillo, *Black Cuban, Black American: A Memoir* (Houston, TX: Arte Público Press, 2000), 30.

3. Armando Mendez, *Ciudad de Cigars: West Tampa* (Tampa: Florida Historical Society, 1994), 168.

4. Rachel L. Swarns, "Hidden in the Past," *St. Petersburg Times*, February 25, 1990, Tampa Section, 3.

5. Francisco Rodriguez Jr., interview by Otis Anthony, May 30, 1978, 1, University of South Florida Special Collections, Department of Anthropology African Americans in Florida Project, Box 11, Folder "Interviews—Transcripts—Rodriguez, Francisco [Jr.] 5/30/1978."

6. Charles Spurgeon Johnson and Lewis Wade Jones, *Statistical Atlas of Southern Counties; Listing and Analysis of Socio-economic Indices of 1104 Southern Counties* (Chapel Hill, NC: University of North Carolina Press, 1941), 77, 80.

7. Nancy Raquel Mirabal, "Telling Silences and Making Community: Afro-Cubans and African-Americans in Ybor City and Tampa, 1899–1915," in *Between Race and Empire: African-Americans and Cubans Before the Cuban Revolution*, ed. Lisa Brock and Digna Castañeda Fuertes (Philadelphia, PA: Temple University Press, 1998), 60.

8. Nancy A. Hewitt, "Becoming Black: Creating a Shared Identity among African Americans and Afro-Cubans in Tampa, Florida, 1880s–1920s," in *Black Women's*

History at the Intersection of Knowledge and Power: ABWH's Twentieth Anniversary Anthology, ed. Rosalyn Terborg-Penn and Janice Sumler-Edmond (Acton, MA: Tapestry Press, 2000), 108–109.

9. Nancy A. Hewitt, *Southern Discomfort: Women's Activism in Tampa, Florida, 1880s–1920s* (Urbana, IL: University of Illinois Press, 2001), 260–262.

10. *Weekly Challenger*, February 16, 1985, clipping, University of South Florida Special Collections, Armwood Family Papers, Box 3, Folder Miscellaneous: No Date General Family Papers.

11. For Armwood's Martí-Maceo membership certificate, invitation, and other biographical information, see University of South Florida Special Collections, Armwood Family Papers, Box 7, Box 5, Folder Organizations: Miscellaneous—Invitations—1920, 1923, 1933, 1937, and Box 3.

12. Leif Bo Petersen and Theo Rehak, *The Music and Life of Theodore "Fats" Navarro: Infatuation* (Lanham, MD: Scarecrow Press, 2009), 10–11.

13. This was also occurring in other ways outside of South Florida. The Tuskegee Institute, for instance, actively recruited Black Cubans during the early 1900s. While they struggled to recruit in South Florida, other Black Cubans joined the institute during this period. See Frank Andre Guridy, "Forging Diaspora in the Midst of Empire: The Tuskegee-Cuba Connection," in *Forging Diaspora: Afro-Cubans and African Americans in a World of Empire and Jim Crow* (Chapel Hill: University of North Carolina Press, 2010), 17–60.

14. Grillo, *Black Cuban, Black American*, 11.

15. Booker T. Washington High School, *Excelsior* (Tampa, FL, 1926), 19–22, University of South Florida Special Collections, Floridiana Collection.

16. Booker T. Washington High School, *Excelsior* (Tampa, FL, 1928), 17, Special Collections, University of South Florida, Armwood Family Papers, Box 3, Folder Armwood—General Family Papers—Yearbook, 1928.

17. Terry Schmida, "Local Teacher Instructed Generations of Key West Musicians," *Key West Citizen*, clipping, Florida Keys History Center at the Monroe County Public Library, African-American History Box 1, Folder "African American—Community and Bahama Village."

18. Terry Schmida, "Theodore 'Fats' Navarro—Key West's Gift to Jazz," *Key West Citizen*, clipping, Florida Keys History Center at the Monroe County Public Library, African-American History Box 1, Folder "African American—Community and Bahama Village"; Petersen and Rehak, *Music and Life*, 12.

19. "Along the N.A.A.C.P. Battlefront," *The Crisis* 43 no. 5 (May 1936), 152; *Key West Citizen*, November 9, 1935, 1.

20. *New York Age*, December 12, 1912, 3, clipping, Florida Keys History Center at the Monroe County Public Library, Box 1 African-American History, Folder Black History File no. 2.

21. "Scholarships for Teachers Are Awarded," *Key West Citizen*, June 12, 1935, 1.

22. "Came Here to Talk on Aliens," *Key West Citizen*, November 11, 1940, 2.

23. The law, also known as the Alien Registration Act of 1940, "required the registration of personal and professional details as well as political affiliations and fingerprinting of all alien residents of the United States from age 14 on" and specifically "made it a criminal offense for any person or organization to advocate the forcible or violent overthrow of the United States government." See Claudia Megele and

Peter Buzzi, "Alien Registration Act of 1940 (Smith Act)," in *Anti-Immigration in the United States: A Historical Encyclopedia*, vol. 1, ed. Kathleen R. Arnold (Santa Barbara: Greenwood, 2011), 8.

24. Quoted in Susan D. Greenbaum, *More than Black: Afro-Cubans in Tampa* (Gainesville: University Press of Florida, 2002), 191.

25. José Fernandez, "Acta No. 8," September 23, 1924, University of Miami Libraries, Cuban Heritage Collection, San Carlos Institute Collection, Unnumbered Box, "Actas of the San Carlos Governing Board, Sept–Oct, 1924."

26. The organization was registered as the Klan of the Keys. See "Imperial Palace, Invisible Empire, Knights of the Ku Klux Klan Charter," February 26, 1921, Florida Keys History Center at the Monroe County Public Library, Box Ku Klux Klan Key West Charter 1921.

27. The names on the charter appear as "J. Y. Porter" and "J. Vining Harris." J. Y. Porter Sr. and J. Vining Harris Sr. also had sons with the same names that resided in Key West. However, the elder J. Vining Harris that was born in 1839 passed away in Key West by 1914. J. Vining Harris Sr., J. Y. Porter Sr., and J. Y. Porter Jr. were all prominent physicians on the island. J. Vining Harris Jr. was a well-known lawyer in Key West. Both families were also active in local politics. For more on the Porter and Harris families, see Jefferson B. Browne, *Key West: The Old and the New* (St. Augustine: Record Company Printers and Publishers, 1912), 134; Gideon Dowse Harris, *Harris Genealogy* (Columbus, MS: Keith Printing Co., 1914), 79–80. Hathitrust Digital Library, https://hdl.handle.net/2027/wu.89066158239; entry for "Jeptha Vining Harris," November 21, 1914, Florida Deaths, 1877–1939, FamilySearch.org.

28. "Hooded Band Goes through in Motorcade," *Tampa Daily Times*, August 7, 1923, 1, 8.

29. "Gangs of Men Whip Three Tampans," *Tampa Daily Times*, November 1, 1923, 1, 11.

30. "Gangs of Men," 1.

31. Stetson Kennedy and Adelpha Pollato, "Enrique and Amanda," January 3, 1939, 12–13, University of North Carolina at Chapel Hill, Louis Round Wilson Special Collections Library, Southern Historical Collection, Federal Writers' Project Papers no. 3709. Wilson Library Special Collections Digital Exhibitions and Collections, https://dc.lib.unc.edu/cdm/ref/collection/03709/id/913.

32. For more on Manuel Cabeza's life and murder, see Florida Keys History Center at the Monroe County Public Library, Box Biographies: Audubon to Morgan, Folder Cabeza/Head.

33. "Norberto Diaz," in *First-Person America*, ed. Ann Banks (New York: Alfred A. Knopf, 1980), 246.

34. Earl R. Adams, "Christmas Eve 1921: A Night to Forget!," *Key West Citizen*, December 23, 1977, Florida Keys History Center at the Monroe County Public Library, Box Biographies: Audubon to Morgan, Folder Cabeza/Head.

35. "Decker, Head Key West Cigar Factory Slain," *Tampa Morning Tribune*, December 26, 1921, 1; *Miami Herald*, December 26, 1921, Florida Keys History Center at the Monroe County Public Library, Box Biographies: Audubon to Morgan, Folder Cabeza/Head.

36. "Head Confessed to Slaying of Decker," *Tampa Morning Tribune*, December 30, 1921, 3; Adams, "Christmas Eve 1921"; "Norberto Diaz," 247.

37. "Gangs of Men," 1.

38. *Key West Dispatch*, quoted in "Celebration of the Civil Rights Bill," *Nassau Guardian*, April 3, 1875, 2; "One Hundredth Anniversary of American Independence!," *Key of the Gulf*, July 8, 1876, 2.

39. "Emancipation Day Celebrated Here," *Tampa Daily Times*, January 2, 1915, "Sporting Section," 2.

40. "Emancipation Day Will Be Observed," *Tampa Sunday Tribune*, January 1, 1928, "Part Two," 7; "Negroes to Celebrate Emancipation Day Here," *Tampa Morning Tribune*, December 31, 1931, 7; "Tampa Negroes Celebrate Their Emancipation Day," *Tampa Sunday Tribune*, January 2, 1938, 13.

41. While changes were made to the park over time, it continues to reside in present-day Bahama Village as Nelson English Park. Regarding the early history of the project, see Jeanne E. English, "English Family Research," 4, Florida Keys History Center at the Monroe County Public Library, Biographical Files D-E, "English Nelson/English James Nelson."

42. "Colored Park Given Name of Nelson English," *Key West Citizen*, August 16, 1934, 1.

43. "To Utilize Park Prize Money for Needed Equipment," *Key West Citizen*, August 18, 1934, 4.

44. "To Utilize Park Prize Money."

45. For the list, see *Key West Citizen*, November 3, 1923, Florida Keys History Center at the Monroe County Public Library, "Key West Qualified Voters 1923 and 1930" Binder.

46. "Total Population—Black," 1920. SocialExplorer.com (based on data from US Census Bureau; accessed December 18, 2020).

47. "Total Population—White," 1920. SocialExplorer.com (based on data from US Census Bureau; accessed December 18, 2020).

48. Hewitt, *Southern Discomfort*, 242–243.

49. Emphasis in original text. See Key West Writers Program, "San Carlos Institute," in *Key West* (Key West: circa 1930s), 237, University of Florida, P. K. Yonge Library of Florida History. University of Florida Digital Collections, https://ufdc.ufl.edu/AA00090265/00001/images/238.

50. R. W. Macdonell, "Our Cuban Work," *Missionary Voice* 1, no. 4 (April 1911): 47.

51. In her analysis of Mexican American women in the early twentieth century, Vicki Ruiz showed how women often made use of religious services and Americanization efforts in a manner that spoke to their own needs and agency. As a result, while many Mexican American women used these services, their participation did not denote a fully assimilationist shift regarding issues like religious conversion. A similar dynamic was likely at play in Cuban South Florida. See Vicki L. Ruiz, "Confronting 'America'" in *From Out of the Shadows: Mexican Women in Twentieth-Century America* (New York: Oxford University Press, 1998), 33–50.

52. Key West High School, *The Conch* 10 (Key West, FL, 1937), Florida Keys History Center at the Monroe County Public Library.

53. Key West High School, *The Conch* 9 (Key West, FL, 1936), 25, Florida Keys History Center at the Monroe County Public Library.

54. "Carlos Recio," Florida Keys History Center at the Monroe County Public Library, Biographical Files RA-RI, "Recio Carlos."

55. Daniel D. Moore et al., *Men of the South: A Work for the Newspaper Reference Library* (New Orleans: Southern Biographical Association, 1922), 286. Hathitrust Digital Library, https://catalog.hathitrust.org/Record/011983877.

56. Harry Gardner Cutler, *History of Florida, Past and Present, Historical and Biographical*, vol. 2 (Chicago: Lewis Publishing Company, 1923), 144–145. Hathitrust Digital Library, https://catalog.hathitrust.org/api/volumes/oclc/1525954.html.

57. The Uhrback surname was from a German grandfather that migrated to Cuba as a sugar planter. Both of Joseph's parents were born in Matanzas, Cuba. Joseph was born in the United States and later served as a US internal revenue collector in Key West. For biographies and the institutional affiliations of Uhrback, Henriquez, Carbonell, and Renedo, see Cutler, *History of Florida*, 290–291, 306–307. Hathitrust Digital Library, https://catalog.hathitrust.org/api/volumes/oclc/1525954.html.

58. Pam Iorio, "Colorless Primaries: Tampa's White Municipal Party," *Florida Historical Quarterly* 79, no. 3 (Winter 2001): 300.

59. Cutler, *History of Florida*, 144–145.

60. Cutler, *History of Florida*, 131.

61. "Mr. Ayala Asks for Fair Play," *Tampa Sunday Tribune*, October 31, 1920, 9; "Florida Still in Democratic Rank, Straight," *Tampa Daily Times*, November 3, 1920, 10.

62. "Day after Tomorrow 'Blue Sunday' according to Chief of Police John Cates," *Key West Morning Journal*, April 5, 1912, 1; "Anuncios Electorales," *Diario de la Mañana*, October 26, 1915, 1, Florida Keys History Center at the Monroe County Public Library, Untitled newspaper box.

63. "Political Announcements," *Key West Morning Journal*, February 19, 1918, 7.

64. "Sen. Arthur Gomez Appointed Judge," *Tampa Daily Times*, May 27, 1937, 16; "Arthur Gomez Now Is Circuit Judge," *Tampa Daily Times*, June 5, 1937, 3; reprinted in "Judge Arthur Gomez Is Dead in Miami," *St. Petersburg Times*, June 3, 1944, 17.

65. Cutler, *History of Florida*, 293.

66. See Gary Mormino and George E. Pizzetta, *The Immigrant World of Ybor City: Italians and Their Latin Neighbors in Tampa, 1885–1985* (Urbana: University of Illinois Press, 1987), 239–240.

67. "Ybor Has Gone to Washington," *Tampa Daily Times*, August 25, 1915, 5.

68. "Cubans Made a Quick Protest," *Tampa Daily Times*, August 24, 1915, 5.

69. "Consul Took Complaint of Discrimination to National Government," *Tampa Daily Times*, August 30, 1915, 7.

70. "El conflicto de Pathé," *El Diario de Tampa*, November 17, 1908, 1; E. F. Tarbel, "A los honorables vecinos de Ybor City y a los bondadosos favorecedores del Teatro Pathé en particular," *El Diario de Tampa*, November 17, 1908, 1–2.

71. As Ian Haney López has noted in his analysis of whiteness within the US legal system, white "does not denote a rigidly defined, congeneric grouping of indistinguishable individuals. It refers to an unstable category which gains its meaning only through social relations and that encompasses a profoundly diverse set of persons." See Ian Haney López, *White by Law: The Legal Construction of Race* (New York: New York University Press, 2006), xxi–xxii.

72. For more on these dynamics, see Gary R. Mormino and George E. Pozzetta,

The Immigrant World of Ybor City: Italians and Their Latin Neighbors in Tampa, 1885–1985 (Urbana: University of Illinois Press, 1987).

73. Ayala was born in Key West in 1888 to Cuban parents. See entry for "Oscar A. Ayala," October 1919, United States Passport Applications, 1795–1925, NARA Microfilm Publications M1490 and M1372, Roll 959, FamilySearch.org; entry for "Oscar Ayala," 1920 United States Census, Sixth Ward, Twenty-Sixth Precinct, Tampa, Hillsborough County, FL, 4B, FamilySearch.org.

74. "Mr. Ayala Asks for Fair Play," *Tampa Sunday Tribune*, October 31, 1920, 9.

75. As Mae Ngai and Ian Haney López have noted, immigrant groups during this period challenged the "black-white paradigm" regarding conceptions of US citizenship. For more on this phenomenon and the Ozawa and Thind cases, see Mae M. Ngai, *Impossible Subjects: Illegal Aliens and the Making of Modern America* (Princeton, NJ: Princeton University Press, 2004), 38–42; Ian Haney López, "*Ozawa and Thind*," in *White by Law*, 56–77.

76. League of United Latin American Citizens, "World War II and Mexican Americans," in *Voices of Freedom: A Documentary History*, 4th ed., vol. 2, ed. Eric Foner (New York: W. W. Norton & Company, 2014), 201.

77. Orozco concedes that whiteness "has some usefulness in the study of LULAC" but also points to the importance of "'Americanness,' 'Mexican Americanness,' and Mexicanness'" to fully understand the group's history. For this and a broader overview of LULAC, see Cynthia E. Orozco, *No Mexicans, Women, or Dogs Allowed: The Rise of the Mexican American Civil Rights Movement* (Austin: University of Texas Press, 2009), 6.

78. "Florida Still in Democratic Rank, Straight," *Tampa Daily Times*, November 3, 1920, 10.

79. "A City within a City, Ybor Is a Live and Very Vital Factor in Progress of Tampa; Making Fine Headway," *Tampa Sunday Tribune*, October 9, 1921, 1B.

80. "City within a City," 4B.

81. "City within a City," 4B.

82. "Ybor Optimist Boys' Center Drive Started," *Tampa Daily Times*, September 15, 1938, 4.

83. "Committee to Be Organized for Latin Festival," *Tampa Sunday Tribune*, December 9, 1934, 2; "Latin Festival Here Will Have Novel Features," *Tampa Sunday Tribune*, December 25, 1938, 10.

84. See Sarah Gualtieri, "Becoming 'White': Race, Religion, and the Foundations of Syrian/Lebanese Ethnicity in the United States," *Journal of American Ethnic History* 20, no. 4 (Summer 2001): 29–58; Earlene Craver, "On the Boundary of White: The Cartozian Naturalization Case and the Armenians, 1923–1925," *Journal of American Ethnic History* 28, no. 2 (Winter 2009): 30–56; Theodore Saloutos, "The Erosion of Hellenic Sentiment," in *The Greeks in the United States* (Cambridge: Harvard University Press, 1964), 232–257.

85. "Adult Classes to Be Opened by Tampa WPA," *Tampa Sunday Tribune*, October 6, 1935, 4; "Interesting Paper on 'Americanization' Read before Tampa Woman's Club," *Tampa Sunday Tribune*, March 4, 1923, 5D; *Tampa Daily Times*, November 22, 1924, 2.

86. "Interesting Paper," 5D.

87. *Tampa Daily Times*, November 22, 1924, 2.

88. "Adult Classes to Be Opened by Tampa WPA," *Tampa Sunday Tribune*, October 6, 1935, 4.
89. "Adult Classes to Be Opened," 4.
90. "Pleasant, Peaceful Observance Fourth," *Tampa Morning Tribune*, July 5, 1921, 7.
91. "Pleasant, Peaceful Observance Fourth," 7.
92. *Florida Times-Union*, quoted in "Making American Citizens," *Key West Citizen*, March 8, 1923, 2.
93. "Latins Organize New Society for Americanization," *Tampa Morning Tribune*, November 16, 1929, 7.
94. "Patriotic Efforts of Leaders of Latin People," *Tampa Daily Times*, January 31, 1922, 4.
95. "Patriotic Efforts," 4.
96. See John F. McClymer, "Gender and the 'American Way of Life': Women in the Americanization Movement," *Journal of American Ethnic History* 10, no. 3 (Spring 1991): 3–20.
97. George J. Sánchez, *Becoming Mexican American: Ethnicity, Culture, and Identity in Chicano Los Angeles, 1900–1945* (New York: Oxford University Press, 1993), 98–104.
98. "Interesting Paper," 5D.
99. "Much Accomplished by Florida's D.A.R.," *Tampa Morning Tribune*, May 16, 1921, 3; "Report on Americanization Work," *Tampa Sunday Tribune*, November 5, 1922, 4A.
100. Neil C. Avery, "Americanization Work in Tampa," *Tampa Morning Tribune*, July 8, 1921, 10A.
101. "Report on Americanization Work," *Tampa Sunday Tribune*, November 5, 1922, 4A.
102. "Report on Americanization Work," 4A.
103. "Mrs. Mederos Told of Club Work in Havana," *Tampa Daily Times*, February 3, 1917, 16.
104. Hewitt, *Southern Discomfort*, 254.
105. Christina D. Abreu, for instance, has shown how some white Cubans in New York City barred Black Cubans from clubs and related gatherings during the middle of the twentieth century. As Tanya Katerí Hernández has noted in her analysis of more recent cases of anti-Blackness in Latino communities and the law, "across diverse geographic locations what remains consistent is the manner in which Latinos regulate public spaces to exclude and demean Blackness. Playing and learning in White-dominated Latino spaces is where Afro-Latinos are taught the rules of Latino racial hierarchies, and African Americans are informed that they are unwelcome." See Christina D. Abreu, *Rhythms of Race: Cuban Musicians and the Making of Latino New York City and Miami, 1940–1960* (Chapel Hill: University of North Carolina Press, 2015), 56–57, 62, 86–87; Tanya Katerí Hernández, *Racial Innocence: Unmasking Latino Anti-Black Bias and the Struggle for Equality* (Boston: Beacon Press, 2022), 55.
106. "Jose Ramon Sanfeliz Album Ybor City Photographs, 1892 to 1920," University of South Florida Special Collections, Tony Pizzo Collection, Box 205, Folder "Jose R. San Feliz Album—Guide."
107. "Jose Ramon Sanfeliz," 1935, 7, University of North Carolina at Chapel

Hill, Louis Round Wilson Special Collections Library, Southern Historical Collection, Federal Writers' Project Papers no. 3709. Wilson Library Special Collections Digital Exhibitions and Collections, https://dc.lib.unc.edu/cdm/ref/collection/03709/id/886.

108. Greenbaum, *More than Black*, 101–102.

109. Stetson Kennedy and Evelio Andux, "Pedro and Estrella," January 1, 1939, 18, University of North Carolina at Chapel Hill, Louis Round Wilson Special Collections Library, Southern Historical Collection, Federal Writers' Project Papers no. 3709. Wilson Library Special Collections Digital Exhibitions and Collections, https://dc.lib.unc.edu/cdm/ref/collection/03709/id/977.

110. Kennedy and Andux, "Pedro and Estrella," 20.

111. Hernández has underscored how this also takes place in Black or multiracial homes. See Tanya Katerí Hernández, *Racial Innocence: Unmasking Latino Anti-Black Bias and the Struggle for Equality* (Boston: Beacon Press, 2022), 16–19.

112. Kennedy and Pollato, "Enrique and Amanda," 3.

113. Kennedy and Pollato, "Enrique and Amanda," 4.

114. Kennedy and Pollato, "Enrique and Amanda," 4.

115. This feeling among Cubans was not necessarily held for poor or working-class Anglos. Aside from being viewed suspiciously as competition in cigar factories, working-class Anglos were sometimes derisively referred to as "crackers," as they were in the "Enrique and Amanda" account.

116. "Minstrels Arrive Today," *Key West Morning Journal*, February 18, 1912, 1.

117. Mario Sorondo, *La Mujer del Buzo*, University of South Florida Special Collections, Cuban Club Records, Box 30.

118. Agustín Rodrígues, *La Loca de la Casa*, University of South Florida Special Collections, Cuban Club Records, Box 33.

119. Antonio López, *Unbecoming Blackness: The Diaspora Cultures of Afro-Cuban America* (New York: New York University Press, 2012), 22.

120. See Jill Lane, *Blackface Cuba, 1840–1895* (Philadelphia: University of Pennsylvania Press, 2005).

121. As Jesse Hoffnung-Garskoff has noted, the plays also had archetypal figures that mocked Black Cubans that aspired to move up in Cuban society. See Jesse E. Hoffnung-Garskof, *Racial Migrations: New York City and the Revolutionary Politics of the Spanish Caribbean, 1850–1902* (Princeton, NJ: Princeton University Press, 2019), 85–86.

122. Grillo, *Black Cuban, Black American*, 7.

123. Grillo, *Black Cuban, Black American*, 9.

124. "Black Cubans—Minority within a Minority," *Tampa Tribune*, September 14, 1977, 1D.

CHAPTER 5: CUBAN AMERICANS, THE DEPRESSION, AND WORLD WAR II

1. Evelio Grillo, *Black Cuban, Black American: A Memoir* (Houston, TX: Arte Público Press, 2000), 103.

2. Grillo, *Black Cuban, Black American*, 103.

3. As Nancy Raquel Mirabal has shown, there was also an increasing number of Cubans—including a "significant proportion of Afro-Cubans"—who migrated to

New York City from Cuba during the early 1900s. Moreover, Christina D. Abreu's work has also catalogued the histories of Black Cubans who moved from Tampa to New York City during the 1940s. See Nancy Raquel Mirabal, *Suspect Freedoms: The Racial and Sexual Politics of Cubanidad in New York, 1823–1957* (New York: New York University Press, 2017), 167; Christina D. Abreu, *Rhythms of Race: Cuban Musicians and the Making of Latino New York City and Miami, 1940–1960* (Chapel Hill: The University of North Carolina Press, 2015), 7.

4. Although few moved to South Florida, many Afro-Cubans migrated to the US during this period. See Mirabal, *Suspect Freedoms*, 169.

5. Jenny Ballou, "Key West Discovers Real Assets Only after Bottom Is Reached," *Jacksonville Journal*, reprinted in *Key West Citizen*, August 3, 1934, 1.

6. For instance, Sarah McNamara has written about Luisa Moreno's organizing in Tampa during the 1930s to underscore women's activism in the region as well as occasional moments of interracial organizing. See Sarah McNamara, "Borderland Unionism: Latina Activism in Ybor City and Tampa, Florida, 1935–1937," *Journal of American Ethnic History* 38, no. 4 (Summer 2019): 10–32.

7. Christina Abreu has also underscored how a similar calendar of events was celebrated in Cuban New York. See Christina D. Abreu, *Rhythms of Race: Cuban Musicians and the Making of Latino New York City and Miami, 1940–1960* (Chapel Hill: University of North Carolina Press, 2015), 83–84.

8. "Marti's Birthday Observed by Unit from San Carlos," *Key West Citizen*, January 29, 1943, 1; "Cuban School Children Visit Bayview Park," *Key West Citizen*, February 24, 1943, 1.

9. As an example, 1932 celebrations of "El Grito de Yara" included representatives from the Cuban consulate, the Emigrados Revolucionarios Cubanos veterans' group, the American Legion, the Instituto San Carlos, and members of the local Marine hospital. See "Cuban Colony Plan for Anniversary Celebration to be Staged on Monday," *The Key West Citizen*, October 8, 1932, 1.

10. See "Key West Administration Has Announced Complete Program Of El Grito De Yara Celebration," *Key West Citizen*, October 6, 1934, 1.

11. "Key West Administration," 1.

12. Ada Ferrer, *Cuba: An American History* (New York: Scribner, 2021), 245–247; Louis A. Pérez Jr., *Cuba: Between Reform and Revolution*, 5th ed. (New York: Oxford University Press, 2015), 214–215.

13. The park's history, and controversies over it, are discussed in the introduction and epilogue of this book.

14. "'El Grito de Yara' Program Sunday—Monday, Announced," *Key West Citizen*, October 4, 1938, 1.

15. "Key West in Days Gone By," *Key West Citizen*, October 6, 1934, 2.

16. USS *Maine* memorials became important both in Cuba and the United States. The most notable memorial was in Havana and was completed before US President Calvin Coolidge's 1928 visit to the island. His speech at the memorial's plaza similarly obscured the tumultuous history between the US and Cuba. See Ferrer, *Cuba*, 224–225.

17. "Mayor Malone and Executive Committee Outline Program on Grito De Yara Celebration," *Key West Citizen*, September 15, 1934, 1.

18. "Mayor Malone and Executive Committee," 4.

19. "Mayor Malone and Executive Committee," 1.

20. "Mayor Malone and Executive Committee," 1.

21. "Velada Closes Yara Celebration Tonight," *Key West Citizen*, October 10, 1938, 1.

22. "Cuban Officials Guests of City," *Tampa Daily Times*, December 6, 1933, 3.

23. "Un lucido recibimiento se hizo ayer a los doctors Capablanca y Lavín, llegados en el American Clipper," *La Gaceta*, December 6, 1933, 1.

24. "Tres recepciones se ofrecieron anoche en el honor de los Comisionados del Gobierno de Cuba," *La Gaceta*, December 8, 1933, 1.

25. "Tres recepciones."

26. Alejandro de la Fuente, *A Nation for All: Race, Inequality, and Politics in Twentieth-Century Cuba* (Chapel Hill: University of North Carolina Press, 2001), 91–92; Melina Pappademos, *Black Political Activism and the Cuban Republic* (Chapel Hill: University of North Carolina Press, 2011), 198.

27. "5,939 Persons Get Books from Ybor City Library," *Tampa Daily Times*, November 20, 1930, 3A.

28. De la Fuente, *Nation for All*, 193, 201.

29. De la Fuente, *Nation for All*, 204.

30. De la Fuente, *Nation for All*, 204–205.

31. "Key West in Days Gone By," *Key West Citizen*, December 8, 1942, 2.

32. Grillo, *Black Cuban, Black American*, 16–17.

33. Roger Daniels, *Guarding the Golden Door: American Immigration Policy and Immigrants Since 1882* (New York: Hill and Wang, 2004), 45.

34. See Daniels, *Guarding the Golden Door*, 45–47; Katherine Benton-Cohen, *Inventing the Immigration Problem: The Dillingham Commission and Its Legacy* (Cambridge: Harvard University Press, 2018), 15, 57; "Act of March 3, 1903 (Re: Codification of Immigration Laws)," "Act of March 3, 1903: Naturalization of Anarchists Forbidden . . . ," "Act of June 29, 1906: Basic Naturalization Act of 1906, Providing for the Naturalization of Aliens throughout the United States and Establishing the Bureau of Immigration and Naturalization," and "Act of February 20, 1907: To Regulate the Immigration of Aliens into the United States," in *U.S. Immigration and Naturalization Laws and Issues: A Documentary History*, ed. Michael LeMay and Elliot Robert Barkan (Westport, CT: Greenwood Press, 1999), 90–99.

35. This also spoke to a broader silencing of labor radicals in South Florida and the Caribbean during this period. Two prominent organizers of this era—the Guatemalan-born Luisa Moreno and the Puerto Rican–born Luisa Capetillo—had long organizing histories that brought them to Tampa during the early 1900s. Both women were later deported—Moreno by the United States and Capetillo by the Menocal administration in Cuba, where she was organizing sugar workers. See Vicki L. Ruiz, "Luisa Moreno and Latina Labor Activism," in *Latina Legacies: Identity, Biography, and Community*, ed. Vicki L. Ruiz and Virginia Sánchez Korrol (New York: Oxford University Press, 2005), 190; Nancy A. Hewitt, "Luisa Capetillo: Feminist of the Working Class," in *Latina Legacies: Identity, Biography, and Community*, ed. Vicki L. Ruiz and Virginia Sánchez Korrol (New York: Oxford University Press, 2005), 131.

36. As Putnam also notes, the Johnson-Reed Act occurred while other regional governments, such as Cuba's, were promoting anti-Black migration measures; Lara Putnam, *Radical Moves: Caribbean Migrants and the Politics of Race in the Jazz Age*

(Chapel Hill: University of North Carolina Press, 2013), 82.

37. This drop was especially notable in Monroe County. During the 1900 census, there were 7,576 foreign-born residents identified in Monroe County and 3,533 in Hillsborough County. Respectively, they made up 42.1 percent and 20.6 percent of the overall county populations. In the 1940 census, there were 1,163 foreign-born residents in Monroe County and 13,352 in Hillsborough County. In 1940, they respectively made up 8.3 percent and 7.4 percent of the overall county populations. While the foreign-born population numbers rose in Hillsborough County, this was largely due to European migration—residents born in Cuba numbered 3,533 in 1900 and 3,483 in 1940. See "Foreign-Born Population 1850–2020," American Panorama, Digital Scholarship Lab, University of Richmond, https://dsl.richmond.edu/panorama/foreignborn.

38. For a brief overview of the Machado era and US-Cuba relations, see Ada Ferrer, "Boom, Crash, Awake," in *Cuba: An American History* (New York: Scribner, 2021), 217–231.

39. Due to ease of travel, Miami became a common tourist destination for middle-class and wealthy Cubans during the 1920s. While the city's Cuban American population would become central in the post–Cuban Revolution period, its roots stem back to this earlier period of the Cuban republic.

40. "Refugees from Cuba Arrive in City Last Night," *Key West Citizen*, November 8, 1932, 1.

41. "Cuban Refugees Arrive in City," *Key West Citizen*, February 4, 1933, 1; "Two More Cuban Refugees Come Here to Join Colony," *Key West Citizen*, January 6, 1933, 4; "Refugees Get Hearing Today," *Key West Citizen*, May 13, 1933, 1.

42. "Cuban Boat Held by Authorities Goes to Havana," *Key West Citizen*, March 30, 1933, 2.

43. "Cuban Refugee Returns to Key West Yesterday," *Key West Citizen*, April 1, 1933, 1.

44. According to one report, he was deported from Key West "because he had no permit from the Secretary of Labor to enter the United States." See "Chocolate Deported for Lack of Permit," *New York Times*, January 20, 1933, 23.

45. Christina D. Abreu, *Rhythms of Race: Cuban Musicians and the Making of Latino New York City and Miami, 1940–1960* (Chapel Hill: University of North Carolina Press, 2015), 72–73.

46. Abreu, *Rhythms of Race*, 59–60.

47. "Cigar Production Hits Highest Mark in Five Years," *Tampa Morning Tribune*, December 31, 1936, 3.

48. "Cigar Industry Here Is Hit by Customs Ruling," *Tampa Morning Tribune*, August 27, 1930, 16; "Would Be Ruinous," *Tampa Daily Times*, May 15, 1931, 8A; "Cigar Factory Here Will Move to New Jersey," *Tampa Times*, October 14, 1930, 3.

49. "Deserves Fair Trial," *Tampa Daily Times*, January 7, 1931, 4A.

50. "A los miembros de la union internacional, que estan sin trabajo," *La Gaceta*, December 6, 1933, 4.

51. Grillo, *Black Cuban, Black American*, 21; Francisco Rodríguez Sr., interview by Fred Beaton and Otis Anthony, August 11, 1978, University of South Florida Special Collections, African Americans in Florida Project. University of South Florida Digital Commons, https://digitalcommons.usf.edu/otis_anthony_ohp/55.

52. Grillo, *Black Cuban, Black American*, 21.

53. "Mercedes Hospital Founded 27 Years Ago Today by 26 Women," *Key West Citizen*, October 10, 1938, 1; for an overview of Gutsens and the hospital, see Consuelo E. Stebbins, "María Valdés de Gutsens 1860–1941: The Soul of Key West's Mercedes Hospital," in *The Variety of Women's Experiences: Portraits of Southern Women in the Post-Civil War Century* (Gainesville: University Press of Florida, 2009), 104–121.

54. Stebbins, "María Valdés de Gutsens," 114–115.

55. See "Makes Report on Hospital Inmates," *Key West Citizen*, November 7, 1934, 4; "Key West in Days Gone By," *Key West Citizen*, February 1, 1936, 2; "Makes Report on Hospital Patients," *Key West Citizen*, July 11, 1939, 4; "Patients at Mercedes," *Key West Citizen*, May 17, 1940, 4.

56. "Council Hears Housing Authority Board Report," *Key West Citizen*, May 5, 1939, 1.

57. "Closing of Mercedes Hospital Attributed to Council Failing to Contribute toward Expense," *Key West Citizen*, August 19, 1943, 1; Stebbins, "María Valdés de Gutsens," 118.

58. Jenny Ballou, "Key West Discovers Real Assets Only after Bottom Is Reached," *Jacksonville Journal*, reprinted in *Key West Citizen*, August 3, 1934, 1.

59. "FERA Extends Period for Enlisting in Key West Voluntary Work Corps," *Key West Citizen*, July 31, 1934, 1.

60. "FERA Would Make Key West Tourist Center, Claims Dr. Newell," *Key West Citizen*, August 17, 1934, 1; "More Forces to Be Employed in FERA on Monday," *Key West Citizen*, March 16, 1934, 1.

61. "FERA to Study Industrial Life of Ybor City," *Tampa Morning Tribune*, February 13, 1935, 3; "Adult Schools Close Tonight," *Tampa Daily Times*, June 28, 1935, 2; "FERA Band Concert," *Tampa Daily Times*, August 8, 1934, 5.

62. Julius F. Stone Jr., "Key West Is to Be Restored by Free Labor of Her Citizens," *New York Times*, August 12, 1934, Section 8, 9.

63. "Adult Pupils End First Year in FERA School," *Tampa Morning Tribune*, June 28, 1935, 9.

64. "Spanish Aviation Class Will Begin," *Tampa Daily Times*, August 3, 1935, 2.

65. "Work to Start Soon on Colored Douglas School," *Key West Citizen*, November 10, 1942, 1.

66. "Work to Start Soon," 1.

67. "Making Plans to Build New School," *Key West Citizen*, January 19, 1943, 1, 4; "Grant for New School Approved," *Key West Citizen*, February 4, 1943, 1.

68. Details on the teams and players were often sparse, but box scores and game summaries of the era recount players such as "E. Suarez," "M. Suarez," and a "Home Run King Gonzalez," among others; "Coconuts Take One Game and Lose Another," *Key West Citizen*, August 20, 1934, 3; Aguilar, "Following Through," *Key West Citizen*, November 9, 1942, 3; "Colored Teams Will Play Here," *Key West Citizen*, April 6, 1939, 3.

69. Aguilar, "Following Through," *Key West Citizen*, November 9, 1942, 3.

70. "Five-Game Series of Baseball Will Start on Sunday," *Key West Citizen*, May 28, 1936, 3.

71. "Negro Theater Guild to Present Program," *Tampa Daily Times*, July 16, 1936, 3.

72. Susan D. Greenbaum, *More Than Black: Afro-Cubans in Tampa* (Gainesville:

University Press of Florida, 2002), 238–239.

73. Greenbaum, *More than Black*, 244.

74. "Today's Program for Tampa Jubilee," *Tampa Morning Tribune*, July 15, 1937, 9.

75. "Dances Open to Public," *Tampa Daily Times*, July 14, 1937, 10.

76. "Program Sunday at Colored Park," *Key West Citizen*, September 29, 1934, 4; "Colored Workers Will Hold Meeting," *Key West Citizen*, November 9, 1934, 4.

77. "Planning Committee Acted on Postwar Projects Last Evening," *Key West Citizen*, June 26, 1943, 1.

78. "Miss Black Was Visitor to City," *Key West Citizen*, January 30, 1941, 4; entry for "St. Elmo Greaux," 1930 United States Census, NARA Microfilm Publication T626, Roll 325, Fourth Ward, Eighth Precinct, Key West, Monroe County, FL, 9A, FamilySearch.org; entry for "St. Elmo Greaux," 1945 Florida State Census, Second Precinct, Key West, Monroe County, FL, FamilySearch.org.

79. "Planning Committee Acted on Postwar Projects Last Evening," *Key West Citizen*, June 26, 1943, 1; "Launch Drive for Colored Hospital," *Key West Citizen*, August 16, 1943, 1; "J. Lancelot Lester," *Key West Citizen*, August 18, 1943, 4.

80. The Island City Civic League sent a letter to Monroe County commissioners, where they described the killing as a "brutal murder." See "Ask Probe in Negro Killing," *Key West Citizen*, July 7, 1943, 1.

81. See Louis A. Pérez Jr., *On Becoming Cuban: Identity, Nationality, and Culture* (Chapel Hill: University of North Carolina Press, 1999), 41.

82. "Several Cases Before Court," *Key West Citizen*, December 14, 1942, 4; "Key West in Days Gone By," *Key West Citizen*, October 3, 1942, 2; "Enrique Esquinaldo, Jr. Named as New Election Commissioner," *Key West Citizen*, October 17, 1945, 1; entry for "Frank J. Fleitas," 1920 United States Census, Sixth Ward, Fifth Precinct, Key West, Monroe County, FL, 1B, FamilySearch.org.

83. "Maximo Valdez Named County Commissioner," *Key West Citizen*, January 15, 1943, 1; entry for "Maximo Valdez," 1900 United States Census, NARA Microfilm Publication T623, Roll 174, Fourth Ward, Key West, Monroe County, FL, A7, FamilySearch.org; "J. Carbonell Is City Head Today," *Key West Citizen*, December 7, 1945, 1; "Proclamation—Navy Day," *Key West Citizen*, October 25, 1945, 1; entry for "John Carbonell Jr.," 1930 United States Census, NARA Microfilm Publication T626, Roll 325, Second Ward, Fourth Precinct, Key West, Monroe County, FL, 5A, FamilySearch.org.

84. "Oscar Herrera Given Hearing," *Key West Citizen*, April 28, 1936, 4; *Key West Citizen*, May 29, 1939, 2; "Judge Carbonell Will Preside at First Case Today," *Key West Citizen*, December 21, 1942, 1; entry for "Raul Carbonell," 1930 United States Census, NARA Microfilm Publication T626, Roll 325, Second Ward, Fourth Precinct, Key West, Monroe County, FL, 3A, FamilySearch.org.

85. "Alberto Camero Seeks Reelection as Police Captain," *Key West Citizen*, October 11, 1941, 1; entry for "Alberto Camero," 1910 United States Census, NARA Microfilm Publication T624, Fifth Ward, Key West, Monroe County, FL, 17A, FamilySearch.org; entry for "Elmer Pino," 1910 United States Census, NARA Microfilm Publication T624, Fourth Ward, Key West, Monroe County, FL, 10B, FamilySearch.org.

86. Little can be confirmed about Valdez's background, but he was killed in the

line of duty in 1946. See "City Receives Check for over Six Thousand Dollars in Lieu of Texas from Housing Setup," *Key West Citizen*, May 2, 1945, 1; "Murder Charges Filed in Killing of Police Officer," *Key West Citizen*, May 13, 1946, 1; "Police Attend Rites for Slain Officer," *Key West Citizen*, May 20, 1946, 4.

87. "Several Cases Before Court," *Key West Citizen*, December 14, 1942, 4; "Negro Now Faces Robbery Charge," *Key West Citizen*, January 2, 1943, 4; "Judge Albury Issues Edict to Loafers; Four Arraigned for Hearing; Bound Over to Court," *Key West Citizen*, February 20, 1943, 1; "Negro Charged with Vagrancy Willing to Return to His Work," *Key West Citizen*, March 27, 1943, 1.

88. "Negro Shot in Mixup Last Night with Policeman," *Key West Citizen*, January 6, 1943, 1.

89. J. A. Murray, "Ybor City Gets in the War, Heart and Soul," *Tampa Sunday Tribune*, magazine features, January 4, 1942, 2.

90. Greenbaum, *More Than Black*, 257; Gary R. Mormino, "Ybor City Goes to War: The Evolution and Transformation of a 'Latin' Community in Florida, 1886–1950" in *Latina/os and World War II: Mobility, Agency, and Ideology*, ed. Maggie Rivas-Rodríguez and B. V. Olguín (Austin: University of Texas Press, 2014), 24.

91. For connections to Latin American populations, see McNamara, "Borderland Unionism," 21–24; Lorrin Thomas, *Puerto Rican Citizen: History and Political Identity in Twentieth-Century New York City* (Chicago, IL: University of Chicago Press, 2010), 129–130, 149–150.

92. "Latin-Americans Are True Americans," *Tampa Morning Tribune*, December 9, 1942, 8.

93. "Latin-Americans Are True Americans," 8.

94. "Ybor Chamber Will Conduct English Classes," *Tampa Morning Tribune*, July 28, 1945, 8; "129 Aliens from Florida Admitted to Citizenship," *Tampa Morning Tribune*, January 20, 1944, 9; "Uncle Sam Gets 145 New Citizens by Naturalization," *Tampa Daily Times*, October 21, 1943, 2; Sarah Worth, "Akerman in Rare Humor as He Admits 44 to Citizenship," *Tampa Daily Times*, January 4, 1943, 3.

95. "Florida U. Student Is First to Enlist in Naval Reserve," *Tampa Morning Tribune*, January 1, 1942, 5; "Marine Corps Enlists 13 at Tampa Office," *Tampa Morning Tribune*, December 30, 1941, 6; "Large Group of Key Westers Enlist at Recruiting Station," *Key West Citizen*, October 6, 1942, 1.

96. "Mendoza Assigned to Local Station," *Key West Citizen*, October 8, 1942, 1; entry for "Charles Mendoza," 1930 United States Census, NARA Microfilm Publication T626, Roll 325, Second Ward, Fourth Precinct, Key West, Monroe County, FL, 1A, FamilySearch.org.

97. "Mendoza Assigned to Local Station," 1.

98. "Tallest and Shortest Men Enlist with Naval Forces in Key West," *Key West Citizen*, October 27, 1942, 1; entry for "Louis Norcisa Jr.," 1930 United States Census, NARA Microfilm Publication T626, Roll 325, Fourth Ward, Seventh Precinct, Key West, Monroe County, FL, 1B, FamilySearch.org.

99. "Call Made for Women to Aid Defense Work," *Key West Citizen*, December 9, 1941, 1.

100. "To Every Woman Who Wants to Do Her Part in This Global War," *Key West Citizen*, February 18, 1943, 1; "WAAC Officer to Arrive Sunday; Will Consider Applications of Women Here Monday and Tuesday," *Key West Citizen*, April

9, 1943, 1.

101. "Colored Youth to Get Training," *Key West Citizen*, October 8, 1942, 4.

102. "Colored Youth to be Trained," *Key West Citizen*, October 26, 1942, 3.

103. Entry for "Merinda" family, 1900 United States Census, NARA Microfilm Publication T623, Roll 174, Fourth Ward, Key West, Monroe County, FL, A7, FamilySearch.org; entry for "Julian Carrera" and "Miranda" family, 1940 United States Census, NARA Digital Publication T627, RG 29, Fourth Ward, Fifth Precinct, Key West, Monroe County, FL, 12B, FamilySearch.org; entry for "Julian E Carrera," November 21, 1942, United States World War II Army Enlistment Records, 1938–1946, NARA NAID 1263923, FamilySearch.org.

104. "Recruiting Colored Women for Service," *Key West Citizen*, January 21, 1943, 2.

105. "Enlistment of Negro Women for WAAC Begins," *Tampa Daily Times*, February 19, 1943, 4.

106. "MacDill Negro Troops Learn Soldiering from A to Z," *Tampa Sunday Tribune*, October 11, 1942, part 2, 8.

107. "Swimming Pool Asked for Negro Soldiers," *Tampa Daily Times*, May 13, 1944, 2.

108. "Blas Sanchez Made Airplane Mechanic," *Key West Citizen*, March 23, 1943, 1; entry for "Sanchez" family, 1920 United States Census, NARA Microfilm Publication T625, Fourth Ward, Fourth Precinct, Key West, Monroe County, FL, 12B, FamilySearch.org; entry for "Blas Sanchez," 1940 United States Census, NARA Digital Publication T627, RG 29, Fifth Ward, Fifth Precinct, Key West, Monroe County, FL, 13B, FamilySearch.org.

109. "Jas. L. Coleman Killed in Action," *Key West Citizen*, March 24, 1943, 1; entry for "Clara C Suarez," 1930 United States Census, NARA Microfilm Publication T626, Roll 325, Third Ward, Seventh Precinct, Key West, Monroe County, FL, 5A, FamilySearch.org.; "Pfc. Ernest Ogden Killed in Action," *Key West Citizen*, May 23, 1945, 4; entry for "Rachel Ogden," 1920 United States Census, NARA Microfilm Publication T625, Fifth Ward, Fifth Precinct, Key West, Monroe County, FL, 21B, FamilySearch.org; entry for "Sanchez" and "Ogden" families, 1940 United States Census, NARA Digital Publication T627, RG 29, Fifth Ward, Fifth Precinct, Key West, Monroe County, FL, 2B, FamilySearch.org.

110. "Marcos Mesa Writes Home," *Key West Citizen*, April 2, 1945, 1; "Mesa Plans Coming Home," *Key West Citizen*, June 21, 1945, 1; entry for "Marcos Mesa Jr.," 1920 United States Census, NARA Microfilm Publication T625, Fifth Ward, Fourth Precinct, Key West, Monroe County, FL, 3A, FamilySearch.org; "Cleveland Henriquez is Prisoner of Japs," *The Key West Citizen*, June 11, 1943, 1; "Cleveland Henriquez, Liberated Jap Prisoner, Says He Was Told United States Had Surrendered," *Key West Citizen*, April 11, 1945, 1; entry for "Henriquez" family, 1930 United States Census, NARA Microfilm Publication T626, Roll 325, First Ward, Third Precinct, Key West, Monroe County, FL, 1A, FamilySearch.org.

111. "Six Key West Youths Enlist in U.S. Navy," *Key West Citizen*, June 4, 1943, 1.

112. Entry for "Ellis" family, 1930 United States Census, NARA Microfilm Publication T626, Roll 325, Fourth Ward, Eighth Precinct, Key West, Monroe County, FL, 9B, FamilySearch.org; entry for "Joseph Ellis" and "Ellis" family, 1935 Florida State Census, Fifth Precinct, Key West, Monroe County, FL, FamilySearch.org;

entry for "Jose Ellis" and "Ellis" family, 1940 United States Census, NARA Digital Publication T627, RG 29, Fifth Ward, Fifth Precinct, Key West, Monroe County, FL, 10B, FamilySearch.org.

113. "Six Key West Youths Enlist in U.S. Navy," *Key West Citizen*, June 4, 1943, 1.

114. Grillo, *Black Cuban, Black American*, 93.

115. See Silvia Álvarez Curbelo, "The Color of War: Puerto Rican Soldiers and Discrimination during World War II," in *Beyond the Latino World War II Hero: The Social and Political Legacy of a Generation*, ed. Maggie Rivas-Rodríguez and Emilio Zamora (Austin: University of Texas Press, 2009), 110–124.

116. See Richard Griswold del Castillo, "The Paradox of War: Mexican American Patriotism, Racism, and Memory," in *Beyond the Latino World War II Hero: The Social and Political Legacy of a Generation*, ed. Maggie Rivas-Rodríguez and Emilio Zamora (Austin: University of Texas Press, 2009), 11–20.

117. Grillo, *Black Cuban, Black American*, 93–101.

118. Frank André Guridy, "Pvt. Evelio Grillo and Sgt. Norberto González: Afro-Latino Experiences of War and Segregation," in *Latina/os and World War II*, 43.

119. "Carbonell Heads Fund Campaign Local Red Cross," *Key West Citizen*, February 11, 1946, 1; "Chairman, Red Cross Fund Campaign," *Key West Citizen*, February 16, 1946, 1.

120. Gerald E. Poyo, "Seeking 'America': A Cuban Journey through the United States and Beyond during the World War II Era," in *Latina/os and World War II*, 228–229.

121. Poyo, "Seeking 'America,'" 230.

122. Lawrence P. Scott and William M. Womack Sr., *Double V: The Civil Rights Struggle of the Tuskegee Airmen* (East Lansing: Michigan State University Press, 1994), 2, 166–167.

123. Francisco Rodriguez Jr., interview by Otis Anthony, May 30, 1978, 7, University of South Florida Special Collections, Department of Anthropology African Americans in Florida Project, Box 11, Folder "Interviews—Transcripts—Rodriguez, Francisco [Jr.] 5/30/1978."

124. "Tampa Attorney Stresses Significance of NAACP," *St. Petersburg Times*, October 26, 1950, 26; Calvin E. Adams, "Southwide NAACP MEET Minutes Received; 142 Delegates Attend," *St. Petersburg Times*, January 29, 1952, 31; Bob Delaney, "Tallahassee Bus Boycott Trial Proceeds in Calm, Orderly Manner," *St. Petersburg Times*, October 21, 1956, 6A; "Leaders Meet to Study School Integration Plans," *St. Petersburg Times*, August 13, 1955, 18.

125. Grillo, *Black Cuban, Black American*, 130–134.

126. Gerardo Castellanos, *Motivos de Cayo Hueso: Contribución a la historia de las emigraciones revolucionarias cubanas en los Estados Unidos* (Havana: Ucar, Garcia y Cía, 1939), 339.

127. Leland Hawes, "Tampa's invisible minority," *Tampa Tribune*, January 28, 1984, 1D, 3D.

128. Francisco Rodríguez Sr., interview by Fred Beaton and Otis Anthony, August 11, 1978, University of South Florida Special Collections. African Americans in Florida Project. University of South Florida Digital Commons, https://digitalcommons.usf.edu/otis_anthony_ohp/55.

EPILOGUE

1. Tom O'Conner, "Italian Club Bars Theater to Leader of Cuban Revolt," *Tampa Sunday Tribune*, November 27, 1955, 1.

2. O'Conner, "Italian Club Bars Theater," 22A.

3. Susan D. Greenbaum, *More than Black: Afro-Cubans in Tampa* (Gainesville: University Press of Florida, 2002), 271–274.

4. Tom O'Connor, "Cubans Here Give Funds to Aid Revolt against Batista," *Tampa Morning Tribune*, November 28, 1955, 12.

5. Frank Bayle, "Air of Mystery Hangs over Marti Dedication," *Tampa Times*, February 29, 1960, 4; "Anti-Castro Cubans Defy Lock to Place Wreath," *Tampa Tribune*, November 28, 1960, 14.

6. "Anti-Castro Rally Erupts into Fight at Marti Park," *Tampa Tribune*, November 27, 1961, 1, 1B; "Two Arrested in Marti Park Fight Get Six Months," *Tampa Tribune*, November 28, 1961, 1B; Jerry Wallace, "Anti-Castro Rally Told Cubans Soon to Be Free Again," *Tampa Tribune*, 1B.

7. Wallace, "Anti-Castro Rally," 1B.

8. Kurt Loft, "Blueprint For Destruction," Baylife, *Tampa Tribune*, April 18, 2006, 4.

9. Robert Samek, "Tampa's Black Cubans Want to Rebuild Clubhouse Patio," *St. Petersburg Times*, February 20, 1989, 8.

10. Applications for the Círculo Cubano, Centro Español, and Centro Asturiano can be found in the National Park Service's Digital Asset Management System. See "NPGallery Digital Asset Management System," National Park Service, accessed August 25, 2022, https://npgallery.nps.gov.

11. Instituto San Carlos, "San Carlos Institute: Restoration of a Precious Legacy," University of Miami Libraries, Cuban Heritage Collection, San Carlos Institute Collection, Unnumbered Box, Unsorted Clippings Bag.

12. Edward Schumacher, "The Long Journey of Hope From Mariel to Key West," *New York Times*, May 20, 1980, B13.

13. Schumacher, "The Long Journey of Hope From Mariel to Key West," 1, B13; John M. Crewdson, "Refugees Straining Center in Key West," *New York Times*, May 6, 1980, 11.

14. Greenbaum, *More than Black*, 296–298.

15. Leland Hawes, "Tampa's Invisible Minority," *Tampa Tribune*, January 28, 1984, 1D, 3D.

16. Hawes, "Tampa's Invisible Minority," 1D; "School Board Candidate Wants Streets Made Safe," *Tampa Tribune*, August 4, 1967, 5B; "Sylvia Grinan de Grillo," *Tampa Tribune*, December 3, 1993, Peninsula 2.

17. Sherri Ackerman and Kathy Steele, "Family Reunion," *Tampa Tribune*, July 30, 2001, 1.

18. Michael Fechter, "One Nationality, Divided by Color," *Tampa Tribune*, February 27, 2005, 9.

19. The Club Civico Cubano was a post-1959 exile group that was founded in part due to initial tensions with the Círculo Cubano. See Kathy Steele, "Picnic Serves Unity for 3 Cuban Clubs," *Tampa Tribune*, 12.

20. See Nancy Raquel Mirabal, "Monumental Desires and Defiant Tributes: Antonio Maceo and the Early History of El Club Cubano Inter-Americano,

1945–1957," in *Suspect Freedoms: The Racial and Sexual Politics of Cubanidad in New York, 1823–1957* (New York: New York University Press, 2017), 193–226; Christina D. Abreu, *Rhythms of Race: Cuban Musicians and the Making of Latino New York City and Miami, 1940–1960* (Chapel Hill: University of North Carolina Press, 2015), 99–104.

21. Susan Clary, "Black Cuban General Will Be Honored Beside Marti," *St. Petersburg Times*, February 29, 1996, 3B.

22. Clary, "Black Cuban General," 3B.

23. Clary, "Black Cuban General," 3B.

24. Tania Spencer, "Statue Unveiling Ceremony Memorializes Cuban War Hero," East Hillsborough, *Tampa Tribune*, June 9, 1996, 8.

25. Instituto San Carlos, "San Carlos Institute."

26. Nancy Klingener, "Slice of Cuban History Makes Proud Comeback," *Miami Herald*, January 4, 1992, 8A, University of Miami Libraries, Cuban Heritage Collection, San Carlos Institute Collection, Unnumbered Box, Unsorted Clippings Bag.

27. "Statue Bound for Key West," *Miami Herald*, January 4, 1992, 8A.

28. Klingener, "Slice of Cuban History," 8A; Instituto San Carlos, "San Carlos Institute."

29. "Adamo Drive Mural Highlights Ybor History and Heritage," *Tampa Bay Times*, December 24, 2012, https://www.tampabay.com/news/adamo-drive-mural-highlights-ybor-history-and-heritage/1267576; "Legend," Ybor Art Project, accessed August 25, 2022, http://yborartproject.com/legend.

30. For local clippings that catalogued Allen's efforts, see Florida Keys History Center at the Monroe County Public Library, Biographical Files D-E, "Dean James."

31. Tom Walker, "Historic Reinstatement Noted on Law Day," *Key West Citizen*, May 2, 2002, clipping, Florida Keys History Center at the Monroe County Public Library, Biographical Files D-E, "Dean James."

32. Walker, "Historic Reinstatement."

33. Nancy Klingener, "Key West Honors Manuel Cabeza Almost a Century after His Lynching," *WLRN*, March 25, 2019, https://www.wlrn.org/local-news/2019-03-25/key-west-honors-manuel-cabeza-almost-a-century-after-his-lynching.

34. For materials related to the 2019 event, see Florida Keys History Center at the Monroe County Public Library, Box Biographies: Audubon to Morgan, Folder Cabeza/Head.

35. Florida Keys History Center at the Monroe County Public Library, Box Biographies: Audubon to Morgan, Folder Cabeza/Head.

36. Fechter, "One Nationality, Divided By Color," 9.

INDEX

Page numbers followed by f indicate images; those followed by t indicate tables.

abolition, 18, 19, 20, 26, 28, 43, 68. *See also* slavery
Abraham Lincoln Masonic Lodge, 35
Abreu, Christina D., 6, 121–122, 138, 172n105, 173–174n3, 174n7
Acción, Facundo, 122
Adams, Charles R., 29
African Americans: and William Artrell, 151n95; and Black Cubans, 6, 11, 88, 89–93, 111, 132; and census of 1885, 151n92; and cigar industry, 34; and Cuban independence movement, 152n127; and Florida constitution of 1885, 66; and IOGT, 151–152n108; and Key West, 5, 25; and Latin community, 144n16; and La Unión Martí-Maceo, 13; marginalization of, 109; post-Reconstruction, 69; and racial discourse, 26; and racial hierarchies, 172n105; and Radical Reconstruction, 19; and voter disenfranchisement, 64; and white Cubans, 39; and World War II, 12, 129
Afro-Bahamians: and cigar industry, 26–27; elected to office, 29; and Island City Civic League, 125; and Key West, 5, 19, 25, 90; and voter disenfranchisement, 64; and World War II, 129
Afro-Caribbean soldiers, 129–130
Afro-Latin@ Reader (Jiménez Román and Flores 2010), 6–7
A. L. Cuesta School, 89
Alfaro, Luis, 110
Alfonso, Evaristo, 84
Alianza Obrera, 53

Alien Registration Act of 1940, 167–168n23
Allen, A. G., 110
Allen, Calvin J., 140
Allen, George W., 31–32
all-white primary systems, 64, 71–72
Alston, Clara, 90
American Federation of Labor, 43, 58
Americanization, 6, 11, 93, 98–99, 104–106, 131. *See also* citizenship
American Legion, 117, 174n9
anarchism, 53, 55, 140
Anglos: and Americanization efforts, 93, 105; and class, 173n115; and Democratic Party, 101; and Republican Party, 9, 68, 78; sensibilities of, 156n95; and US centennial, 30–31; and white Cubans, 11, 88, 98–99, 100, 102, 111, 131
anti-Blackness: and Cuban independence movement, 37–38; and family, 109; and Instituto San Carlos, 78; and Johnson-Reed Act, 175–176n36; in Latino communities, 172n105; and legislation, 66, 175–176n36; and popular culture, 110–111; and post-Machado Cuba, 119; and violence, 25, 85; and white Cubans, 6–7
Arenas, Crecencio, 89
Armwood, Levin, 70
Armwood, Levin Jr., 90
Artman, Estella Rebecca nee Recio, 100
Artman, Policarp, 100
Artrell, William, 27, 29, 30, 31, 35, 70, 151n95, 151–152n108
"Atlanta Compromise" (Washington 1895), 81

185

186 • INDEX

Autobiography of an Ex-Colored Man (Johnson 1912), 28
Avellanal, José Ramón, 164n106
Ayala, Oscar, 100, 102–103, 171n73

Baez, Juan, 35
Bahama Village, 169n41
Bahamian Conchs, 38–39
Bahamian Republican Club, 29
Bahamians, 19, 26, 149n65, 152n124
Bakunin, Mikhail, 53
Balsero Crisis (1990s), 136
Bandera, Quintín, 75
Barrett, James R., 166n1
baseball, 104, 116, 124, 161n48, 177n68
Batista, Fulgencio, 1, 115–117, 133
Batrell, Ricardo, 75
Bayview Park, 118f
Beatty, Blanche Armwood, 90, 91f, 167n11
Black Bahamians. *See* Afro-Bahamians
Black Cubans: and African Americans, 88, 95; and agency, 6; associations of, 10, 48; and celebrations, 118–119; and Cuban identity, 131–132; and Cuban independence movement, 19, 154n31; and Cuban War of Independence, 75; and James Dean, 67–68; disenfranchisement of, 163n83; in early twentieth century, 89–93; and fraternal orders, 35; and Great Depression, 112, 124–125; and history, 120, 134, 137, 140; and independence movement, 2; and influenza pandemic of 1918, 64; institutions of, 44; and Instituto San Carlos, 79f; and interracial organizing, 43, 80; and interracial republic, 62; and Jim Crow system, 12, 74, 111; and labor-independence movement ties, 56; and labor unions, 42, 52; and Gerardo Machado, 174n4; marginalization of, 109; and José Martí, 56; José Martí on, 49; migration of, 121–122; and multiracial democracy, 86; and mutual-aid societies, 76–77, 102; and newspapers, 45; and New York City, 173–174n3; and PIC, 11, 81–85, 165n124; and PRC, 47; and public school, 164n101; and "raceless" society, 51–52; and racial separatism, 141–142; and racial solidarity, 23; and radicalism, 54; returning to Cuba after independence, 62; and segregation, 3, 65, 78; "self-making" among, 153n13; silences of, 166n131; and *teatro bufo*, 110, 173n121; Diego Vicente Tejera on, 50; and Ten Years' War, 46; and Tuskegee Institute, 164n105; and voter disenfranchisement, 64, 72, 96–98; and Weight Strike (1899), 58; and World War II, 114–115, 126–127, 129–130; and Ybor City, 103
blackface, 110
Black newspapers, 27
Black troops (World War II), 129–130
Black voters, 97t; and Democratic Party, 37, 68–69, 72, 100; and Monroe County elections, 39, 96–98; and Republican Party, 161n57. *See also* voter disenfranchisement
"Blancos y Negros" (Tejera 1897), 23
Bonilla, Juan, 23, 44, 45
Booker T. Washington High School (Tampa), 90, 92, 95
Borrego, Carlos, 31, 150n79
Borrero Echeverria, Esteban, 45
Boy Scouts, 117
Bradwell, William, 25
Brito, Cornelio, 46
Broward, Napoleon, 73
Brown, Canter Jr., 149n62
Brown, Charles, 105
Browne, Jefferson, 96
Bush, Jeb, 140
Butler, Robert W., 29

Caballeros de la Luz, 100
Cabeza, Manuel, 94–95, 140–141
Call, Wilkinson, 71
Calle, Tomas, 136
Camero, Alberto, 126
Capetillo, Luisa, 175n35
Capó, Julio Jr., 145n27
Caraballo, Martin, 100

Caraballo Muller, Dalia Antonia, 7, 144n13
Carbonell, Juan, 100
Carbonell, Juan Jr., 125
Carbonell, Raul, 125–126
Carbonell, Ygnacio, 130
Caribbean South, 7–8, 30, 39, 85
Carrera, Julian, 128
Casanovas, Joan, 22, 146n13
Casellas, Juan, 119
Casellas-Allen, Belinda, 138, 142
Castellanos, Gerardo, 131
Castro, Fidel, 1, 133, 134, 135, 136, 143nn3–4
Catholic Woman's Club, 106
Cayo Hueso, and Black Cubans, 104, 120; and Cuba-US relations, 117–118, 174n9; and Instituto San Carlos, 115–116; and Jim Crow system, 6, 93–94, 95; and La Unión Martí-Maceo, 125; and US centennial, 30–31. *See also* Key West celebrations
Centro Asturiano, 102, 135
Centro Español, 135
Céspedes, Carlos Manuel de, 20, 30
Céspedes Hall, 77
Céspedes y Céspedes, Carlos Manuel de, 9, 30, 31, 32f, 35, 98, 125, 150n81
Chambers, Glenn, 14
Chávez, Ernesto, 14
Chinese-born cigar makers, 21
Chinese Cubans, 51
cigar industry: and Cuban émigrés, 18; and Cuban South Florida, 2, 4, 7, 132; and Great Depression, 12, 114; hierarchical nature of, 23; and independence movement, 40; and Jacksonville, 28; and Key West, 21; and labor unions, 52–56, 56–58; and *lectores*, 22; multiethnic work force in, 33–34; and political discourse, 115; and race, 93; and Tampa, 157n115; and women, 147n23. *See also* Clear Havana cigar industry
Cigar Makers' International Union (CMIU): after Cuban independence, 62; and American Federation of Labor, 57; and Great Depression, 122; and La Resistencia, 58, 60; and racial tropes, 10; strategies of, 157n104; and women, 61
cigar workers, 21–23, 34, 52–54, 57
Círculo Cubano: and Americanization efforts, 105; and Black Cubans, 77; and Fidel Castro, 133; and Club Nacional Cubano, 108; and Cubans of color, 81; and influenza pandemic of 1918, 63–64; and Jim Crow system, 76; and La Unión Martí-Maceo, 93, 119, 138; and other mutual-aid societies, 102; and segregation, 13; and *teatro bufo*, 110; and urban renewal, 135
Círculo de Trabajadores, 54
Citizens' Committee (Tampa), 60, 61, 157n115
citizenship, 9, 14, 29, 39–40, 103–106, 171n75. *See also* Americanization
civil rights: after Cuban independence, 52; and Blanche Armwood Beatty, 91f; and Caribbean South, 39–40; and Cubans of color, 89; and La Resistencia, 60; and PIC, 81–82; and public solidarity, 95; and Republican Party, 68; and World War II, 115
Civil Rights Act (1875), 29, 95
Clara Frye Hospital, 64
Clealand, Danielle Pilar, 49–50
Clear Havana cigar industry: and cigar workers, 55; and CMIU, 57; decline of, 87; as economic driver, 4; and Great Depression, 12, 122; and Key West, 21; and race, 64; and Ybor City, 9. *See also* cigar industry
Club Emilio Nuñez, 45–46
Club Mariana Grajales de Maceo, 46
Club Nacional Cubano, 64, 77, 108
cohabitation laws, 67
Cold War, 133–134
Colegio Unificación, 33
Coleman, James Leonard, 129
Comite Busto Antonio Maceo, 138–139
Communist Party, 119
Conch yearbooks, 99
Congress of Industrial Organizations, 133

188 • INDEX

Cookman Institute, 78
Coolidge, Calvin, 174n16
Creci, Enrique, 53, 55–56
Cuba: after independence, 74–76; and anti-Black migration measures, 175–176n36; and Black leaders, 62; and Black rights, 70; and Luisa Capetillo, 175n35; and Cuban Americans, 115–122; and insurgency of 1868, 19; and integrated public school, 80; migrants from, 114; and James K. Polk, 17; and race, 65, 141; and racial discourse, 81; and racial politics, 13
Cuba Lodge No. 15 of the Independent Order of Odd Fellows, 35
Cuban American National Foundation, 140
Cuban Club, 124, 138
Cuban Democratic Club, 36
Cuban émigrés: communities of, 146n10; and Cuban independence movement, 20–21; institutions of, 44; and Key West, 25; and newspapers, 45; and racial disparities, 87–88; and Republican Party, 9, 71; and revolutionary publications, 23; and Ten Years' War, 18. *See also* exiles
Cuban independence movement: and Black Americans, 27–28; and Black Cubans, 2, 75; and cigar industry, 55; color-blind ideology of, 6; and Cuban émigrés, 5, 93; and Democratic Party, 37, 69; ideals of, 4; and Instituto San Carlos, 3, 24; and interracial collaboration, 62, 141; and interracial politics, 40; and Key West, 18; and labor unions, 52–56; and multiracial alliance, 51; and James K. Polk, 17; and race, 43–44; and women, 45–46; and Ybor City, 1
Cuban Little War, 44
Cuban republic: and Black Cubans, 41–42, 47–48, 51, 56, 62; flag of, 17; and Great Depression, 114; and inequalities, 65, 75; and Instituto San Carlos, 24; and Key West, 40; José Martí on, 49; and Martín Morúa Delgado, 23, 44; and PIC, 81–82;

and political discourse, 115–116; and racial democracy, 80, 85–86; and racial ideology, 164n100
Cuban Republican Club, 32
Cuban Revolution, 1, 8, 134, 135–136, 139, 143n3, 176n39
Cuban Revolutionary Party. *See* Partido Revolucionario Cubano (PRC)
Cubans of color. *See* Black Cubans
Cuban War of Independence: and Black Cubans, 41, 45, 65, 75–76; and Black leaders, 85; and cigar unions, 10; and Enrique Creci, 55–56; and exiles, 56; and Florida celebrations, 116; and multiracial coalitions, 74; and USS *Maine*, 117

Daniels, Roger, 120
Daughters of the American Revolution, 106
Davis, Ben, 104
Dean, James, 10, 39, 66–68, 67f, 140, 159n20
Decker, Samuel, 94
Deisher, Stella B., 100
de la Cruz, Manuel, 51
de la Fuente, Alejandro, 85, 164n100, 164n101
de la Grana, Frank, 127
Delgado, Alfred, 33
Delgado, Margaret, 33
de Loño, Angel, 35, 36, 37, 69
del Pino, Elmer, 126
Democratic Party: and all-white primaries, 72; and Black Americans, 38; control of Florida by, 66; and Cuban vote, 36–37, 71; and Enrique Esquinaldo Jr., 125; and Jim Crow system, 3, 10, 39, 64; and Key West, 26; and local politics, 101; and Angel de Loño, 69; and voter disenfranchisement, 96, 98; and white Cubans, 9, 14, 65, 88, 100–102
Directorio de Sociedades de la Raza de Color de Cuba, 47–48
Discípulas de Martí, 45–46
Domínguez, Teófilo, 44
Dortas, Armando, 133

Dosal, Paul, 138
"Double V," 130
Dred Scott v. John F. A. Sandford (1857), 82
Dueñas, Mercedes, 46
DuPont, Charles, 39, 70

Echemendia de Mederos, Susana, 107
education: and Americanization efforts, 98–99, 104–105, 106; and Black community, 27; and Black Key West, 34–35; and multiethnic Black community, 89–91; and PIC, 81–82; and segregation, 77; Diego Vicente Tejera on, 24; and whiteness, 146n34
El Centro Español, 102
El Diario de Tampa, 80, 82
Elks, 100
Elliott, Robert B., 29
Ellis, Jose Camacho, 129
Ellis, José (Joseph), 129
El Partido Revolucionario Cubano (Cuban Revolutionary Party), 4
El Pueblo, 23, 45
El Republicano, 22
El Separatista, 23
El Sport, 44
El Yara, 22
Emancipation Day, 95
Emigrados Revolucionarios Cubanos, 174n9
English, James D., 26, 96
English, Nelson, 26, 92, 95–96
Esquinaldo, Enrique Jr., 125
Estenoz, Evaristo, 81
Estrella Solitaria, 46
European immigrants, 102
Excelsior yearbooks, 92
exile newspapers, 44
exiles: and activism, 162n75; and Cuban independence movement, 19; and Cuban Revolution, 133–134; and Instituto San Carlos, 139–141; and Key West, 18, 40; and Antonio Maceo, 138; and Mariel boatlift, 136; and José Martí, 135; and "raceless" society, 51–52; and radicalism, 56. *See also* Cuban émigrés

Federación Local de Tabaqueros, 54
Federal Emergency Relief Administration (FERA), 95–96, 116, 123–124
Federal Works Agency (FWA), 124
Federal Writers' Project (FWP), 108–109
Fernandez, Frank, 99
Fernández, Frank, 56
Fernández-Armesto, Felipe, 145n25
Ferrer, Ada, 37, 75, 152n119, 154n31, 154n35, 163n83
Fidel Castro, 136
Figueredo, Candelaria, 20
Figueredo, Fernando, 71
Figueredo y Cisneros, Pedro "Perucho," 20
Figueroa, José Juan, 29, 149n62
filibusters, 17–18, 28
Fleitas, Juan Francisco, 125
Fleming, Francis, 67
Fletcher, Rosa, 67
Flores, Juan, 6–7
Florida: and Black officials, 149n62; and Black voters, 72; and Caribbean migration, 8; and cohabitation laws, 67; and constitution of 1885, 66, 77; and history, 145n25; and Jim Crow system, 3; and Reconstruction, 25–28; and voter disenfranchisement, 96
Florida A&M College, 93
Florida Emergency Relief Administration (FERA), 93
Foreign Women's and Mothers' Clubs, 106
Foy, Annie, 69
Franco, Francisco, 127
fraternal orders, 6, 14, 35, 100. *See also specific orders*
Frederick Douglass School (Key West), 27, 30, 34–35, 69, 91, 124

Gabriel, Robert, 26, 27f, 34, 38, 70
Galleani, Luigi, 53
gender, 22–23, 57, 62. *See also* women
Gibbs, Jonathan C., 25
Girl Scouts, 117
Golden Eagles, 100
Gomez, Arthur, 101
Gómez, José Miguel, 82, 83, 165n111

Gómez, Juan Gualberto, 45, 47–48
Gómez, Laura, 14
Gómez, Máximo, 78
Gómez, Rogelio, 121, 125–126
Gonzales, Antonio, 66–67
Gonzalez, Carlos, 138–139
Gonzalez, Julian, 44
Gonzalez Mendoza, Charles, 127
González, Norberto, 129–130
Gordon, Dexter, 92
Granados, Joaquín, 23, 44, 45, 46, 54, 56
Grau San Martín, Ramón, 115
Great Depression, 12, 87, 114, 121, 122, 124–125
Greaux, St. Elmo, 125
Greenbaum, Susan, 4, 5, 108, 137
Grillo, Evelio: and Facundo Acción, 122; on African Americans, 92; on Black Cuban history, 120; as community organizer, 131; on interracial friendships, 111; and segregation, 3, 89; and World War II, 113–114, 115, 129
Griñan, Sylvia, 89, 111, 137
"Grito de Baire," 93, 116, 174n7
"Grito de Yara," 20, 30, 93, 116, 117, 174n9
Guerra, Lilian, 47
Guridy, Frank Andre, 6, 7, 8, 164n105
Gutierrez, Aurora, 100
Gutiérrez, Margarito, 23, 44, 45
Gutsens, María Valdés de, 123, 159n20

Haitian refugees, 8
Haitian Revolution, 82
Haitians, 83
Harris, J. Vining Jr., 168n27
Harris, J. Vining Sr., 168n27
Harrison, Will, 69
Havana, 21, 52, 53, 60, 174n16
Havana Woman's Club, 107
Hayes, Emelina Teresa nee Recio, 100
Hayes, John Alexander, 100
Haymarket massacre, 50, 105
Helg, Aline, 65, 164n100
Helping Hand Day Nursery, 90
Henriquez, Cleveland, 129

Henriquez, Rafael, 100
Hepburn, George Charles, 125
Hernández, Tanya Katerí, 7, 109, 172n105
Herrera, Luz, 61
Hewitt, Nancy, 4–5, 156n95
Hillsborough County, 70, 72f, 90, 100, 102–103, 104–107, 176n37. *See also* Tampa
Hispanic Commission, 139
Hoffnung-Garskoff, Jesse, 6, 35, 49, 153n13, 165n130, 173n121
Horr, John F., 159n26
Hurricane Maria, 8

identity: and Americanization efforts, 98–99, 105; and Black Cubans, 4–5, 42, 88; and Cuban holidays, 116; and integration, 43; perception of, 159n23; and race, 12–13, 131–132; and *teatro bufo*, 110; and white Cubans, 7, 15, 102; and whiteness, 6, 103; and World War II, 126, 130
Ignacio Agramonte club, 56
immigration quota system, 120–121
influenza pandemic of 1918, 63
Ingalls, Robert, 157n104, 157n115
Instituto San Carlos, 79f; and Americanization efforts, 98; and anti-Black racism, 110; and Black Cuban history, 120; and Black student photo, 163n92; and Cuban identity, 131; and Cuban independence movement, 24; and Cuban Revolution, 135–136; and Cuban state, 114, 115; and Cuba-US relations, 12; as cultural center, 143n7; and education, 34; founding of, 2; and Grito de Yara celebrations, 116, 174n9; and integration, 98; and interracial collaboration, 32, 80; and Jim Crow system, 76, 77–80; and La Resistencia, 61; and Eugene Locke, 71; and Antonio Maceo, 120; and Juan Pérez Rolo, 143n6; and race, 93–94; and Republican Party, 31; restoration of, 139–140; and segregation, 3, 88, 91, 93–94; and Rafael Serra, 44, 52; and *teatro bufo*,

110–111; and theater, 150n86; and white Cubans, 88
interethnic marriage, 15, 100
interethnic organizing, 144n16
interethnic relationships, 33
interethnic schools, 89–90, 99
International Order of Good Templars (IOGT), 151–152n108
International Trades and Labor Assembly of Tampa, 58
interracial democracy, 3, 5, 18–19, 42, 56, 86
interracial marriage, 66, 140, 160n34
interracial organizing, 94, 144n16, 174n6
interracial relationships, 33, 94–95, 140–141
interracial schools, 3, 136
Iorio, Pam, 161n57
Island City Choral Singers, 92
Island City Civic League, 125
Ivonnet, Pedro, 81

Jacksonville, 28
James, Winston, 4, 5
Jim Crow system: antecedents of, 38; and baseball, 124; and Black Cubans, 4, 13, 86, 87, 89–93; and cigar industry, 74; and Cuban American agency, 6; and Cuban South Florida, 11; and Democratic Party, 10, 39; enforcement of, 126; and Florida state government, 66; and Great Depression, 123–124; and history, 137, 140; and influenza pandemic of 1918, 63–64; and lynching, 140–141; and multiracial coalitions, 74–75; and multiracial Cuban enclaves, 3; and mutual-aid societies, 76–77; and power dynamics, 96–98; and public transportation, 73; and racial separatism, 141; scholarship on, 4–5; and South Africa, 113; Diego Vicente Tejera on, 50; and US labor movement, 58; and voter disenfranchisement, 71–72; and white Cubans, 103. *See also* segregation
Jiménez Román, Miriam, 6–7
Johnson, Frank, 99
Johnson, James Weldon, 28
Johnson, Sylvanus, 69–70
Johnson-Reed Act (1924), 120, 175–176n36
Jones, Jennifer A., 12, 145n29

Kennedy, Stetson, 108–109
Key, Jack, 99
Key of the Gulf, 32, 36–37
Key West: and Anglos, 88; and Black community, 27; and Black officials, 149n62; and Caribbean migration, 8; Caribbean population of, 149n65; census of 1885, 147n22, 151n92; and cigar industry, 34; and "Conch," 152n124; and Cuban celebrations, 116, 117–118; and Cuban community, 150n79; and Cuban history, 131; and Cuban independence movement, 18, 44; and Cuban nationalism, 4; and Cuban refugees, 121; and Cuban Revolution, 134, 135–136; and James Dean, 66–68; and Angel de Loño, 69; demographics of, 33; and Great Depression, 12, 114, 122, 123, 125; and history, 118f, 137; and Instituto San Carlos, 2–3, 24, 32, 139–140; and interracial collaboration, 141; and interracial marriage, 6; and KKK, 94; and labor unions, 54; and La Resistencia, 61; and La Unión de Tabaqueros, 53; and *lectores*, 22; list of qualified voters in, 97t; and local politics, 100–101; and multiethnic Black community, 90–93; and multiracial democracy, 28–32, 39–40, 80; and mutual-aid societies, 78; and PIC, 65; police department of, 126; and Porter and Harris families, 168n27; and post-Reconstruction politics, 159n26; and race, 9, 159n20; and racial discourse, 23; and racial divides, 95–96; and racial terminology, 15; and Radical Reconstruction, 19; and railcar boycott, 73; and Reconstruction, 5, 25–26; scholarship on, 144n16; and Tampa, 7; and *teatro bufo*, 110; and Ten Years' War,

20; and theater, 150n86; and white Cubans, 14, 98; and working-class Cubans, 21. *See also* Monroe County
Key West Citizen, 96
Key West Cornet Band, 29
Key West Democrat, 36, 37, 38
Key West High School, 99
Key West National Guards, 117
Key West News, 27
Knights of Columbus, 100
Knights of Labor, 57
Knights of Pythias, 100
Kropotkin, Peter, 53
Ku Klux Klan (KKK), 25, 85, 87, 94–95, 119, 166n132, 168n26
Ku Klux Klan Kubano, 119, 166n132

labor organizing: and cigar industry, 21, 52–56; and cigar workers, 56–58; decline of, 75; and interracial collaboration, 62; and KKK, 94; and race, 9, 42; and violence, 60. *See also* unions
labor radicalism, 52, 105, 115, 120, 175n35
La Concha, 129
La Discusión, 80
La Fraternidad, 23
Lago, Elizabeth, 33
Lago, José, 33
La Loca de la Casa (Rodrígues), 110
La Lucha, 80
La Mujer Del Buzo (Sorondo), 110
La Resistencia, 59f; and CMIU, 60; critics of, 62; and interracial collaboration, 79–80; and multiracial organizing, 57–58; and José Ramón Sanfeliz, 108; and strike settlement, 157n124; and US labor federations, 43; and violence, 61
La Revista Popular, 23, 45
La Revolución Cubana y la raza de color (de la Cruz 1895), 51
Latin-American Festival, 104
Latin identity, 15, 102
La Unión de Tabaqueros, 21–22, 53, 54
La Unión Martí-Maceo, 84f, 91f; and African Americans, 111; and Blanche Armwood Beatty, 167n11; and Black Cubans, 13, 42; and Fidel Castro, 133; and Círculo Cubano, 81, 93; and Cuban history, 132; and Cuban representatives, 119; and demolished building, 134, 135; and education, 90; founding of, 77; and Great Depression, 124–125; and history, 137–138; and Jim Crow system, 5, 10, 64; and PIC, 83; and *Previsión*, 165n130; and respectability, 88; and World War II, 127; and Ybor City, 103
Lavin, Pablo, 119
League of United Latin American Citizens (LULAC), 103, 171n77
lectores, 22, 23, 87, 147n17
Legionarios de Martí, 119
Leon, Jorge R., 100
Lester, Herminia nee Recio, 100
Lester, Joseph Lancelot, 100
LGBTQ communities, 145n27
Liceo Cubano, 44, 61
Liga Obrera de Trabajadores de Tampa, 54, 156n79
Livingston, L. W., 38–39
Locke, Eugene, 71
Long, Thomas W., 25
Lopez, Andrew L., 101
López, Antonio, 110
Lopez, Clayton, 140–141
López, Ian Haney, 171n70, 171n75
López, José A., 80–81, 85
López, Lydia, 74
Lopez, Manuel, 99
López, Narciso, 17–18, 20, 69
Los Vengadores de Maceo, 108
Louisiana, 162n75
Lucumí people, 75
L'Unione Italiana, 53, 102, 133, 135
lynching, 70, 140–141

MacDill Air Force Base, 128
Maceo, Antonio: and Cuban independence movement, 64–65; and history, 140; and Instituto San Carlos, 24; legacy of, 45, 120, 138–139, 143n4, 148n38; mother of, 46; and Parque Amigos, 1–2
Maceo, Remember, 138, 139

Macfarlane, Hugh, 60
Machado, Gerardo, 114, 115, 119, 121
Malatesta, Errico, 53
Mallea, Juan, 137
Malone, William H., 117
Maloney, Walter C., 149n62
Mariel boatlift, 134, 136
Martí, José: and cigar makers, 10; and cigar workers, 55–56; and Club Mariana Grajales de Maceo, 46; and Cuban émigrés, 5; and Cuban independence movement, 18; and Instituto San Carlos, 3, 139; legacy of, 135, 143nn3–4; official uses of, 117; and Parque Amigos, 1; and Paulina Pedroso, 2; and PRC, 47; and "raceless" society, 48–49; and racial unity, 154n35; on racism, 51; and Rafael Serra, 52; statue of, 118f; on US life, 50
Martínez, Altagracia, 61
Martull, Guillermo, 124
Marxism, 135
Mas Canosa, Jorge, 140
Mascotte, 52
Masons, 100
McGhee, Howard, 92
McKay, D. B., 100
McNamara, Sarah, 174n6
Meacham, Robert, 25
Menard, John Willis, 27–28, 35, 38
Mendez, Armando, 89
Menendez, Ricardo, 137
Mercedes Hospital, 123, 159n20
Mesa, Marcos Jr., 129
Messonier, Enrique, 53
Mexican Americans, 14, 129, 169n51
Miami, 8, 121, 134, 141, 145n27, 176n39
migrant networks, 4
Milian, Francisco, 61–62
minstrel shows, 110
Mirabal, Nancy Raquel, 4, 5, 6, 138, 166n131, 173–174n3
Miró, José, 45
Miró Cardona, José, 135
miscegenation laws, 69–70
mission schools, 106

Monroe County: and Black officials, 39, 70; and James Dean, 66–68; and Democratic Party, 37, 38; demographics of, 29; elections in, 150n80; foreign-born population of, 176n37; list of qualified voters in, 96–97; and local politics, 101; and multiracial democracy, 28; and José G. Pompez, 71; and Republican Party, 31; and voter disenfranchisement, 72f; and white Cubans, 125–126. *See also* Key West
Montejo, Esteban, 75, 76
Moragues, Frances, 100
Morales, Edward, 92
Morales, Richard D., 100
Moreno, Luisa, 174n6, 175n35
Mormino, Gary, 137
Morris, George, 92
Morúa Delgado, Martín: after Cuban independence, 62, 76; on Black Cubans, 19; and Cuban independence movement, 44–45, 64–65; and Juan Gualberto Gómez, 47–48; on integration, 23; and PIC, 82; on socialism, 54
Morúa Law, 48, 82
Muerte del General Maceo (Miró), 45
multiracial democracy: decline of, 81; and early Cuban republic, 80, 85–86; ideals of, 11; and Key West, 28–32; and Reconstruction, 13; and white Cubans, 39
mutual-aid societies: and cigar industry, 21; and Great Depression, 125; and influenza pandemic of 1918, 63–64; and Jim Crow system, 76–77; and segregation, 10, 13; and World War II, 127
Mutual Mercantile Company, 70
"My Race" (Martí 1893), 49

NAACP, 70, 72, 90, 92, 128, 130–131
National Register of Historic Places, 135
naturalization, 103, 104–106, 120, 126, 127
naturalization classes, 92–93
naturalization laws, 39–40

Navarro, Theodore "Fats," 91–92
Nelson English Athletic Field, 95–96
Nelson English Park, 124, 125, 169n41
Neutrality Act, 18
New Deal, 95–96, 123–124
New Orleans, 14, 113, 114, 146n34
New York Age, 38
New York City: and anti-fascist organizing, 127; and Black Cubans, 49, 114, 172n105, 173–174n3; Cuban enclave in, 4, 174n7; and Cuban independence movement, 44; and Antonio Maceo, 138; and race, 107; and revolutionary publications, 23; and Félix Varela, 139; and white Cubans, 21
Ngai, Mae, 171n75
Norcisa, Luis Jr., 128
Noriega, Isabel Alyce, 92
"Nuestra America" (Martí), 117

Odd Fellows, 100
O'Farrill, Alberto, 110
Ogden, Ernest, 129
Olivette, 52
Orozco, Cynthia, 103, 171n77
Ortiz, Paul, 144n16, 151n95, 152n127

Padilla, J. G., 60
Pagés, Ramón, 162n75
Palacios, Grace, 92–93, 95, 125
Palomares, Bernice, 90
Palomino, José de C., 159n23
Pan American Airways, 118–119
Parque Amigos de José Martí, 1–2, 117, 135, 138–139, 143n3
Partido Independiente de Color (PIC / Independent Party of Color): and Black Cubans, 165n124; controversy over, 81–85; founding of, 11; and José Miguel Gómez, 165n111; violence against, 65, 164n100
Partido Revolucionario Cubano (PRC): and cigar workers, 55; and Cuban War of Independence, 41; decline of, 62; and interracial collaboration, 47; and José G. Pompez, 161n48; and radicalism, 56; and Rafael Serra, 52; and women, 45
Paschel, Tianna S., 12, 145n29
"Pasó en Tampa" (Rodríguez), 121–122
passing, 89, 99
Pathé Theater, 101
Pedroso, Paulina, 47f; after Cuban independence, 62, 76; and Cuban independence movement, 44, 64–65; and history, 140; life of, 143n5; and José Martí, 2, 46, 56
Pedroso, Ruperto, 2, 46, 56
Peñalver, Rafael Jr., 139
Pendleton, C. B., 70
Pérez, Lisandro, 48, 144n13
Pérez de Alderate, Jorge, 121
Pérez Díaz, Eliseo, 80–81, 85
Pérez Rolo, Juan, 20, 143n6
Philbrick, John Jay, 31
Pizzo, Tony, 1
Planas, Emilio, 23, 24, 44, 45, 46, 78, 84
Plant Steamship Company, 155n65
Platt Amendment, 48
Plessy v. Ferguson (1896), 74, 162n75
Polk, James K., 17
poll taxes, 66, 71, 72, 72f, 96
Pompez, Alejandro (Alex), 161n48
Pompez, José G., 71, 161n48
Pompez, Loretta Pérez, 161n48
Porter, J. Y. Jr., 168n27
Porter, J. Y. Sr., 168n27
Portuondo Linares, Serafín, 76
Poyo, Gerald, 55, 130, 144n16
Poyo, José Dolores, 130
Poyo, Sergio, 130
Pozzetta, George E., 53
Previsión, 84, 165n130
Proudhon, Pierre-Joseph, 53
Puerto Ricans, 8
Pujol, Tete, 139
Putnam, Lara, 120–121, 175–176n36
"Que Que Que" letters, 94, 95
Quevedo, Manuel, 1
Quitman, John, 18

Rabí, Jesús, 45

race: and Afro-Latinos, 172n105; and Caribbean migration, 144–145n19; and cigar industry, 22–23; construction of, 37; and Cuban émigrés, 144–145n19; and Cuban independence movement, 42, 43–44; and Cuban South Florida, 5; debates over, 65; hierarchies of, 62; ideas about, 145n29; and identity, 12–15; and insurgency of 1868, 19; and labor unions, 54, 57; and marriage, 66; José Martí on, 55; and José de C. Palomino, 159n23; and PIC, 65, 165n111; and political power, 35–36; and PRC, 47; Diego Vicente Tejera on, 50; and US centennial, 30–31; and violence, 60, 150n74; and voter disenfranchisement, 96–98; and voting rights, 36–37
"raceless" society, 48–52
racial democracy. *See* multiracial democracy
racial discourse, 44, 103
racial equality, 23, 26, 42–43, 78, 85, 164n100
racial formation, 6
racial hierarchies, 172n105
racial ideology, 164n100
"racial innocence," 7
racialization, 8, 166n1
racial politics, 3–4, 12–13, 40, 94
racial separatism: and Black Cubans, 74; consequences of, 141; and Cuban independence movement, 35; and Cuban Key West, 9; and history, 140; and Key West, 19; and public transportation, 162n68; and white Cubans, 37–38, 107–108. *See also* segregation
racial terminology, 13–14, 15
racism: in Cuba and US, 76; and Cuban communities, 4, 141; and Cuban independence movement, 40; and early Cuban republic, 80, 164n100; and education, 78; and fraternal orders, 35; and Latin community, 6–7; and New York City, 107; and PIC, 83; and "raceless" society, 49–51; and *teatro bufo*, 110–111; tropes of, 82; and war effort, 113, 115, 130
Radical Reconstruction, 18–19, 29, 39–40, 70. *See also* Reconstruction
Recio, Carlos, 35, 99–100
Recio, Emeline, 100
Reconstruction: and interracial collaboration, 141; and interracial schooling, 24; and Key West, 5, 8–9, 25–26, 144n16; and Redeemer ideology, 65; and Republican Party, 159n26; and voting laws, 28. *See also* Radical Reconstruction
Red Cross, 92, 130
Redeemers, 39, 65
refugees, 8, 117, 121, 136
Renedo, Joseph M., 100
Republican Party: and Black officials, 25, 38; and Black politics, 96; and Black voters, 161n57; and Cuban vote, 36–37; and James Dean, 68; leadership structure of, 31; and local politics, 101; and multiracial coalitions, 28–29; and José G. Pompez, 71; and Radical Reconstruction, 19; and Reconstruction-era coalitions, 9; white leadership of, 159n26
Revista de Cayo Hueso, 45, 147n24, 148n38
Revista de Florida, 54
Rivera-Rideau, Petra R., 12, 145n29
Rivero, Ramón, 46
Rodrígues, Agustín, 110
Rodríguez, Alejandro, 60
Rodríguez, Arsenio, 121–122
Rodríguez, Francisco Jr., 13–14, 15, 89, 130–131, 132
Rodríguez, Francisco Sr.: and cigar industry, 122; and Cuban history, 132; and interracial collaboration, 43–44; interview of, 152n1; and Jim Crow system, 62; and La Unión Martí-Maceo, 13; life of, 41–42; migration of, 56; on Paulina Pedroso, 46; on race relations, 77
Rodriguez, Isidore, 99
Roediger, David, 166n1

Roig San Martín, Enrique, 53, 55
Rosa, Enrique, 94
Rosa Valdés Settlement, 106
Royal Knights of America, 105
Ruiz, Vicki, 169n51
Ruth Hargrove Institute, 98–99

San Carlos Rescue Committee, 139
Sánchez, Blas, 129
Sanchez, Ellen, 92
Sánchez, Rachel, 129
Sanfeliz, José Ramón, 59f, 108, 164n99
San Mateo hospital, 64
Sardiñas Montalvo, Eligio "Kid Chocolate," 121
Schomburg, Arturo, 82
Scott, Rebecca J., 83, 162n75, 164n100, 165n111
Scottish Rite, 100
segregation: and ancestry, 137–138; and Cuban identity, 131–132; and Cuban South Florida, 15; and education, 99; and fraternal orders, 100; and Great Depression, 124; and identity, 88; and influenza pandemic of 1918, 64; and multiracial populations, 66–68; and private schools, 164n101; and public school, 80; of public transportation, 73; and US military, 129–130; and voting rights, 96–98; and white Cubans, 10. *See also* Jim Crow system; racial separatism
Segura, Francisco, 54
Seidenberg, Samuel, 55
Semper Paratus Always Ready (SPARS), 128
Serra, Rafael, 13, 24, 44, 48, 51–52, 64–65, 86, 154n31
Shofner, Jerrell, 151n95
Shriners, 100
slavery: and Bahamians, 26; and cigar industry, 21; in Cuba, 19; and Cuban independence movement, 20; debates over, 13; and filibusters, 17, 18; and Grito de Yara, 20; and Spanish repression, 25; and Ten Years' War, 75. *See also* abolition
Smith Act (1940), 93

socialism, 53, 54, 140
Sociedad Cuba, 77
Sociedad de Socorros La Caridad, 46
Sociedad El Progreso, 150n79
Sociedad Patriotica Cespedes de West Tampa, 77
Sola, Disdiero, 84
solidarity, 23, 28, 56, 83, 95, 119
Sorondo, Guillermo, 19, 33, 54, 56, 62, 156n79
Sorondo, Mario, 110
South Africa, 113
Soviet Union, 136
Spain, 17, 18, 53, 65, 110, 131
Spaniards, 99, 100
Spanish Americans, 127
Spanish colonialism, 24, 145n25
Spanish Empire, 18, 20
Spelman Seminary, 90
steamship routes, 52–53
Stebbins, Consuelo, 159n20
stemmers, 23, 34, 58, 61, 147n23
St. Francis Xavier's School, 35, 90–91
St. Joseph's School, 90–91
St. Michael's Lodge of the Grand United Order of Odd Fellows, 35
Stone, Julius F. Jr., 123–124
St. Paul African Methodist Episcopal Church, 95
St. Paul's Episcopal Church, 35
St. Peter's Claver Elementary School, 90
St. Peter's Claver Episcopal Church, 160n34
St. Peter's Parish, 35
strippers. *See* stemmers
Stubbs, Jean, 21
Suarez, Clara, 129
Suarez, Joseph, 128

Takao Ozawa v. United States (1922), 103
Tampa: and Americanization efforts, 104–106; and Anglos, 88; and anti-Black racism, 78; and anti-fascist organizing, 127; and Oscar Ayala, 102–103; and Blanche Armwood Beatty, 90; and Caribbean migration, 8; and Fidel Castro, 133; and

Citizens' Committee, 157n115; and Cuban independence movement, 44; and Cuban nationalism, 4; and Cuban refugees, 121; and Cuban Revolution, 134; and Emancipation Day, 95; and Great Depression, 12, 114, 122, 123, 124–125; and history, 137; and influenza pandemic of 1918, 63–64; and Jim Crow system, 76; and Key West, 7; and labor radicals, 175n35; and labor unions, 42, 54; and La Resistencia, 43, 57–58, 157n124; and Latin community, 53, 100, 102; and Antonio Maceo, 138–139; and José Martí, 48–49; and Francisco Milian, 61–62; multiethnic work force in, 33; and multiracial families, 108–109; and PIC, 65; and race, 9, 142; and racial discourse, 81; and segregated public transportation, 73; and segregation, 3; and steamship routes, 53; and urban renewal, 135; and violence against labor, 60; and white Cubans, 14, 98; and White Municipal Party, 72; and women's activism, 174n6. *See also* Hillsborough County

Tampa Bay Area Cuban Exile Council, 138–139

Tampa Electric Company, 73, 74

Tampa FERA Orchestra, 123

Tampa Latin Clubs, 127

Tampa Sunday Tribune, 103–104

Tampa Tribune, 46

Tampa Urban League, 90

Tampa Woman's Club, 106, 107

teatro bufo, 110–111, 173n121

Tejera, Diego Vicente, 19–20, 23–24, 43, 50–51

temperance organizing, 35

Ten Years' War: and Black Cubans, 46, 75; and cigar industry, 21; and Cuban émigrés, 2; and Grito de Yara, 30, 116; and insurgent debates, 146n13; and Key West, 8–9, 18, 20; and *lectores*, 22; and race, 43, 146n7

Terpsichorean Circle, 92

Teurbe Tolón, Miguel, 17

Texas, 72

Thurston, Sarah, 107

Treaty of Guadalupe Hidalgo (1848), 14

Trelles, Jorge, 119–120

Tuskegee Institute, 164n105, 167n13

Uhrback, Joseph F., 100, 170n57

Unión Cubana, 78, 83

unions: conflicts among, 58; in Cuba and US, 21–22; and Cuban independence movement, 10; decline of, 75, 87; inclusiveness of, 23, 42–43, 57; international nature of, 52–53; and interracial collaboration, 9, 93, 95, 110–111; strikes by, 54. *See also* labor organizing; *specific unions*

United Republican Club of Monroe County, 70

United States: and Fulgencio Batista, 117; and citizenship, 171n75; and immigration law, 167–168n23; and Luisa Moreno, 175n35; Diego Vicente Tejera on, 50; and USS *Maine*, 42; and whiteness, 170n71. *See also* US-Cuba relations; US immigration policy; US occupation

United States v. Bhagat Singh Thind (1923), 103

University of South Florida, 137

Urban League, 125

urban renewal, 135

US Bureau of Naturalization, 106

US centennial, 30–31

US-Cuba relations, 85, 116, 118f, 133, 176n38. *See also* United States

US immigration policy, 120–121. *See also* United States

US occupation, 65, 80, 163n83, 164n105. *See also* United States

USS *Maine*, 42, 117, 174n16

vagrancy, 61, 126

Valdes, Jose de Jesus, 67

Valdez, José, 126, 178–179n86

Valdez, J. R., 100–101

Valdez, Maximo, 125

Vanguardia de Crombet, 56

Varela, Félix, 139

Veracruz, Mexico, 4

veterans, 130
violence: against labor, 9, 10, 43, 60–62; anti-Black, 25, 85; anti-PIC, 65, 81; and Manuel Cabeza, 140–141; and KKK, 94; and labor radicals, 105; and Gerardo Machado, 121; racial, 150n74; and Tampa, 157n115; and work competition, 151n95
V. M. Ybor School, 106, 124
voter disenfranchisement, 64, 65, 66, 68–69, 71–72, 96–98. *See also* Black voters
voting rights, 6, 35–36, 71

Walls, Josiah T., 25
Washington, Booker T., 81, 164n105
Weight Strike (1899), 58, 59f, 79–80, 108
Welters Cornet Band, 92
Welters, Frank, 92
West Tampa: and Americanization efforts, 106–107; and Cuban officials, 71; and FERA, 124; and independence movement, 5; and KKK, 94; and Francisco Milian, 61–62; and segregation, 74, 77, 89
West Tampa Woman's Club, 107
white Cubans: and Anglos, 11, 37; and anti-Black racism, 6–7, 172n105; and cigar industry, 23; and class, 15; and Cuban identity, 131; and Democratic Party, 9, 65, 88, 100–102; and education, 99; and European immigrants, 102; and FERA, 124; and fraternal orders, 35; and Great Depression, 125–126; and identity, 6, 12; and Jim Crow system, 4, 85–86; and passing, 67; and PIC, 81, 83; politics of, 39; and power structures, 114; and "raceless" society, 49–50; and racial discourse, 43–44; and racial hierarchies, 107–108, 109; and racial separatism, 76, 141–142; and racial solidarity, 23; and segregation, 3; Rafael Serra on, 52; and Ten Years' War, 46; and voting rights, 72–73, 96–98; and white allies, 111; and whiteness, 14; and World War II, 126, 128–129, 130
white Latinos, 7
White Municipal Party, 72, 100
whiteness: and Americanization efforts, 104–105; between Cuba and United States, 8; and Black Cuban identity, 6; and Cuban Americans, 98–99; evolution of, 14; and Latin Americans, 146n34; and LULAC, 171n77; and power structures, 126; shared concept of, 101–102; and US intervention, 163n83; and US law, 170n71
white supremacists, 25
white supremacy, 66, 85
Wicker, Frank N., 31
Williams, Andrew, 94
Wilson, Helen, 92
"With All, for the Good of All" (Martí 1891), 48–49
Wolff Mission, 107
Wolff Mission School, 98, 106
Woman's Council of the Methodist Episcopal Church, 106
women: and activism, 4–5, 11, 45–46, 79–80, 92–93, 106–107, 174n6; and Americanization efforts, 169n51; and charity work, 147n24; and cigar industry, 23, 34, 147n23; and community institutions, 92–93; and Helping Hand Day Nursery, 90; and La Resistencia, 58, 60–61; and La Unión Martí-Maceo, 165n130; and World War II, 128. *See also* gender
Women Accepted for Voluntary Emergency Services (WAVES), 128
Women's Auxiliary Army Corps (WAAC), 128
Woodcock Foundation schools, 27
working-class Cubans: and Americanization efforts, 107; and dating, 109; discrimination against, 101; and Great Depression, 122–123; and immigration law, 120; and Instituto San Carlos, 3; and Jim Crow system, 126; and Key West, 18, 19; and labor movement, 62; and José Martí, 56;

and race, 111; and Ten Years' War, 21; and voter disenfranchisement, 72, 96, 100; and whiteness, 14–15
Works Progress Administration (WPA), 104, 105, 108, 125
World War II, 6, 12, 114–115, 126–130

Xavier University of Louisiana, 113, 114

Ybor, Rafael, 83, 101–102
Ybor, Vicente, 48
Ybor City: and Facundo Acción, 122; and anti-Cuban discrimination, 101; and cigar industry, 41; and Clear Havana, 9; and education, 90; and European immigrants, 102; and FERA, 124; and Great Depression, 123; and history, 140; and independence movement, 1–2, 5; and influenza pandemic of 1918, 63–64; and KKK, 94; and Latin community, 103–104; and La Unión Martí-Maceo, 134; and José Martí, 56; multiethnic work force in, 4, 33; and multiracial families, 108–109; and segregated public transportation, 74; and *teatro bufo*, 110; and urban renewal, 135
Ybor City Businessmen's Association, 103–104
Ybor City Chamber of Commerce, 104, 127
YMCA, 105